Praise for
Running on Empty

"Marshall is The Man. Definitively. His run across America at the age of fifty-seven sealed that distinction forever. He's living proof that endurance never sleeps, never gets old, never tires. Nothing can stop him, and that gives us all hope, gives us resolve to keep trying."
—DEAN KARNAZES, acclaimed endurance athlete and bestselling author of *Ultramarathon Man: Confessions of an All-Night Runner*

"Marshall and I go way back to the first Eco-Challenge in 1995. An athlete of astonishing grit both then and now, he never fails to push the limits of his sport, no matter what extreme endurance event he's chosen. *Running on Empty* tells the story of Marshall's greatest test: reading it, you get a sense of how tough this man is, but there's also a bit of Everyman in Marsh. He's an inspiration to all of us."
—MARK BURNETT, Emmy Award–winning producer of *Survivor, Eco-Challenge, The Apprentice, Are You Smarter Than a 5th Grader?* and other programs

"Riveting—the man has endured more, experienced more, accomplished more than you can imagine. You have to read it to believe it." —AMBY BURFOOT, winner of the 1968 Boston Marathon and editor at large, *Runner's World*

"You can learn from every race, even the ones you read about instead of run yourself. Marshall is a master of mental toughness, an endurance legend, and exactly the kind of example our country needs right now." —KARA GOUCHER, American middle- and long-distance runner, Olympian and World Championships medalist

"I'm always secretly envious of guys like Marshall, who run for adventure and cover extreme distances. What goes on inside their heads? How do they keep going, on and on, into the night, for days on end? What do they experience that the rest of us don't? *Running on Empty* tells it all, giving a rare glimpse into the world of ultrarunning and into the life of a man who epitomizes his sport's doctrine of 'never say quit.'" —RYAN HALL, first U.S. runner to finish the half-marathon in under an hour and current U.S. record holder

Running on Empty

To Kinsey & Diana,
So grateful to
have met you! Here's
to great adventures
in the future!
Dig deeper &
love more!
Marsh & Heather

July 25, 2019

Running on Empty

An Ultramarathoner's Story of Love, Loss, and a Record-Setting Run Across America

Marshall Ulrich

AVERY

a member of Penguin Group (USA) Inc.

New York

AVERY

Published by the Penguin Group
Penguin Group (USA) Inc., 375 Hudson Street, New York, New York 10014, USA • Penguin Group (Canada), 90 Eglinton Avenue East, Suite 700, Toronto, Ontario M4P 2Y3, Canada (a division of Pearson Penguin Canada Inc.) • Penguin Books Ltd, 80 Strand, London WC2R 0RL, England • Penguin Ireland, 25 St Stephen's Green, Dublin 2, Ireland (a division of Penguin Books Ltd) • Penguin Group (Australia), 250 Camberwell Road, Camberwell, Victoria 3124, Australia (a division of Pearson Australia Group Pty Ltd) • Penguin Books India Pvt Ltd, 11 Community Centre, Panchsheel Park, New Delhi–110 017, India • Penguin Group (NZ), 67 Apollo Drive, Rosedale, North Shore 0632, New Zealand (a division of Pearson New Zealand Ltd) • Penguin Books (South Africa) (Pty) Ltd, 24 Sturdee Avenue, Rosebank, Johannesburg 2196, South Africa

Penguin Books Ltd, Registered Offices: 80 Strand, London WC2R 0RL, England

Excerpt from "Desert Places" from *The Poetry of Robert Frost*, edited by Edward Connery Lathem. Copyright 1947, 1969 by Henry Holt and Company. Copyright 1975 by Lesley Frost Ballantine. Reprinted by arrangement with Henry Holt and Company, LLC.
   Excerpt from "Living Like Weasels" from *Teaching a Stone to Talk: Expeditions and Encounters* by Annie Dillard. Copyright 1982 by Annie Dillard. Reprinted by permission of HarperCollins Publishers.
   Excerpt from "The Shore and the Sea" from *Further Fables for Our Time* by James Thurber. Copyright 1956 by Rosemary A. Thurber. Reprinted by arrangement with Rosemary A. Thurber and The Barbara Hogenson Agency. All rights reserved.
   The poem "Running America" was written in Marshall Ulrich's honor by Joanne Gabbin, Ph.D, director of the Furious Flower Poetry Center at James Madison University in Harrisonburg, Virginia. Copyright 2009 by Joanne V. Gabbin. Reprinted with her permission.
   The guidelines for the world-record attempt (fastest crossing of the United States on foot) have been provided courtesy Guinness World Records Limited.

Most Avery books are available at special quantity discounts for bulk purchase for sales promotions, premiums, fund-raising, and educational needs. Special books or book excerpts also can be created to fit specific needs. For details, write Penguin Group (USA) Inc. Special Markets, 375 Hudson Street, New York, NY 10014.

Library of Congress Cataloging-in-Publication Data
Ulrich, Marshall.
Running on empty: an ultramarathoner's story of love, loss, and a record-setting run across America / Marshall Ulrich.
   p.   cm.
ISBN 978-1-58333-423-2
1. Ulrich, Marshall.   2. Long-distance runners—United States—Biography.   3. Long-distance running—United States.
I. Title.
GV1061.15.U47A3   2011   2010044849
796.42092—dc22
[B]

Printed in the United States of America
10   9   8   7   6   5   4   3   2

BOOK DESIGN BY NICOLE LAROCHE

A portion of the proceeds from the sale of this book will go to support the Religious Teachers Filippini, a not-for-profit humanitarian organization devoted to empowering women and children around the world.

Penguin is committed to publishing works of quality and integrity.
In that spirit, we are proud to offer this book to our readers;
however, the story, the experiences, and the words
are the author's alone.

To Mom, who let me dream

Dad, who taught me discipline

Rory, my biggest fan

and Heather, who held me up

Contents

PART III
Liberty

Foreword

Marsh, honey, you're running in your sleep again. Rest, sweetheart.

—Heather Ulrich, late one night during
Marshall's dramatic race across America

The problem with the best Marshall Ulrich stories is that you never seem to hear them from Marshall Ulrich. He's one of America's greatest living adventurers and an expert without peer in human endurance, yet most Ulrich lore is passed along only by spoken word, making him a hero in other people's Greatest Hits collections and a figure who comes across less like a real human and more like a mythological creature who ferries drowning men to shore before vanishing back into the sea. Travel around the Rocky Mountains or Death Valley at the right time of year—the right time, of course, being 4:00 a.m. in a hailstorm or high noon on a 120-degree day—and you'll find endurance daredevils testing themselves against tales like these:

"You know the Pikes Peak Marathon? Thirteen miles straight up the side of a 14,000-foot mountain and thirteen miles back down again. You can't do Pikes *and* the Leadville Trail 100 in the same year when they're both on the same weekend, because you'd never be able to complete the hundred and then get to Colorado Springs in time, much less do the mar-

athon. Then one summer, just as they're counting down for the start at
Pikes, a Datsun comes roaring up and screeches to a stop. This guy
comes tumbling out, all caked in trail dust and grime. He jumps into the
race just as the gun booms. Marshall had finished the hundred-mile
Leadville race in under twenty-four hours, then floored the three-hour
drive to Colorado Springs because the race director was a buddy of his.
No one else has ever done it. I don't think anyone else has even *tried*."

"Know how Marsh spent his fiftieth birthday? Raising money for orphans by running across Death Valley—four times *in a row*. That's nearly
six hundred miles, back and forth across the hottest place on earth and
up and down Mount Whitney. He challenged the course, both the desert
and the mountain, another time by stuffing his gear and water in a hot
dog cart so he could run across Death Valley alone."

My favorite is one I heard from Frank McKinney, a Florida real estate
developer with heavy-metal hair and an ocean-view treehouse for an
office. McKinney wasn't a runner—he preferred tennis, if anything—
and he knew nothing about mountains or desert heat. But he found out
about the Badwater Ultramarathon and got the idea that running 135
miles in awful desert heat would be kind of a kick. Somehow he got in,
so off he set on race day, trotting through the salt flats in his head-to-
toe sun whites. By mile seventy-five or so, McKinney had gotten the fun
smacked out of him; head spinning, muscles knotting, he was a panting
mess by the side of the road. He lay in the shade of his support team's
van, mustering the strength to get inside and head the hell home. He
wasn't just exhausted and overheated—he was *scared*. People die in Death
Valley all the time, their brains slowly convection-cooking inside their
skulls.

And that's when a shadow blocked out the sun. A man stood over him,
then squatted down. His voice was calm, quiet, lighthearted. He wasn't
trying to buck McKinney up so much as talk the race down. Not a big
deal, he told McKinney; get some water down your throat, maybe some

tapioca pudding, and then look around. Isn't this place awesome? How many other people get a chance to see this? We're a couple of lucky guys, you and I. . . . Did you finish that pudding? Good, try a banana. . . .

The year before, Marshall had come straight to Badwater after reaching the top of Mount Everest. Marshall had always wanted to make the climb, and the only window had opened before Badwater. Rather than choose between the challenges of a lifetime for anyone else, he'd once again decided to just live a little harder than anyone else. He knew the consequences: No matter who you are, you're half the man you were by the time you get down from Everest. You've lost at least one-third of your muscle mass, and count yourself lucky if you're not dehydrated, frostbitten, malnourished, and snow-blind. Somehow, Marshall had managed to hustle his muscle-depleted self off the Himalayas, and then, for good measure, he headed to Russia to reach the summit of Mount Elbrus before returning halfway around the globe to complete Badwater.

The year he met Frank McKinney was mild by Marshall's standards; all he'd done was complete the Seven Summits, including climbing Mount Vinson in Antarctica, before coming here to squat on 200-degree asphalt with some guy who really wished he'd go away.

Marshall chatted with McKinney for an hour. A full hour, in the middle of a race that he'd won four times and exactly at a time when he should have been worrying about title number five instead of teaching Badwater 101 to an inexperienced freshman. But it worked; bit by bit, McKinney began to feel better. He got to his feet and tested his legs. Not *totally* like wet newspaper. He began to shuffle, then jog, then run—and he kept going until he crossed the finish line more than a day later.

When I finally got the chance to ask Marshall about it, I had one question: "Why?" Every second you spend under the Death Valley sun increases your risk of ending up in the hospital with an emergency IV in your arm, and no one knew that better than Marshall. Once, he'd watched Lisa Smith-Batchen, the supertalented desert specialist and a former winner of a six-day race across the Sahara, get pulled from Badwater and rushed to the ER. So why was he risking his race—potentially, his *life*—for this guy?

Marshall didn't know. And that's when I discovered, absolutely by accident, the key to his superhuman strength: Marshall keeps going forward because there's no looking back. He kept running, adventure racing, and climbing because those activities demand movement in a single direction. Even in his sleep, as his wife would discover, Marshall can rest only if he's in motion. You can answer *why* only with a look in the rearview mirror, and those were two things—rear views and mirrors—that Marshall absolutely did not deal with.

That's how it was when I met him in 2005. I'd had the spectacular luck to attend a running camp in Idaho's Grand Tetons organized by Marshall and Lisa. He was awe-inspiring: kind, funny, happy-go-lucky, insightful, a sharp mind with a keen biomechanical eye. Two of the greatest gifts you can give an endurance athlete are the chance to run with Marshall Ulrich and the chance to pick his brain, and I was delighted to get one because I knew the other was off the market.

And then, something happened. After almost thirty years of keeping his eyes drilled forward and his thoughts to himself, Marshall woke up. He realized, with one of those bursts of clarity that are so frightening that you hope you never have one again, what had happened to him. All those stories he'd spent a lifetime avoiding were locking together into a tragically disturbing pattern. *If only he'd realized it before . . .*

So what was it? What was it that brought Marshall Ulrich back to the world, and what has happened since then? Ordinarily, you'd have to wait for the story to pass from mouth to mouth, making the rounds of the rumor circuit. But now, for the first time, Marshall can tell you for himself.

CHRISTOPHER McDOUGALL

author of *Born to Run*

Prologue

Born on the fourth of July, I was always suitably independent. Stubborn, too, and competitive. By the age of ten, I'd already figured out that when my older brother and I got into trouble, whomever Dad caught first was going to get it the worst. If I could outrun Steve, sometimes I could avoid a lickin' altogether. Dad's legs weren't in the best shape—he'd fought in World War II and still suffered the effects of injuries he'd sustained at the Battle of the Bulge—and I was usually way out in front of both of them, racing across the fields at top speed. Sorry, Steve.

My family lived in a simple ranch-style house in the middle of an eighty-acre dairy farm near Kersey, Colorado. We kept a herd of about sixty cows and grew corn and alfalfa to feed them. Mom, Dad, my sister, Lonna, Steve, and I all worked to keep things going, but my brother and I were constant companions, laboring together in the fields and at the barn from the time we were big enough to wield pitchforks. At the ripe old age of eight, I taught myself to drive a tractor when Dad wasn't looking, and after that, Steve and I were in business. Three or four times a year, the alfalfa had to be cut, dried, baled, loaded onto a "sled" we pulled behind the tractor, then stacked in the back of a truck. In our teen years, as we grew stronger, it was a badge of honor to be able to tell our parents what we'd accomplished in a day. All on our own we could, for example, put up more than two thousand square bales—that's a couple hundred bales, at seventy pounds each, per hour. It was hard but gratifying labor, and although our parents didn't materially reward us for it, we certainly felt their approval.

Sometimes it was fun, too. Steve and I made most chores into a contest: "Who can bale and stack the most hay today? Ready, set, go!" He almost always beat me at this, which I hope in some way compensates for all the punishment he took on my behalf.

We worked seven days a week, before and after school, and all day Saturday, but Sunday afternoons were my own. My comic books, sketchpad, and adventure novels kept me company on the back porch, my refuge year-round, even in winter when it wasn't heated. Engrossed in a tale like *The Call of the Wild*, I could feel the chill and indulge myself in the fantasy of being Buck, the noble sled dog, braving the frigid Yukon. I also loved to draw, especially my comic book heroes as they performed superhuman feats, and Mom always encouraged these interests—reading and art—by keeping me in good supply of books and pencils and paper.

The fictional stories fired my imagination, while TV coverage of the true-life exploits of the early Everest mountaineers made me want to test my farm-hardened strength against the natural world. I was two years old in 1953 when Edmund Hillary and Tenzing Norgay ascended the 29,035 feet, the first men to reach the top and come back alive. Before my adolescence, more than a dozen summiteers had conquered Mount Everest, and many, many more have done it since. Not without paying a price, however. Images of their hands, so dramatic on our black-and-white television's screen, fascinated me: Nails and knuckles swollen and darkened by severe frostbite, they had clawed their way down the mountainside as the wind blew, sounding an unyielding, eerie, and violent noise. Indeed, many climbers returned with fingers and toes frozen off, sacrificed to the gods of great adventure on the highest mountain on earth. Clearly, not just anyone would do this, but it was equally evident to my young eyes that it could be done. Besides, Mom was always telling us kids that we could accomplish *anything*. At five years old, I'd already decided that I wanted to climb mountains. Someday, I'd be one of the elevated few, keeping company with those exceptional people who brave the elements, tough it out, go the distance. Someday, I'd be a man who, as Jack London put it, "sounds the deeps of his nature."

Yet the demands of the farm kept me in the here and now. There was *always* work to be done. Crops to be tended, harvested, stored. Cows to be milked, fed, moved. Sheds to be cleaned and filled with straw. Machinery to be maintained, fixed, and, on incredibly rare occasions, junked. Dad, a real no-nonsense businessman in addition to being a farmer, was loath to throw anything away or buy anything new. The one time we told him about our neighbors' suggestion that we get a new conveyor chain for the manure spreader, because they replaced theirs every couple of years and never had trouble with breakdowns, he looked at us like we'd lost our minds. His stern expression said it all: "You boys get on out there and use the links I bought you to fix that chain we've got."

When I graduated from high school, in 1969, no one was surprised that I'd achieved less than a 2.0 grade-point average. Homework had always been a low priority, somewhere between visits to the barbershop and cleaning my room. In other words, I rarely studied, and my results reflected my schoolwork ethic.

That August, a month after my eighteenth birthday, a dairy farm much larger than ours was home to the Woodstock Festival in New York. No, I didn't attend, but I was well aware that we were in an era of free love and draft cards. By then I was seeing Jean Schmid, a girl I'd met a couple of years earlier on a blind date at a church hayride, and we'd go into Boulder to listen to the Freddie Henchie Band and gawk at all the hippies on "The Hill," which was Colorado's answer to Haight-Ashbury.

Jean and I had fallen in love quickly, proving that opposites attract: She was as socially outgoing as I was shy. She had a crackerjack mind, hazel eyes, and an infectious laugh. She also knew what she wanted, enjoyed a joke, and was nurturing in a way I'd never experienced—all traits I found irresistible. A slight young woman at four feet, eleven inches and eighty-seven pounds, she'd climbed onto my lap on our second date and started making out with me, letting me know exactly how she felt. I was completely taken with her, and by the time we were seventeen, I knew I wanted to spend the rest of my life with Jean.

A few years later, after I'd done my time in a junior college, and put in a year of basic training with the Air National Guard, she agreed to marry me. She transferred to the University of Northern Colorado in Greeley, where she continued to study journalism and I went into the fine arts program. In June 1974, we received our diplomas, tied the knot, and started my first business, all in the same week.

Although I'd spent the last few years working on weaving, sculpture, and painting, I'd decided to go into the family business, and opened a rendering plant. Buying cattle carcasses and processing the dead animals to make dog food, I jokingly referred to myself as a "used cow dealer."

Because I was so busy with the new operation and Jean was pursuing a law degree, we put off having children for a while, but as soon as she had that locked up, we were ready. In fact, Jean sat for the bar when she was eight months pregnant, and as expected, she handily passed the exam.

Life seemed full of promise. Both of us had worked hard for what we'd achieved, and with a baby on the way we felt as if we had everything we'd ever hoped for. In 1979, after twelve hours of labor, Jean gave birth to our daughter by cesarean section. It was considered unorthodox at the time, but I was allowed in the operating room when the doctors pulled our girl, healthy and squalling, from her mother's womb, and I took many, many photographs of the birth. Calling such a moment miraculous hardly describes the joy and intimacy of it, but that's what it seemed to us. Our parents, siblings, and friends came by to celebrate our baby daughter, Elaine, the first grandchild for both sides of the family. I was sure life couldn't get any better, and I was right. Everything was perfect.

A year later, just after we'd bought our first house and little Elaine was starting to toddle around the yard, we got the devastating news: Jean had invasive breast cancer, which had already spread to her lymph nodes. Telling us about it, the doctor tried to remain professionally detached but was visibly rattled by what he'd seen on the mammography films. He scheduled Jean for surgery immediately, and within just a couple of days, she underwent a double mastectomy. By the week's end she began chemotherapy.

During Jean's first treatment, she made small talk with the chemo-therapist and mentioned that we were looking forward to having more children; little ones make life so rich, take you outside yourself, and help you to keep things in perspective—they even make trials like this one bearable. Tending to her IV, the doctor offhandedly told her we should wait. Well, of course, we'd hold off until Jean was feeling better . . . No, that's not what he meant. He explained that he didn't know if she'd be around to raise them. That stunned and silenced her, and I could imagine what she was thinking: Would she live to see Elaine get out of diapers, much less become an adult?

We were both quiet during the seventy-mile drive back home from the hospital. Neither of us could say it out loud: We might never have another child, and Elaine might grow up without a mother. *Jean might die.* What we'd heard in that sterile room overwhelmed my wife; although she'd known, on some level, that her cancer could be deadly, she hadn't really accepted that fact until she realized that her future as a mother was threatened. The realization knocked Jean off-kilter for a few days, but she eventually regained her footing, deciding that what she needed to do was take this one step at a time, try to get well, and then we'd figure out what to do next. Everything had become incomprehensibly complex.

After Jean healed from the surgery, our lives changed, but not as drastically as you might expect. We kept up our normal routine as much as possible: Jean went to her office and continued to practice law five days a week. I took Elaine with me to Fort Morgan early every morning, left her with a friend, and then put in a long day at the rendering plant. Sometime around six or seven o'clock, I'd pick up Elaine and head back to our house; occasionally, I'd stay later than that and Jean would get Elaine, or I'd go back to the plant in the middle of the night, depending on my workload. Jean never brought work home, so she could focus her attention on the family, and was always eager to have our daughter back in her arms. We dealt with this crisis by compartmentalizing: There was home, work, and the medical merry-go-round—which we desperately hoped would solve this problem for us. We tried to keep it all as separate as possible, acting as if everything would be okay if we kept moving forward, just as Jean had resolved, taking one step at a time.

She was a trouper, although it's true what they say about cancer: Sometimes the treatment is as awful as any illness might be. Jean lost both of her breasts and some tissue under her arms to the radical mastectomy, and then her hair fell out from the chemotherapy. She was often weak, nauseated, and off balance, and she had no appetite, so she dropped weight, yet she was puffy from taking prednisone. She worried about what I thought of her appearance. Honestly, I couldn't have cared less about that and was simply grateful to have her home with us, no matter how much this cruel disease might change her. It did make me sad and angry that cancer could attack my wife so viciously, so senselessly, and there was nothing I could do to stop it.

Jean was mad, too. "Why me? I don't smoke or drink. What have I ever done to bring this on myself?"

Staring blankly, I was completely incapable of answering her, but I could empathize. "I understand. I'd be furious if it was me."

And what if it *was* me . . . next? I couldn't help wondering. Her illness made me acknowledge my own mortality, along with my powerlessness and the vulnerability of everyone around me. If this could happen to Jean, such a good person, so smart and loving and health conscious, who was safe? What about Elaine? Could I really protect anyone I loved?

Once, when Jean went to the hospital for a spinal biopsy, a long procedure that involved an intimidating surgical drilling device and a lot of waiting, a nurse took my blood pressure to kill some time. She deftly avoided telling me my results but talked with Jean about it later. The numbers were through the roof, something like 160/110. My wife urged me to see our family physician.

The doc confirmed my hypertension and had one piece of advice: cardiovascular exercise. The problem was stress-induced, as my blood pressure had been rock solid until then. I was extremely fit from my work at the rendering plant and from my fairly recent foray into salt-curing hides, demanding physical work that had given us the money we needed to put Jean through law school. At five feet, nine inches and 148 pounds, I was lean and muscular, but the pressures of my personal life were squeezing my heart.

My brother Steve liked to run and would enter a few races here and there. Jean's boss at the law firm was a runner, too, and he encouraged me to get outside and blow off some steam.

"It'll do you good."

So I pulled on a pair of low-top canvas Converse shoes I'd had since I was thirteen, and I stepped out the front door of our house to go on my first jog. No music to accompany me, of course; this was 1980. (Not even an early-model Walkman, as Sony hadn't introduced portable cassette players to U.S. markets yet.) I listened to the sound of my breath, pulling hard through my mouth, my jaw tight. As I picked up the pace, my heart pounding, I wondered why the hell any adult would run if he didn't have to. I didn't like that feeling of gasping for air, my leg muscles straining, my feet slapping the pavement until I turned off the road and into the woods, where at least the ground was softer. I ran a couple of miles.

The next day I was sore and uninterested in ever doing that again.

But I did do it again, of course. I took a break for one day, and then I got back out there because I knew I had to. After a week of off-and-on "training," I entered my first race, the Fort Morgan Times 5K, and got done in just over twenty minutes—once again ahead of Steve, who was unamused. At the finish, I congratulated him, and he gave me a dead-eyed stare, then walked away into the crowd of runners, distraught. Soon after that, he quit running altogether, for which I sort of blame myself.

Running provided an excellent distraction from my life, which was filled with the stress of my business, my little girl's confusion about what was happening to her mom, doctor's appointments, and the looming threat of death, coupled with the effort of maintaining my denial. While running, I could focus on something else: It provided mental relief and emotional release, an escape into physical effort. Sometimes, the real world would catch up with me, and I'd duck behind a bush and allow myself to indulge in sorrow and self-pity, crying openly, something I never did at home. But most of the time, I kept plugging along, fantasizing about something completely unrelated to my existence at the moment. In my mind, I explored other continents, scaled Everest, trod the jungles of Borneo and the Australian outback, paddled the rivers of Patagonia.

In short order, the regular cardiovascular exercise worked to bring my blood pressure down and keep it in check. Nearly every day started with an early-morning run, which I finished by about 6:30 a.m. so that I could get back to the house for Elaine and then on to work for the day. It was also good for me to be able to go off on my own, both physically and mentally, whenever I'd reached my emotional limits. When I'd feel as if I was going to break down in front of Jean, who I believed needed me to be unfailingly positive and strong, I'd head out for a run, where I could think about her, admit my sadness, let the tears flow, dwell on something else for a while, and then come back to the house in better shape to care for my wife and child. I felt guilty about spending time away from my family, but I also knew I was literally running for my life.

Jean's treatments seemed to do the trick, at least for a while. But less than a year after her surgery, the cancer returned with a vengeance, and she stopped working as the disease consumed her body. She sought comfort in being with family and friends, spent time reading the Bible. Her doctors tried an experimental treatment that brought her white blood cell count down to dangerous levels, leaving her susceptible to infection. Any visitors had to wear face masks, and Elaine was banned from the room. Many times before, though, when Jean had been in the hospital and in better health, Elaine had played on the white bed, chattering and singing and showering her mother with kisses. Now, when I had to come alone, the pleasant distraction was gone and the disease became more present, the nearness of Jean's death more real. At these times, we'd talk about Elaine's future, and what we wanted for her. During one of these hospital-room discussions, Jean asked me to promise that I'd secure a place for Elaine at a college on the East Coast, where Jean imagined she would have gone had she not decided to put our romance and then our family first. (Not that she had any regrets, she assured me. She wanted Elaine to have opportunities she might have pursued herself.) She especially liked Wellesley College, a school she believed would help our daughter become the kind of person we both aspired to raise: an educated, self-possessed, strong woman with a dedication to and passion for her life's work. Of course, I promised Jean I would do all I could, though I insisted she'd be around to do it herself.

It had become obvious that Jean was dying, but I couldn't confront that reality. I sought solace in increasing distances and thinking about faraway places. The mounting mileage was intimidating but exhilarating, and on race days, I was regularly finishing in the top 5 or 10 percent. As the distances grew, I spent even less time at home. I ran until I was emptied out, and then I ran some more. Until I could come back to my wife and not start screaming or crying or explode into a million pieces at the sight of what the cancer was doing to her.

Jean was supportive, as she could see that this outlet was becoming increasingly important to me, giving me a way to cope. In June 1981, I competed in an especially tough race, a 14.5-mile slog on the highest paved road in the United States, running up nearly four thousand vertical feet—my first attack on serious elevation gain—and Jean came out to cheer me at the finish. Atop Mount Evans at 14,264 feet and weak from a recent chemotherapy treatment, she still jumped up and down, excited for my achievement; I'd earned the Mount Evans Trophy Run prize for those of us who finished in the top 10 percent, a chunk of rock with a plaque commemorating the effort. Seeing her this way was incredible: It looked to me as if she'd finished America's highest road race herself. In those moments, she was vibrant, happy for me, alive.

There was one day, though, when Jean lay in her bed at home in a darkened room, battered and exhausted from all that the disease was doing to her. The gloomy scene made me claustrophobic: my wife wasting away in a lightless cavern.

I wanted to run and told her so.

"How can you leave me right now? How can you be so callous? I need you. I'm so tired. Please stay."

I have to run.

"Don't go! Please. God, I'm so alone . . ."

I looked at her, desperate to go.

"Marshall."

I left.

I did: I ran, and I still regret it. I never could admit and talk honestly about my own fear of being left alone, without her, although both of us knew how sick she was. I'm embarrassed to admit that the one time she asked me, straight out, if I thought she was going to die, I couldn't bring myself to say yes.

"No." It felt like a betrayal, but I lied to her anyway, and I tried to lie to myself.

The cancer metastasized to her brain and crossed her eyes, then ravaged her lungs, her bones, and finally her liver. In November 1981, when the doctors said there was nothing more they could do, we took Jean home to her parents' place in Greeley, where we stayed for a couple of weeks, her pain mitigated by morphine shots a hospice nurse taught me to give her. One night I carried her into bed, and we lay down together for the last time. At about one o'clock in the morning, I heard an unearthly gasp as my thirty-year-old wife took her last breath.

In the days after, our family surrounded Elaine and me. I never talked with anyone about it, but my mind was racked with despair and fear: *Why did this happen to Jean? What am I supposed to do now? How will I take care of Elaine by myself? Will I be the next to die? Is life even worth living?* Although I agonized in private, it was clear to everyone around me that I felt lost and was struggling to feel whole again. In the last couple of weeks, I'd dropped ten pounds, and I looked gaunt. With a sunken chest, a collapsed face, and an eerie emptiness in my eyes, I must have appeared a shrunken shadow of my former self.

Ever the practical person, my mom counseled me to move on. It's time to get on with your life, son. Put away your tears. Be a man. Stand on your own two feet. Depend upon yourself. What you need to do is get back to work.

So that's what I did.

PART I
Desert

They cannot scare me with their empty spaces . . .
I have it in me so much nearer home
To scare myself with my own desert places.

—Robert Frost, "Desert Places"

1.

As Far As I Can, As Fast As I Can

During the two years that our family lived with Jean's cancer, the 5Ks became 10Ks, which became ten- and thirteen-milers, and then I graduated to mountain races and marathons. After my wife died, I pushed beyond these distances to elite courses and ultrarunning races. They were the most punishing, and they made me feel the most alive.

Hills became my proving ground, and although I had yet to realize my dream of climbing Mount Everest, I conquered more modest elevations. As a boy in Greeley, Colorado, I'd looked longingly at the Rocky Mountains from the valley of our family farm, and in my thirties I was finally exploring them, running on the local territory and running over my own persistent sense of loss. I missed Jean, and my life after her was lonely despite my attempts to rebuild it.

In 1982, I remarried, and I also ran my first Pikes Peak Marathon in the front range of those mountains, completing the prestigious race in 5:40:37. It was a respectable time, and I felt honored to have competed in one of the oldest marathons in the country, severe in both elevation and terrain. Established in 1956, it began as a challenge between three smokers and ten nonsmokers. None of the smokers finished the course. Adding to its colorful history, in '59, Arlene Pieper ran the Pikes Peak race, making it the first U.S. marathon venue ever to host a woman, and she became the first woman ever to complete such a race.

I felt an urgency to accomplish as much as I could as quickly as possible, to not put off the pursuit of any goal. Who knew how long I'd be around? I needed to hurry up and get things done. I adopted a new motto: "As far as I can, as fast as I can." It's how I articulated my mixed feelings from having faced death: the impulse to make the most of every minute and the fear that my time could run out any day. It didn't matter that I was healthy, loved my wife and daughter, and owned a flourishing business. I needed to do more, as much as I could, *now*.

So as soon as I'd succeeded at Pikes Peak, I was looking for the next big challenge. Ramping up my daily mileage, I prepared for greater distances. Sixty to eighty training miles per week, and less than a year later, I ran my first ultra, the Rocky Mountain 50, a hilly fifty-mile course on dirt and gravel roads from Laramie to Cheyenne, Wyoming, and finished with fifth place in 7:51:53. Having given it my all and feeling completely wrung out at the end, I thought I'd completed the ultimate endurance race.

Just a few months later, my son, Taylor, was born. Life goes on, yes? And nothing affirms it as joyfully as the healthy yell of a newborn. With my family growing, I had every reason to spend more time at home and no real excuse for taking on bigger challenges. Yet I kept up my rigorous running schedule, continuing my early-morning training year-round, racing in local 10Ks whenever they were on (most weekends) and in half-marathons and marathons during the fall and spring.

My motto manifested itself not just in my running but also in my pursuit of material success. I invested in a car wash in New York and bought a condo in Steamboat Springs because they came at a good price. And I continued to work long hours, expanding our family business into

Nebraska. I went to the plant six days a week, pushing to be the best and take down the competition with an unparalleled work ethic. Year by year, we picked off the other local rendering operations by giving better service. We were the first in our area to pay for the remains we hauled away, and I was one of the few "dead truck" drivers around who didn't insist that the farmers pull their animals out of the corral. I'd drive right through the open gate, engage my winch, secure my load, and then go on to my next stop quickly, if I was lucky enough not to get stuck in the mud and manure on my way out.

The costs of my amateur athletics could easily have outstripped my professional profits—if I'd taken time off from work, flown to events around the country, stayed in nice hotels, and paid for other luxuries—but I've always been frugal by nature, and kept a keen eye on the bottom line of both ventures. I'd drive to races relatively close to home, sleep in my car if necessary, and always make it back in time to start the work-week. There was a price, though, and my family picked up the tab. They had a good provider, a man who took his responsibilities and commitments seriously. What they didn't have was a husband and father who made being at home with them a priority.

Although it wasn't a conscious decision, I kept my distance.

Sometime in 1987, I was reading an article in *Runner's World* by George Sheehan that described a monster of a California trail race, the hundred-mile Western States Endurance Run, and I was completely taken aback. Wait. What? People run a hundred miles in a race? How had I never heard about this before? It was probably because ultramarathoners didn't bother with publicity back then; they were a bunch of guys (mostly) who were willing to go insane distances and didn't care if anyone else knew about it. The accomplishment was the thing. There wasn't big prize money, or stadiums of adoring fans, or even an ultrarunner's club—

just bragging rights whenever you made it to the finish. George Sheehan wrote about the silver belt buckle that served as the sole prize for completing the Western States 100 in under twenty-four hours, the outrageously beautiful and brutal landscape of the Sierra Nevada Mountains, the small number of participants, and the sometimes eccentric personalities of the competitors. I wanted in.

Without consulting the family, and now considering myself in training for the Western States, I started looking for a relatively flat course where I could push beyond my fifty-mile distance before taking on the greater challenge of the California race, which was coming up in June 1988. It just so happened there was an appropriate event in New York. Score! I had to visit the state anyway, to check on the car wash and meet with my partner there. I signed up for the twenty-four-hour run in Buffalo, which would be held in a park on a one-mile bike path loop, during which participants would circle the course as many times as they could in the time allotted.

So, at the age of thirty-six, I set my sights on running at least one hundred miles in twenty-four hours. The math seemed solid: If I could average just under fifteen minutes per mile, I'd achieve my goal. I had no reason to believe I could pull it off—I'd never run that far or that long—but I felt confident: Just as Mom had taught us kids, I believed I could do anything if I applied myself. Knowing nothing about training for this distance, I figured I'd ramp up my mileage bit by bit. So I increased to eight miles every morning with a twenty- or thirty-mile run on the weekends. As presumptuous as it sounds, I have to admit that I never questioned myself in this, never asked myself if I should try.

Why *not* do it?

Sure, I was scared, but I didn't let myself think about that until I was standing at the starting line, and then it hit me: *Oh, shit. What have I gotten myself into?* But by then it was too late to turn back, and soon after the gun went off, the jitters fell away, and my practiced focus and concentration kicked in. To my great surprise, I completed 122 miles, won the race, and set a course record.

Even more confident than before, I ran the Western States 100 for the first time just a month later. Two months after that, I completed my first Leadville Trail 100 in Colorado, and a month after that won a silver medal at the U.S.A. 24-Hour Run Championship with a finishing distance of over 133 miles.

Totally unexpected: I had a natural talent for these extreme distances. When others slowed down, I held steady, even sped up. I could take the discomfort of running hour after hour, beyond soreness and fatigue and even pain. Sometimes, I'd run negative splits—come back faster than I went out—so I could catch up to and keep pace with 2:30 and 2:40 marathoners at the tail end of races over fifty miles. My iron gut was suited to these tests, too. I was able to eat on the go, get the calories I needed, and keep on running. It's not uncommon for people to throw up what they've just eaten because their systems are too delicate to ingest, digest, and exert energy at the same time. But I was able to keep anything down, metabolize it, and burn that fuel efficiently until the end of the course. Mentally, I'd been prepared by my upbringing to work hard until the job was done, no matter how long it took. My mother had insisted to all us kids that we always hold our heads high, keep our backs straight, move with assurance; it says something about a person, how he carries himself. All good lessons for running, besides. A stickler for form, I trained my body to become more and more efficient in the sport, conserving energy and covering the ground economically. Even if injured, I did my damnedest not to alter my stride, never hung my head or slouched forward. Giving in to the pain would mean breaking form and potentially creating a secondary problem, so I steeled myself against it.

On I ran, racking up some first-place wins at elite races, earning more medals, setting more records. I ate hills for breakfast. I learned how to deal with the mental torture of great distances, how to compartmentalize my physical anguish across the miles, how to push through the injuries and exhaustion, how to strategize my races and overcome my opponents. Running, I invited pain, embraced it, made it my own.

Not long before my third child, Alexandra, was born in 1990, I discovered the notorious Badwater Ultramarathon, which *National Geographic* has ranked as the toughest footrace in the world. The magazine called it that because of the desert's scorching temperatures (up to 130 degrees Fahrenheit), drastic changes in elevation on the course (from 282 feet below sea level at the start to the top of Whitney at 14,496 feet), and the extreme distance. That July, the first time I ran it, the race was 146 miles from the lowest point in the Western Hemisphere to the highest point in the contiguous United States. (They've shortened the course to 135 miles since then, and it now stops at the Whitney Portal, at 8,360 feet.) The next year, in 1991, the same month I turned forty, I set the 146-mile course record to the top of Whitney, which at the time of this printing still stands as the fastest.

After three more Badwater wins, I got creative. In addition to the organized ultrarunning races, I started inventing extreme challenges that no one had ever attempted before. It was my way of making a personal statement, of adding something significant and unique to the sport. I felt that I'd mastered "conventional" ultrarunning and was ready to break previously conceived barriers, to prove that the body—even a middle-aged one—could go farther and recover faster than anyone else had thought.

So I devised combination challenges no one had ever tried before and few others were likely to attempt after me. Running the Pikes Peak Marathon four times in a row. Doing the Leadville Trail 100 and Pikes Peak Marathon in the same weekend. Completing the Badwater solo, self-contained and unaided, hauling my water, food, clothing, and medical supplies in a cart that weighed more than two hundred pounds.

All these unusual accomplishments garnered recognition from others in the ultrarunning world; the invitational Badwater, in particular, became a kind of homecoming for me every year. Early on it was just about a dozen runners who'd show up, and each time about half came back from prior years, and there were always more, a growing number of us ready to kick up some dust across Death Valley, to test ourselves against uncompromising desert heat, extreme elevation changes, and the punishing distance. I found friends there, people driven by their own demons and dreams, men and women of extraordinary grit and drive and determination.

Despite my achievements in business and sports, my family life remained challenging, owing mostly to my unresolved grief and the ripple effects it caused in my marriage. Continuing to use my athletic endeavors as an escape and proving ground, I was convinced that the best way to prevent getting crushed by another tragedy was to achieve greater and greater self-sufficiency. I guarded against intimacy to protect myself from the pain of losing anyone I loved again. Ironically, though I suppose predictably, Danette and I divorced when I was in my early forties. Elaine and I moved out, and a joint custody arrangement dictated that Taylor and Ali lived with their mom but stayed overnight with me every other weekend.

In 1995, I started adventure racing, participating in team expeditions that took me to remote jungles and deserts in Africa, Australia, and Asia, as well as here in the United States. Yes, I would finally explore the outback, paddle in Patagonia, trek the Himalayas, but my first experience with one of these multidisciplinary, multiday sporting events was an Eco-Challenge in Utah. Created by Mark Burnett, it required a five-person coed team, and by the time we were done, two other racers and I were calling ourselves "Team Stray Dogs." It turned out to be fitting; in adventure races we entered after that, we'd pick up one or two other elite athletes with the right skills and temperament to round out the group. These contests require diverse skills: some combination of endurance disciplines like trail running and hiking, climbing with fixed ropes, riding a bike (or a horse or a camel), swimming, and paddling, so you want teammates who are strong in the areas where you aren't.

Adventure racing provided opportunities for me to conquer old obstacles, particularly my fear of heights and water (not phobias, but definitely weaknesses), as well as a contrast to ultrarunning: with the team, it was better to be less intense, have a sense of humor, try to relax and enjoy what we were doing. I didn't train specifically for any of these events, and instead relied on my endurance and my team to carry me through whatever we might encounter, wherever we might go. As amazing as most of the locations turned out to be, these adventures weren't vacations in a traditional sense (and we sure as hell were *not* catered to in any way—think *Survivor* without the amenities), but they were about working together, having a good time, trying new things. The looser we were, the more we seemed to do well.

In time, when we started posting some respectable finishes in or near the top ten, Team Stray Dogs attracted a sports agent to represent us, which meant sponsorships. Early on, single-event entry fees started at about $15,000 per team, and during the late 1990s they steadily rose to about $25,000 per team. We were grateful to have corporate support from Pharmanex (a division of Nu Skin) for our Morocco and Patagonia adventures and later from DuPont, which underwrote numerous races and for which we tested clothing and fibers. Incidentally, there was no financial profit in it for us athletes—not that we cared, as we were doing what we loved on someone else's dime. But the agent made some good money, and the corporate sponsors got exposure when MTV, the Discovery Channel, USA Network, ESPN, or Nat Geo broadcast the Eco-Challenges or Raids Gauloises.

Altogether, the running and the adventure racing took me away from home and work three to six weeks out of the year, not an unreasonable amount of time, I thought. Still, training runs and local races that ranged from fifty kilometers to one hundred miles consumed most of my "downtime," leaving little for family or a social life. It was extremely rare for me to read a book, go to the movies, or watch TV. Today, it surprises me when I discover some sitcom of which I was completely unaware during the eighties. I still find "new" episodes of *Seinfeld* hilarious.

So I worked. I spent time with my kids. I ran. I raced. And I thought up new ways of torturing myself, wanting to do something each year that no one else had ever done before.

It felt as if 120-volt shocks probed my legs with every step. Arriving at the top of Towne's Pass in Death Valley National Park, I'd already been running for five days straight, more than three hundred miles across the desert floor and up Mount Whitney—and I still had over two hundred miles and another summit of Mount Whitney to go. People surrounded me, giving me advice. But I was in a fog, stumbling around in my own world with memories and voices from the past floating through the haze. Self-doubt clouded my mind: *I can't do it anymore. The pain is too much. I have to stop.*

In July 2001, in honor of my fiftieth birthday, I was attempting to complete the first-ever Badwater Quad: running the Death Valley course four times in a row, plus tacking on a few extra miles so I could climb the mountain twice. When I was done, it would be four crossings, 584 miles, and a total elevation change of 96,000 feet, essentially nonstop.

A little more than halfway through and after 130 hours, I was feeling completely used up, suffering from severe tendonitis. No wonder. During one course completion at Badwater, your feet strike the ground more than three hundred thousand times, absorbing the impact of four million pounds—the equivalent of hitting the pavement after falling three thousand feet, or being struck in a head-on collision with a jumbo jet. Ask around at your local running shop, and they'll tell you runner's tendonitis is a "typical overuse injury." Well, sure, I was in a state of overuse, but that's where ultrarunners live, in that place where you feel as if there's nothing left, no more energy, no more reason, no more sanity, no more will to go farther. Then you push forward anyway, step after step, even though every cell in your body tells you to stop. And you discover that you *can* go on.

At this time in my life, I was running on empty in a larger sense, too, still punishing myself, still trying to prove that I could survive just about anything, still trying to outrun my mortality. In the twenty years since Jean's death, I'd racked up a list of accomplishments as I'd strived to fulfill my definition of success and compensate for what I perceived as my personal shortcomings. Nearly all of my family relationships were strained. My dad, brother, and sister thought I was crazy for all the time I devoted to running, and they didn't like that it took me away from our business. Dad had loaned me start-up money, and since then Steve and Lonna had bought into the business and were working in Greeley while I took care of things in Fort Morgan, so they each had a vested interest and strong opinions. I'd married and divorced Danette, then done it all over again with another woman, and I considered all three of my marriages failures—I was alone, wasn't I? My relationship with Danette was tense, and my children (now eleven, eighteen, and twenty-three), resented all the time I'd spent away from them.

So, sure, I'd raced at all the major events, won some, and broken records. In my thirties, I'd discovered my talent for ultrarunning; in my forties, I'd taken it to another level with my creative extremes, and diversified with adventure racing; now, as I entered my fifties, I was something of a celebrity among endurance athletes. *Trail Runner* magazine would call me one of the legends of the trail, *Outside* would crown me "Endurance King," and *Adventure Sports* would highlight me as an athlete "Over Fifty and Kicking Your Butt."

Good for me. I was a badass.

At least my exploits had taught me ways to get myself through tough spots like the one I was experiencing on Towne's Pass, such as using my athletic pursuits to raise money for a charity I cared about, a religious order of sisters serving women and children. On that day, I pushed through the pain by reminding myself that I wasn't doing it only for me. My suffering had a purpose. Anyone who's walked or run a few miles to benefit a cause knows how motivating this can be. Just when you start to feel as if you have nothing left to give, you remember how difficult someone else's life is, and you can keep going. Perspective does wonders. (I love this sign, spotted at a marathon to benefit cancer research: "Blisters don't require chemo.") So I strapped a bag of ice onto each shin and slogged it out for the final 232 miles, my legs the center of my universe, tormenting me for the next five days, all the way to the finish.

Badwater Quad, check. Now just a couple of goals nagged at me still, like some kind of extreme bucket list. Before I departed this earth, I wanted to climb Mount Everest and realize my boyhood dream. And I had this other ambition to run across the United States, something I considered the ultimate ultra: more than three thousand miles from shore to shore, across all kinds of terrain. It would be the run of a lifetime, the most extreme challenge I'd ever attempted. In the same way I'd thrilled to the early stories of the Everest mountaineers, I found the travails of those who'd managed to cross our country on foot completely riveting. I wanted to experience all of that for myself, firsthand.

The month after my Badwater Quad, I was still so burnt from it that I couldn't compete in that year's Leadville Trail 100, so I was happy to help a friend get the job done. When I first started ultrarunning, there were no coaches, no experts, no manuals, no playbooks. Sometimes, there wasn't even a marked course—you just had to get yourself from point A to point B, from starting line to finish line, however you saw fit to go. Forget frequent water stations and cheering onlookers. Ultrarunning is all about going it alone—or, if you're smart, you might draft a friend or two to pace you by running alongside you, or to "crew" you by providing first aid or any other assistance you might need, from blister care to icing you down. When you're out in the middle of nowhere, with runners miles apart and covering extreme distances on trails few other folks ever get the chance to see, it's an advantage to have someone else with you, ideally someone with endurance and experience.

Although by 2001 the Leadville race had become more organized, Theresa Daus-Weber had asked me to crew and then pace her back over Sugar Loaf Pass because of my wealth of experience on the Leadville course. Waiting for her to arrive at an aid station, I met Theresa's friend, Heather Vose, who introduced herself and her dog. While Ripley sniffed me out, Heather told me she'd gotten to know Theresa at their place of work, an environmental consulting firm in Denver. She'd come out to watch Theresa and was curious about "this ultrarunning thing," which she'd heard of only recently.

Smart and sexy, Heather intrigued me. She was also younger than I, at least ten years my junior if I guessed right. Maybe more. *Does it matter?* Over the next fifteen hours of the race, I thought about that. And her. A lot. So I was pleased when I saw Heather again as Theresa crossed the finish line, making her one of only two women who've completed the course eleven times. Heather and I quietly celebrated our friend's victory, and I found myself growing more and more attracted to her. What an extraordinary woman!

Years ago, I'd decided I wasn't marriage material: With my track record, I didn't want to subject any more women to being tied to me that way. But who'd said anything about marriage? I just wanted to talk to Heather again. Sadly, I anticipated I'd never get the chance. As we said our good-byes, I hugged her and kissed her lightly on the cheek.

After the race, though, Heather and I exchanged some e-mail messages, and a few months later, I joined her, Theresa, and another friend for Christmas dinner in the mountains near Leadville. We went snow-shoeing, shared some laughs, and told stories while Heather and I checked each other out surreptitiously. At the end of the day, I drove Heather home, we stood on her doorstep, and feeling uncharacteristically bold, I took her in my arms for our first kiss. As she returned my embrace, Heather's snowshoes clattered to the ground, and that was the beginning of our romance.

In April, Heather asked if she could move in with me; we were spending so much time together that it just made sense. I hadn't expected to be ready for something like that so soon in our relationship, or ever—hell, I was fifty and set in my ways—but this straightforward, passionate woman brought out feelings long dormant in me, and I agreed, happy to have her near.

A month later, she kissed me good-bye when I left to embark on my first mountaineering experience. Sometime before, professional mountaineer Gary Scott had called me after reading an article in *Outside* magazine that mentioned my desire to scale Mount Everest. We'd never met, but he was interested in helping me gain some experience, and he advised me that although I was already skilled with some climbing from my adventure racing, I'd better go up a few seriously big mountains before attempting Everest. He'd be happy to guide me, he said, and then suggested we put together a team to climb Denali; at just over 20,000 feet in elevation, it's the highest peak in North America, the perfect place to start my training, and we could do this expedition inexpensively. Great! As usual, I'd lucked into the cheapest way possible to try something new. I contacted some friends I knew from adventure racing, Charlie Engle and Tony DiZinno, and Gary contacted a young man with some mountaineering experience, Aron Ralston. We got sponsors, too, who gave us backpacks and climbing gear, and Gary led us to the top. When I handled the altitude well, it gave me the confidence I needed to climb Aconcagua, the highest peak in South America, less than a year after that. I was on my way to Everest, mountain by mountain, now determined to climb all Seven Summits.

In another year, I'd changed my mind completely about getting married again, and on Christmas Day in 2002, I gave Heather a stuffed moose with an engagement ring hung on a gold chain around its neck. At first, she thought the moose was all there was to it, but then she noticed the ring and I made my proposal. To my relief and excitement, she said yes. With a wink at my checkered romantic past, we exchanged our vows on April Fools' Day, 2003, and enjoyed a delayed honeymoon trip to Africa in July, where we summited Kilimanjaro together. I'd found a partner in her, a woman who loved me in spite of my flaws and who was even willing to join me in a few of my obsessions. We'd both entered this relationship with serious misgivings, but by the time we were standing on that mountaintop together, we'd let the walls down. I'd come to understand what made her who she was, and what she'd been through in her own life, and I'd shared my own story. She'd already convinced me that I wasn't unfit to be her husband, and was helping me to finally deal with my grief over Jean's death and my shortcomings as a father. Through my guilt and regret and other messy feelings, she was undeterred. She'd become emotional ballast for me, my refuge and my rock.

A year after our summit of Kilimanjaro, I was making plans for us to climb Mount Elbrus, the highest peak in Europe, when I came across something startling, a website for "Everest 10000." *What's this?* Sitting at my computer, I read about a Russian adventure team, led by Alex Abramov, and its Everest expedition, which would cost me $10,000 (a bargain!) to join if they accepted me. I called Alex right away to express my enthusiasm, share my athletic résumé with him, and ask for a place on his team.

"One spot open, sure. You send money right away."

Four weeks later, I was sitting in base camp in Tibet at 17,160 feet with the Russians, ready to attempt the climb to summit the highest mountain in the world.

Mount Everest, check. I came home with all ten toes and fingers but lost a few brain cells to sleep deprivation and oxygen deprivation. Despite temperatures that plummeted well below zero, winds that whipped us at thirty or more miles per hour, claustrophobia, weight loss, and nearly being swept away in a torrential glacial stream, I made it back down alive, my lifelong dream fulfilled. Heather met me on the trail just outside base camp, where she'd waited for my return with her father. We held each other quietly. Nothing else mattered to me in that moment but that we were together, and even Everest seemed suddenly insignificant.

2.

Legacy

- ☑ "The Last Great Race"—complete all six hundred-mile trail races in one season *(finished in the top ten in five of them, first person to do so)*
- ☑ Badwater 146 *(many times, four wins and course records, current record holder for the summit of Mount Whitney)*
- ☑ Pikes Peak Quad *(one of the first, and only person to do it twice)*
- ☑ Run across Colorado *(three times, current record holder)*
- ☑ Leadville Trail 100 and Pikes Peak Marathon in the same weekend *(only person to do it)*
- ☑ Eco-Challenges *(one of only three people to compete in all nine)*
- ☑ Badwater solo, unaided and self-contained crossing *(first and only person to do it)*
- ☑ Badwater Quad *(first person to do it)*

☑ Summit Mount Everest *(reached the top of all Seven Summits on first attempts)*

☐ Run across America

Now, there was just one item remaining unchecked on my extreme to-do list: the transcontinental run. At almost sixty years old, if I didn't get moving soon, would I ever do it?

Like my dream of climbing Mount Everest, I'd been thinking about this for a long time, always intrigued by the pioneers who'd made their way across the United States in covered wagons. Stories of the western expansion, with its hardships and the people's perseverance, had riveted me since childhood. Captains Lewis and Clark, Davy Crockett, Daniel Boone, Kit Carson, and others: legends, every one, but real men, just the same. In imaginary play as a boy, my brother and I had become them, wearing faux coonskin caps and firing cork rifles through the bushes and around the corners of our house. Some part of the frontier character cried out for expression in my adulthood, too. Back in my early forties, I'd signed up to do the "Trans Am '92," an organized race that would follow a historic route and pit me against a few other acclaimed ultra-runners, but in the end, I'd decided not to go, because of family and work obligations. At the time, my kids were too young for me to take off for two months, plus I was in the process of getting my first divorce and still actively building my business.

By 2006, though, I'd resigned from managing Fort Morgan Pet Foods, my youngest, Ali, was nearly driving age, and I had Heather by my side. The timing just might be perfect.

Besides, I was gripped by my recent conversations with Ted Corbitt, my mentor and a modern pioneer, one of the founders and architects of ultrarunning. He'd described in depth a transcontinental race held in 1928, nicknamed the Bunion Derby—the very race that had inspired the Trans Am from which I'd had to bow out. Among the Bunion Derby's 199 starters were sons of clergy and sons of former slaves, men who were known for their prowess as runners and men who'd never run much at all, guys of all ages, ones who came with financial backing and ones who came only with the clothes on their backs.

As an African-American born in 1919 in South Carolina, and a child when the bunioneers made their cross-country trek, Ted was especially impressed by how egalitarian that footrace had been—no one was excluded. Growing up and becoming an elite athlete, he'd experienced plenty of racism and been banned from a few competitions because of his skin color. Although Ted recalled his own trials with humor and grace, he didn't discount how significant it was that the field of runners in 1928 was composed of people from all walks of life. The Bunion Derby, with its diverse competitors, had sparked something in him, an ideal that kept him going when he faced obstacles of his own.

Like me, Ted had started running on his family farm. As an adult, he'd competed in the 1952 Olympics, helped found the New York Road Runners Club, set standards for course measurements, organized a thirty-miler in the five boroughs that was the precursor to the New York City Marathon, held distance records throughout his running career, and even coined the term *ultrarunning*. He achieved idol status in the admittedly small world of ultramarathons, especially for his athletic achievements after age forty, when he was competing in the masters' category. At age eighty-three, he walked 303 miles in a six-day running race, covering just over fifty miles a day. His accomplishments earned him the titles "father of ultrarunning" and "spiritual elder of the modern running clan."

Ted was in his late eighties when we met, and he told me that he'd long dreamed of running across America himself, although he was never in a position to make an attempt. Finances and work had kept him from it, but the extreme distance and the athleticism required to pull off a record-setting finish fascinated him. We talked about this, and about how those guys in 1928 had run across a still-segregated country mostly on dirt and gravel, wearing leather-soled shoes and street clothes. One wore flannel underwear.

Of course, there were others who came before and after. Walkers, runners, people who crossed east or west in pursuit of, well, a different objective for each of them, I suppose. Like Ted, I wanted to retrace these people's steps, too. In places where the land remained unchanged, I wanted to see what they'd seen. Where modernization had won out, I wanted to marvel at our inventions and consider whether so-called progress had, indeed, moved us forward. I wanted to meet people as I ran, get a sense of the American character, if there really was such a thing. I was itching to get out there on our nation's roads and test myself against the elements that had battered my forerunners, and I wanted to prevail. I wanted to set a new world record.

THE REQUIREMENTS

Guinness World Record Guidelines

This record is for crossing the U.S.A. in the shortest time on foot—the participant may run or walk as desired.

The attempt should start at City Hall New York and finish at City Hall Los Angeles or San Francisco (or vice versa). The mileage covered is not relevant to the attempt—it is up to the participant to choose the most suitable or shortest route between these two points.

1. The run should only proceed on roads where it is safe and/or legal to run. The breaking of any laws during the journey will result in disqualification.

2. The record will be timed from the moment the runner sets off to the moment he/she arrives at their final destination. Breaks may be taken as desired, but at no time will the clock stop.

3. The runner is allowed the benefit of a support team, but at no time may he/she be transported towards his/her destination by the support vehicle. Each leg of the journey should resume at the exact point at which the last leg ended.

At the beginning of 2007, I clicked through the Guinness World Records site to receive information about qualifying for an attempt to break the transcontinental record. I knew I wanted to do it, but I hadn't figured out the particulars yet. Who would finance it? I doubted I could foot the bill all by myself for the route detailing, support team/crew, food, lodging, vehicles, gas, medical care, and whatever else we'd need.

That winter, it was as if someone fired a start gun when I heard that Charlie Engle (my Denali climbing teammate, with whom I'd also adventure raced in Fiji and Vietnam) was running across the Sahara Desert with another friend, Ray Zahab, as well as Kevin Lin. Their 4,500-mile journey was being underwritten by a documentary of their experience, which would be titled, simply, *Running the Sahara*. Narrated by Matt Damon, it would capture the spirit of the three runners, the desert environment, and the obstacles they'd face, and it would bring awareness to the water crisis in that area. *Running the Sahara* would be in the tradition of other great extreme sports films—as could be a film about my own transcontinental run, I imagined. It would be like the 2005 BBC documentary I'd watched fairly recently, about a group of men who re-created Robert F. Scott and Roald Amundsen's treks to the South Pole, racing each other and using Greenland as a backdrop. Or like Jon Muir's tale, made into the film *Alone Across Australia: A Story About a Man*

Who Takes His Dog for a Walk. (Don't let the title fool you, as this is an amazing adventure, a 2,500-mile, self-sufficient crossing of the Australian outback—even the dog dies!) There'd been a few films about ultrarunning, such as *The Distance of Truth* and *Running on the Sun,* both about the Badwater 135. But I envisioned something on an epic scale that would be about more than running.

Extreme sports documentaries were becoming more and more popular, and I knew a transcontinental run could make a great addition to the genre. My theory was that people would love to see a film about unadorned athleticism that would also be positive and motivational, and this one would reveal the many faces of America, its landmarks and landscape, some running history, and even a bit of what our pioneers experienced in their push westward. What better way to do all that than to film a run nearly straight across the whole damn U.S. of A.?

Because Ray was more accessible by e-mail than Charlie while they were in the Sahara, I sent a message through him to ask Charlie if he'd be interested in brokering a deal with any of his film or corporate contacts so that I could gain media interest, financing, or product support for a run across America. I suspected that this idea of a transcon—and of me doing it at my "advanced age"—might catch Charlie's eye; he respected me, I believed, plus he had a reputation of being a smooth operator, someone who could sell ice to an Inuit, exactly the kind of guy I wanted on my team if I was going to get the cross-country ultrarun under way *now.*

I laid it all on the line. At the end of my e-mail, I revealed my thoughts about challenging the record:

> . . . That would involve running at least sixty-eight miles per day (or more) for a forty-four-day finish. The old record is sixty-seven miles per day for forty-six days. Publicly, I would say I'm going for the Grand Masters (over fifty years old) men's record of sixty-four days, completing forty-five miles a day. Confidentially, I would be going for the overall record—at least giving it a shot. . . .

I realize that it would be a huge effort, and I don't take this
lightly. What you guys are doing is unbelievable—keep it up!!!

Marsh

Calling a transcontinental run a "huge effort" wasn't hyperbole. If anything, I was underplaying it. This would be the biggest thing I'd ever done, the hardest, the longest, with the most potential for both injury and enlightenment, my magnum opus. At the time I wrote that note, I didn't fully grasp the impending transformation, the personal revelations that would turn something I'd believed for my whole life upside down. How it would completely alter my sense of reality and relationships, my definitions of independence and self-reliance. How the distance would chastise my body and the experience would scald my soul.

But I wouldn't fully understand that until later, during the run. What I did understand, even just contemplating this, was the intense effort it had taken Frank Giannino, who'd set the record with his second attempt in 1980 at the age of twenty-eight.

When I'd contacted Frank, some months before I wrote to Ray and Charlie, and asked his advice about challenging his record, he had been encouraging and told me to go for it. He'd also admitted how difficult it was, during his first crossing in '79 (coincidentally, the same year I started running), to start out with a friend, have that friend falter and drop out, and watch his crew disintegrate. It ruined the friendship, and he wasn't satisfied with his finishing time.

The next year, he'd come back with his mother, father, and brother to crew, run alone, and set the record on his own, completing the course in a little more than forty-six days. Frank counseled me to get into a routine as soon as possible, as I'd need to have small, consistent things to look forward to as I ran. He never said anything about how physically demanding the run would be. That was understood, a basic fact, an undeniable reality of what would come.

I also understood there'd be no second chance for me: Unlike Frank, I didn't have the youth, the money, or the heart to put my family through this ordeal twice. As with Everest, I was going to succeed, or fail, in one try.

It took Ray a while to get back to me. He and Charlie were busy putting in forty-mile days across the largest desert in the world. But when I heard from him, Ray's news was positive. Yes, Charlie was interested. In fact, Charlie decided later that he'd like to attempt the run with me, to take his own crack at the transcon record set in 1980.

Would I like some company on the road?

Sure, I said. Let's do this thing.

We'd have to map out a course, sticking to legal pedestrian roads, per the Guinness World Record guidelines, choosing the most direct, legal route. We'd both need to recruit our own crews, two separate groups of people who'd take care of us on the way. We'd have to secure some vehicles, product sponsors, and financial backing. We'd have to train. Hard.

It was all coming together: Charlie was on board and would pitch my idea to his movie contacts, plus he thought that a documentary would help attract sponsors. A race director and close friend of mine had offered to underwrite the run, so we just had to go and meet with her to see how she felt about a two-man attempt on the record and get her blessing to proceed.

One hitch: After the three of us met in New York, she told me that although she was still willing to finance the run, and she could see great reasons to do a two-man race, she didn't like my choice of running mate. To be blunt, she couldn't stand Charlie, didn't trust him, and didn't think much of his résumé.

She had good instincts, but I thought she was wrong about him. Sure, he was less experienced than I, but he was also a tough competitor and I'd watched him keep a sense of humor under some tense circumstances during the adventure races we'd done together. Yes, he could be volatile: I'd seen him blow up before. When we'd climbed Denali together, I'd been clipped to a steep-incline rope above him and our guide, Gary Scott, when the two of them got into a heated argument over I don't remember what. That had been unnerving, and I'd wondered if they were going to start punching each other out while we all dangled there. Thank God they didn't. And true, Charlie had hollered at me on the phone once, angry when I'd told him it was time to pay back some money he owed me, threatening to kick my ass or beat the shit out of me (one or the other) the next time we crossed paths. He just didn't like to be called on his bad behavior. And sure, there were . . . other times, other trivial arguments, other things that showed me that Charlie could be a powder keg. But I felt sure I could handle whatever might come up. Under all that bluster, I believed, was a good guy who had what it would take to run across the country. He also brought a lot to the table with his media and sponsorship contacts.

We would have to find a different backer. I couldn't, in good conscience, take my friend's money when she didn't feel a hundred percent confident in the venture. Besides, I was squeamish about putting her personal funds at risk. What if something went sideways and it ruined our friendship? Not worth it.

By then, it seemed chances were good that Charlie could come through with a viable documentary deal, get us involved with producers who would make a film that could fulfill my grandiose vision. And with the right production company, we could pursue big-name sponsors and serious money. That was a better plan all around—less risk—so I thanked my friend profusely for her offer, and then explained that she wouldn't have to put even one cent of her own cash on the line.

"Don't worry. I'm still going to run across the country."

———————

There was one more problem, though. In passing, I mentioned my brewing plans to Heather, who shot me a pained look. Usually supportive of my exploits, she nonetheless rejected this idea.

"What?! You never told me about this . . . no. No, no, no. You can't."

She knew the price Everest had exacted—temporary cognitive problems and permanently impaired concentration—and worried that a run of this magnitude would be like that multiplied many times over. The numbers were dizzying, unimaginable: 3,063 miles, 117 marathons back to back over more than 40 consecutive days of running. The farthest I'd ever gone was for the Badwater Quad, nearly six hundred miles that took me more than ten days and pushed me to my limits mentally, emotionally, and physically. This would exceed five times that distance and grow exponentially more difficult as we neared the end. Any suffering I'd experienced in my earlier pursuits, including Everest and the Badwater Quad, would seem transient and insignificant by comparison. She also knew my history, including how my compulsion to keep going farther had contributed to the demise of my second marriage and still affected my relationships with all three of my children, Elaine, Taylor, and Ali. Extreme sports had been a wedge between my family and me, and it looked as if I was going to repeat that pattern all over again.

She fought me for a year. As plans progressed, she fought harder. She didn't understand why I was still so compelled to do this, and she wasn't buying any of what she called my "bullshit reasons." She fought me right up until about two weeks before we were supposed to go to the San Francisco starting line, and then she finally acknowledged the inevitable: I was going to traverse the United States, from San Francisco to New York City, on my own two legs. Starting in mid-September, I'd begin to run the equivalent of more than two marathons and a 10K every day, chasing autumn from west to east for at least six weeks.

3.

It's Just Who I Am

Some people find my feet fascinating because I have no toenails. Magazine and newspaper folk have interviewed me about them and photographed my toes, which friends have described as little bald-headed men, or ten nursing piglets. Why, reporters always ask, would a man go so far as to have his toenails surgically removed? What kind of person alters his anatomy for sport?

Look, the toenails are the least of it. The kind of sacrifices you make when you're running hundreds of miles are considerably more profound than whether you'll ever get a proper pedicure again. But I understand the freak-show quality of my feet. It's like the Everest mountaineers' blackened, frozen fingers that mesmerized me years ago: It symbolizes something, says something about a person's commitment. What that something is—unlimited human potential and extraordinary daring, or something darker, like madness and obsession—seems a mystery.

The real sacrifices? Family relationships often suffer in the ultrarunning community; clearly, mine are no exception. The time away from home, the solitariness, the stubborn self-reliance all take their toll. Marriages are ruined, children alienated. During the races themselves, people battle dehydration, salt loss, sleep deprivation, blisters that make the most hardened athletes buckle, trashed knees, pulled hamstrings, acute tendonitis, and more. In the face of all this pain, ultrarunners also tend to develop a morbid sense of humor. Dr. Ben Jones used to bring a coffin, fill it with ice, and submerge himself to cool off during the Badwater Ultramarathon. (Ben is a coroner, but still.) Actually, it's rare for someone to die doing this sport, but it's not at all rare to want to. Once, I asked a physician friend of mine, a cardiologist, if a person could run himself to death—I wanted to know how hard I could push myself. No, he told me. Your body is smarter than you are and will "put you down" first, meaning you'll drop from dehydration, or pass out or something, before you can run yourself to death.

Why do we go the distance? Is it a cult? An addiction? Some kind of penance? Do we have something to prove? What do we get out of it? The answers to these questions are nearly as individual as the runners themselves. Charlie Engle, for example, would say yes, it's like an addiction—he traded cocaine and alcohol for competition. Ray Zahab would tell you that he started running for his health, dropped a pack-a-day smoking habit, and then got hooked by the personal discovery that comes from covering long distances in exotic lands, and finding opportunities to connect with and contribute to people from different cultures.

As for me, sure, there's an underlying compulsion: survivor's guilt and a need to punish myself, to prove myself, to face down my own mortality, to defy death. But my running is also a reflection of my upbringing, a work ethic, a personal challenge. My love of history gets interwoven, too—the feats of other people in other times—coupled with the alluring possibility that I might be able to go farther, faster, *today*.

In the fall of 2007, I began training for the transcon and reaching out to friends in the running community to ask them to crew for me. Charlie and I had decided to make our record attempt in the spring of 2008 and were also working out the details of the route, securing funding, and seeking sponsorship. A few of my longtime supporters came on board, most notably ENGO/Tamarack Habilitation, the company that makes ENGO blister patches, which provided both products and money for the run; as well as GoLite, Injinji, LEKI, Pacific Outdoor Equipment, Pearl Izumi, Sportslick, and Zensah—all of whom stocked us up with most of my favorite gear.

Charlie came through in a big way. He signed us a documentary deal (he became one of the producers, too) for the transcontinental run. The production company—NEHST, the same folks who'd bought distribution rights for *Running the Sahara*—decided to title the film *Running America*. This was huge, as NEHST helped promote the event with a Running America '08 website, which they launched in July 2008, and no doubt the documentary did help attract additional big-name corporate sponsorship. NEHST would manage the finances for this two-month adventure, taking receipt of sponsorship money and establishing a budget for everything from hiring the filmmakers to feeding us to providing us with two RVs (a place to cook, sleep, have medical care, and house off-duty crew), as well as two vans, one for each crew to stock and drive.

The crews would be paid little and work hard, staying within a mile of their runners on the road. Charlie and I might start out together, but we were sure to get separated, due to varying paces, possible injuries, and any other obstacles each of us might face on our own. So we'd need at least four or five people to staff each crew: one to drive each runner's RV, which would be stationed for long stops, where we'd need a kitchen and a place to sleep; one to drive each runner's crew van, which would go a mile ahead of the runner, stop, and prepare to meet him as he passed to deliver whatever he needed (from food and drink to encouragement and changes of clothing), then do it all over again, every mile of the way; plus one or two more for medical support and miscellaneous duties.

NEHST would take care of feeding and providing lodging for these folks, and pay their small stipend.

Among the sponsors Charlie and the producers secured were Super 8, which would provide some funds and hotel rooms for the production crew (and for us and our own crews, if we ever desired); VQ OrthoCare, who'd make a huge financial contribution and supply both equipment and a representative from the company to assist during the run; AXA Equitable, which would give funding and arranged to have its logo "wrapped" on one of the RVs; Vita-Mix and Crocs, both of whom would give us money and products to use on the road; plus SpinVox, Champs, and SPOT, who'd give us products and services. We had a stellar lineup of sponsors and underwriting.

But all of that didn't come together before the spring start date, so it was postponed from March to May, and then again to August. Finally, everything was set up for September 2008, so it turned out that we had about a year to train for this event. Early on, I consulted with Ray, asking him to give me the benefit of his experience with having just run thousands of miles to help me get ready for my own cross-country journey. We talked about how the surface would make running America particularly challenging. We'd be on pavement, and the pounding would surely take its toll. But the biggest physical challenge, and Ray understood this better than most anyone else, would be the high daily mileage. We'd be attempting to log seventy miles—essentially two and a half marathons—every day, for well over forty days. (He also, gently, questioned whether Charlie was the right man to attempt this with me. He didn't tell me about it, but I suspected something had happened out in the desert that had left a bad taste in Ray's mouth. I assured him that I knew how Charlie could be, but that I also felt confident I could handle whatever might set him off, plus I respected Charlie as one of the toughest athletes we knew.)

In the training schedule Ray devised, he demanded of me a kind of rigor that suited my body type: sturdy, strong, compact, "a tank," some say. It was also made to capitalize on my many years of experience with extreme endurance sports, and to help me adapt to the particular demands of running across the country, mostly on asphalt and concrete. Specifically, the schedule was designed to improve my agility and occasionally give me a break from the pavement with trail running, my core strength using tire drags and cross-training, my leg strength with hill repeats, my speed with tempo runs, my endurance with long runs and multiple runs in a day, as well as long runs, back to back, on consecutive days. We would also further train my digestive system to accept food every mile, a few mouthfuls at a time. At my peak volume, I was running up to two hundred miles per week, a mixed bag of long runs, peak runs, strength training, and cross-training.

I had my moments of doubt. Ray's schedule taxed me, took me to my physical and mental limits over and over again. At the end of 2007, as a training exercise, I participated in a seventy-two-hour run with the goal of completing seventy miles a day for three consecutive days, the same daily mileage we hoped to cover once we began the "real" event in California. About ten hours into the first day of the race, as I circled the looped course, I was right on schedule with more than fifty miles behind me, when I began to question myself. *Why am I doing this? What's the purpose? Do I really want to be here? This is incredibly hard, and I don't want to be out here for another sixty-two hours.*

I'd had enough.

I quit.

When I told Heather that I was through, that I was done with the whole endeavor—forget this race, this insane training schedule, and running across America—she didn't believe me, however much she may have hoped it was true. Quitting was out of character, out of the blue. But, I insisted, I'd been thinking about it for a full hour before I stopped. I wasn't ready to carry this burden.

Everyone goes through these periods, not just in athletic pursuits but also in life, and we all find our way through them somehow, even if they last longer than we want. We call on our friends. We lean on our spouses and ask them not to worry too much. Ultimately, we suck it up and start talking ourselves out of whatever tailspin we've been in. It took me a good month to get over it, to regain my confidence and motivation after quitting; it took the people I love counseling me to accept what I was going through and give myself permission to let it be; it took one of my closest friends telling me that it didn't matter if I never ran another step and that everyone loved me for myself, even without the running; it took my coach, Ray, telling me that it would pass and not to force it.

It took me realizing that it was okay to lose the battle so I could come back to win the war. I could be kind to myself about a temporary "failure" to complete, and it served to save me, psychologically, for the times when it would be *really* important to continue no matter what.

Ultimately, the start-date delays allowed me to train hard and taper several times before we got to the starting line in San Francisco. During this time, I also devoted an hour or two each week to phone sessions with a friend and mentor for toughening up and steeling myself never to quit during the transcon. We'd talk about the upcoming race. We'd talk about Ted Corbitt and the bunioneers. We'd talk about heroes and history, about myth and mystery, about the rigors of the road and what it would take to march my body across the entire United States. These conversations were designed to prepare me mentally, just as Ray's training plan was designed to prepare me physically, for the upcoming ordeal, to give me the strength and stamina to deal with whatever might happen once we were under way.

Yet all during that training period, from October 2007 to September 2008, Heather and I had more immediate hardships to confront. There was her resistance, and my insistence. There was also a string of personal tragedies that pushed us both to the outer edges of loss and sorrow, as well as some moments of brilliance and hope and inspiration. All of this, too, may have been preparation for what was to come.

—————

"The best I can figure is that we've been told too many times that adventure just isn't in the cards for everyday folk like you and me. It's reserved for the people we read about in books and magazines, not mere mortals like us. Well, I'm not buying it."

Chris Douglass was always saying things like that, getting himself and other people inspired to do what's out of the ordinary. He'd competed in marathons and an ultramarathon, struck out on wild adventures he called "small world treks," written charming vignettes about the people he'd met and the places he'd seen in the world, and recently embarked on a new interest, short films.

That's why he called me in May 2008, four months before the start of my run across America, to introduce himself and request an interview. He told me that he admired me, that he was preparing for his own cross-country trip (walking from Colorado to Maine), and that he wanted to talk with me, get to know me, pick up a few of my "secrets," and put together a promotional clip I could use, gratis. At twenty-eight, he came across as incredibly warm, friendly, and enthusiastic about this project and the kind of life he'd carved out for himself. I could tell, already, that Chris was my kind of guy, a kindred spirit, and I wanted to meet him, too.

"Sure, come on over to the house and we'll interview each other." I thought it would be fun if he asked me whatever questions he had, and then we'd flip the camera around and I'd return the favor.

After a lively afternoon together, filming mostly on my back deck in Idaho Springs, Colorado, we said our good-byes and Chris promised to send me a finished clip in a couple of days. When he left, Heather turned to me, an odd look on her face. "My god, Marshall. That was what I imagine it would have been like if I'd met you twenty years ago. Those intense blue eyes. His build. His dreams and energy."

To tell the truth, the similarities were eerie, except Chris exuded positivity in a way I never had. That's not to say he was some airheaded Pollyanna. He had a way of sharing his ideas and experiences, displaying a groundedness that was invigorating and reassuring at the same time.

What a breath of fresh air! Heather and I had been through the wringer ever since I'd decided to do the transcontinental run, and meeting him gave us a lift we desperately needed. For months, we'd faced some agonizing twists and turns. Heather had continued to worry that I was going to permanently damage myself physically or psychologically in attempting this feat, and I'd had a hard time envisioning such a journey without her support. I'm not sure she was able even to consider giving it to me, however. In the spring of 2007, her father had been diagnosed with stage-IV kidney cancer, and she'd made him her first priority. We'd fully expected him to be gone within a few months, but we'd gotten lucky, and Rory was given more time than that.

Even as Heather was being frustrated in her attempts to talk me out of running across America, Rory was cheering me on. "Tell me what you're doing again?"

Despite his own suffering, he wanted to hear about my training regimen, which I'd begun that fall over Heather's protests. We always called Rory my biggest fan, because he made sure I knew how proud he was of me, and not just for the athletic achievements, but also for my character. The feeling was mutual. I admired his intellect, valued his opinions, and connected with this respected biologist's affection for the outdoors. In short, I loved Rory. We were friends, and at only ten years older, he was basically a contemporary of mine. I remember him telling me when we met that it was okay for me to date his daughter "as long as you don't call me 'Dad' and I don't have to call you 'son.'"

Deal. We understood each other. Still, when he became so ill, I couldn't help feeling as if I was losing a father figure. Nor did it keep me from resenting the time Heather was spending away from home to care for him. As much as I loved Rory, I wanted to be her first priority, and this was, understandably, the cause of even more friction between us.

Somebody once said that adversity doesn't build character, it reveals it, and that's certainly been true for me, for better and worse.

When winter of 2007 came, we heard that Ted Corbitt had died of complications from prostate and colon cancer. It struck me not just as a personal loss, but also a calamity for our sport. My grief was intensified by a feeling that we were burying an icon, a standard bearer. He stood for a kind of sportsmanship that seemed to be waning, one marked by ethics, doing what you say you'll do, and setting an example for the up-and-comers. With Ted gone, it felt as if the torch of the elder American ultrarunners had been passed to me, and just two months into my training for running across America, I made a silent promise that I'd hold that torch high in his honor.

Then, in April 2008, while we were at Rory's house with Heather's mom, taking care of him after a serious setback in his declining health, I got a call from my own mother.

Your dad's not doing well, son. He's in intensive care at the hospital.

What? This was too much. "What's wrong, Mom?"

My father had prostate cancer, had had it for thirteen years and told no one except my mom, who alone looked after him, though he wasn't exactly giving in to the disease. She'd even had to trick him into going to the hospital when he clearly needed emergency care. (She'd pretended to be driving him to work.) Assured that Rory was stable enough for us to leave him, Heather and I both went to see my dad at the Northern Colorado Medical Center, where he faced death like the old soldier he was. Compared with the horrors he'd observed during World War II, our life—by no means luxurious—must have seemed like a dream to him, and Dad knew how to appreciate it. So when he passed away, at age eighty-five, he had no regrets. I know because my daughter Ali, then eighteen, had offered to go out and do anything that her grandpa felt he'd left undone, and he'd patted her hand and told her no, there wasn't a thing. My dad died at peace with what he'd accomplished in his life.

There were things Dad never told us and that we discovered only after his passing. We knew that he'd risked his own life to carry a wounded soldier off the battlefield, not because my dad talked about it, but because the man he'd pulled to safety kept in contact with our family for the rest of his life. But it turns out that Elmer Ulrich had also participated in the liberation of survivors from the Buchenwald concentration camp. He never spoke of it. My cousin had found out only because she'd recently interviewed Dad for a school project and asked pointed questions.

I talked about this, and the father I knew, when I delivered his eulogy on a wind-whipped spring day.

We returned to Winona, Minnesota, to help Heather's mom, Janis, care for Rory, and just three weeks later, on May 10, he died, tearing Heather's world apart. I found myself reverting to an old role, trying to stay strong and positive in the face of what was becoming an avalanche of loss.

That's the emotional landscape onto which Chris had walked, and we drank in his youthful exuberance like two thirsty travelers who've finally wandered out of the desert and found water.

The short film he made about me was posted on YouTube within a few days, just as he'd promised. (You can watch the clip, and others he made, at http://www.youtube.com/user/ChristopherEDouglass.) We were so impressed with what he'd done that we showed it, like proud parents, to lots of our friends, including one who did not disperse praise liberally. Someone who was more likely to designate something as "complete shit" than a treasure, she loved what Chris had produced, thought it was fantastic, and wanted to be introduced to him right away so she could discuss some projects they could do together.

On May 28, Chris called us from his car while he was driving to the start of his Colorado-to-Maine adventure, just to let us know how thrilled he was to have met us, how flattered he was that my friend liked his short film, and how he looked forward to working with her as soon as he got home. He was sure life couldn't get any better than this.

Thirty minutes later, Chris was dead, killed in a car accident.

His mother called to tell us what had happened, and a few days later, shocked and further numbed by our compounding grief, Heather and I traveled to Maine to attend our third funeral in two months. Although I'd known Chris for only a short time, his parents told me that I probably understood him better than anyone else, that Chris had called me his hero, and they asked me to deliver Chris's eulogy. While we were there in his hometown, we stayed in his room, slept in his bed.

I quoted Chris during that eulogy, repeated his rejection of the idea that adventure wasn't in the cards for ordinary folk. Chris had embodied a philosophy the two of us shared: that living life to its fullest is what it's all about. Yes, there may be suffering—in fact, it's certain there will be—but it serves to heighten our joy. It makes us grateful to be alive.

Without question, I was grateful to have met and known Chris, if only for a few weeks. Although his death pained me, I felt something extraordinary had transpired between us, and I cherished it. His vibrancy of spirit, like that of the other men who'd recently passed into memory, redoubled my commitment to carry out the transcontinental adventure. I was determined to go.

We were at it again, arguing about the impending run, which was now only a few weeks away.

Why? Heather was asking me for the who-knows-how-many-eth time. With all we'd been through, with all I was sure to go through, why? Why? *Why?* Worn down from more than a year of this, I said the only thing that made sense to me anymore.

"It's just who I am."

It's also just what I needed: to get outdoors, to clear my head, to allow myself the time to think about what I'd experienced and then think about something else for a long, long time. I needed to run, to empty out the accumulated emotion, to strip myself of comfort and grieve the loss of these four men at my own pace, in my old, familiar fashion. As with

Jean's death, running would provide a way for me to both deal with and avoid the emotional pain.

"Well, finally." Heather took a deep breath. "The truth."

My simple declaration had hit a nerve, and she knew that we'd reached the bottom of my particular mystery. All the other reasons I'd given her were versions of the truth, but this was new, truth with a capital T. It was then I began to see some kind of acceptance. She was going to give me her blessing; she knew that taking on these extreme tests of endurance, ones that demand not just athletic rigor but a unique brand of mental toughness, had become woven into the fabric of my being.

The transcontinental run would be about so much more than breaking a record, reliving history, or attempting some kind of extreme sightseeing trip. It would transcend the homage to my predecessors, although they were certainly on my mind. It would be a personal reckoning, an accounting of my character, that was sure to leave me scoured of everything but the essentials. It would mean running through the emptiness, beyond any pain, facing unimagined hardships, and on to . . . what? I didn't know. But I wanted to find out.

"You have to come with me." I'd said this many times before.

Heather could see how much I wanted her to be a part of this endeavor, to support me in it not just with her words but with her presence. Truly, I didn't believe I could do it without her, and she knew that. She also knew, without me saying so, how cathartic this could be for me, what an incredible accomplishment it would be if I made it, and what it might cost us as a couple if she denied me.

She said yes, although she had no idea what she was signing up for.

Despite my background, neither did I, really. What we did know for certain was that it would be grueling, fraught with harsh realities, and incredibly hard on my fifty-seven-year-old body. And we knew I had to do it.

4.

Fool's Errand

Days 1–2

Before the start of the race on September 13, 2008, when Heather and I arrived before dawn at San Francisco City Hall, I felt sick to my stomach whenever I thought about the impending grind. Everyone was making their last-minute preparations, especially confirming the day's route. (Our plan for leaving City Hall had been worked out the night before, a last-minute scramble caused by miscommunication or a lack of communication or someone dropping the ball, depending on whom you ask about it.) I tried to distract myself by cracking dumb jokes, giving my crew a hard time, and watching Charlie sign shoes and shirts for about a dozen guest runners who'd registered on the Running America website to come out and be a part of the start of this . . . thing.

Oh, shit. What have I gotten myself into?

I always say the only limitations are in your mind, and if you don't buy into those limits, you can do a helluva lot more than you imagine. So I let my mind wander away from my doubts and rest in my immediate surroundings. It wasn't yet fully light out, there wasn't much traffic, and the only people nearby were part of our deal. Guest runners stretching and warming up. The film crew getting ready to catch the beginning of what they expected to be an epic story. Charlie's and my race crews climbing in and out of the RVs and vans, double-checking supplies and reviewing the route.

With the buzz of all this activity below me, I walked up the broad stairs to the city hall's main entrance and considered how much this imposing white building, with its enormous dome and soaring pillars, looked like so many other U.S. government centers, not so different from the one in lower Manhattan that would serve as our finish line. This architectural connection struck me as symbolic—another continuity across the vast distance we'd cover—but, to be honest, it didn't calm my jangling nerves. Trying to stay positive, I reflected on my original concept for the run and how it had all finally materialized with Charlie's efforts; the support of our sponsors who'd given equipment, gear, and money; and the keen interest of this talented documentary team hired by NEHST. Together, we'd see America one mile at a time, honor the history and diversity of our country, raise money and awareness for the United Way's campaign against childhood obesity, and literally follow in the footsteps of those who'd done this before. I'd had the lofty idea, too, that we'd somehow reintroduce America to Americans, showing how similar we all are while also celebrating the differences among the people we'd meet and the dramatically changing landscapes we'd traverse.

Now standing in front of the immense doors of City Hall, I waited for everyone to finish their preparations so we could get moving. This is where it would all begin. You could feel the excitement in the air—and the pity, too.

Welcome to California!

"The Golden State"

Arrival date: 9/13/08 (Day 1)
Arrival time: 5:03 a.m.
Miles covered: 0
Miles to go: 3,063.2

Finally, just after five o'clock in the morning, Charlie and I stepped off the starting point together, chatting about the road ahead. He's taller than I am, slightly stooped, with broad shoulders and long legs, but I have a huge stride, so I had no trouble going alongside him. We traveled briskly up and down the hills on city streets, remaining intentionally oblivious to what lay beyond the next streetlight illuminating the long road ahead. We both knew this would be an ordeal, yet we felt some security in our partnership. With two runners, we'd increase our chances of at least one man making it into New York City, and if we could go all the way together (even if we finished separately), the ongoing competition would push us to set a new record. If one of us had to drop out, then he'd be there for the other guy, support him the rest of the way by sharing crew, gear, or whatever the remaining runner needed.

By about mile five, I settled into my own pace and moved away from Charlie and his group. A good friend, Chris Frost, stayed with me, and within hours of leaving City Hall, we'd run along the waterfront and crossed the Golden Gate Bridge, where another friend surprised us and ran with Chris and me through Sausalito.

I had company on and off for the rest of the day, even horsed around with Charlie on the Richmond–San Rafael Bridge, cutting up for the cameras with him while we waited for a prearranged police escort.

We'd gotten off to a decent start together, despite tension that had developed between us during the months prior to the race. The guy could work a room, for sure, but his braggadocio and craving for the limelight had begun to rub me the wrong way. He'd neglected to include me or even mention my name in most of the pre-race publicity and sponsorships, and he'd made promises he'd failed to keep. Heather and I had begun to joke that I was the "invisible man." On one hand, his disregard for my part in this event rankled. Yet he'd been instrumental in making it all come together, and once we were under way, I was grateful to him for keeping most of the attention on himself. I had enough to do, just staying focused on the run and not letting my concerns about the mileage get in my way, without having to worry about looking good for cameras or anyone else.

It took fifteen hours of active running to log the requisite seventy miles on that first day. My nerves had finally settled down by the time we'd goofed around on that bridge, and not long after that we'd finished our first marathon, stretched, and then cruised by the beautiful countryside of Napa Valley, stopping for the night in Fairfield a few hours after marathon number two. Heather and I bedded down in the RV with our friend and RV driver, Roger Kaufhold, and everyone else—the rest of my crew, Charlie, his crew, and the documentary team—drove many miles away to stay in the nearest Super 8 hotel, so I didn't get to hear about how he was doing, but my group felt good about the day's effort, with growing confidence that I could do this. I was tired, but not *that* tired. I was sore, but not *that* sore.

The next morning, Charlie started a few miles behind me, having staked out his finish short of the full seventy miles on day one, but I didn't know if he was already having trouble or just being smart. My own legs felt heavy as I started off again on day two, a familiar feeling for any ultrarunner. My world was narrowing, too, another usual effect of long

distances. The day before, I'd been keenly aware of the details of the landscape through the Bay Area, in particular certain smells that had marked our progress: first the urban aromas at City Hall, then the salty-fishy air of the wharf and the eucalyptus as we approached the Golden Gate Bridge, and then the distinctive fumes of the oil refineries as we headed out of town. But now I was less alert, not so attuned to whatever existed outside the five-foot bubble in which I was running. Like a horse with blinders on, most of my attention was on the terrain under my feet. Still, I heard the wind generators south of Highway 12 at the early-morning start, and although it was pitch-dark as I ran by them, I felt their huge mechanical presence dwarfing me and the nearby cattle, which I could faintly make out as they calmly grazed below the massive, whirring blades.

Once the sun came up, the pastureland surrounding Rio Vista showed itself, golden with the fading grasses of early fall. As the sun rose higher in the sky, I felt the temperature rising, climbing to about ninety-five degrees Fahrenheit, and my crew brought me a short-sleeved shirt. Continuing on, I breathed in the dust kicked up by a dry crosswind, and with essentially no shoulder to run on, I'd flinch as the trucks whizzed by, creating vortexes of dirt and hot air that regularly ripped my hat off my head and occasionally threatened to pull me into their path. Any kind of traffic was a menace, and it became clear that one of the major dangers during this race would be the chance of getting hit. We needed to run on the highways—they were legal routes and most often the shortest distance between two points—but on them I felt vulnerable to the elements and the environment. Doubt made itself at home in my psyche. More than once, I wondered, *What the hell am I doing?* The thought would surface, I'd let it go, and then I'd drift back into my "road trance."

When a harbor seal swam by in the Sacramento River upstream from the Bay, a solitary figure cutting through the water about ninety miles inland, I felt a certain kinship with him. Some part of my brain was always looking for something to relate to—a seal, a tree, a rattlesnake, a rock. It lifted the burden somehow, knowing that others had been out of their element and suffered a private hardship, too. Yet I was hardly alone. Heather was somewhere nearby, now completely in my corner. I didn't know exactly how she'd convinced herself, but she was one hundred percent on board, working with the crew and taking shifts in the van, which always stayed within a mile of me to make sure I had everything I needed to keep going. She'd also station herself in the RV, our rolling headquarters, at mealtime and physical therapy time and bedtime, because she knew how much it meant to me just to see her face, touch her hand, lie down with her if only for a quick break.

She was indispensable to me, even though we had an all-star crew. How lucky we were to have found such experienced and expert people who were willing to take a pittance in pay and time off from their regular lives to assist me: Jesse Riley, a friend who'd run across the United States in 1997 and Australia in 1998, and directed the Trans Am '92, was a key resource to me, providing crucial insight and counseling, as he understood these megadistances. Our neighbor, Roger Kaufhold, who at the tender age of sixty-seven had climbed Kilimanjaro with me, would drive the RV and perform other countless K.P. and organizational tasks. He was invaluable not only for his services but also for his unfailingly good company, as Heather and I always felt we could be ourselves and at ease with Roger. Kathleen Kane was our massage therapist, her hands a moving balm to my legs and back. And Dr. Paul Langevin, a Wyoming orthopedist Heather and I had met at an ultrarunning training camp in Switzerland, was our doc on the road. Heather's job was to act as the "runners' advocate," carrying Charlie's or my requests to the production crew, assisting with communications from the road, and being my chief moral support. She wasn't technically on my crew, but she was a critical member of this operation.

Five people to support me. It's one of the aspects of ultrarunning that goes against my nature, but I'd learned to accept (up to a point) that if I was going to cover the miles, I'd need help. Anytime you're going as far

as we planned to go, at the pace we intended to keep, you don't just throw on a pair of shoes and head out the door. A group of people like this makes all the difference: people who understand an athlete's needs, and can anticipate them and satisfy them even before the runner recognizes there's any need at all.

Here, Marsh, take a drink of this milk shake. Turn here, Marsh, and head that way for about fifty miles. Come over here and lie down, Marsh, and I'll stretch your legs for you. Here are your meds and lip stuff, Marsh.

(All right, we actually called it "lipshit," rhymes with *dipshit*. We had silly names for everything, including my "murse" (man purse) and the RV that I nicknamed "The Starship" at the same time I dubbed Roger "Captain Kirk.")

Besides, as we got closer to Nevada, I was losing my ability to make good decisions for myself. Given the seventy-mile-a-day gambit, I was catching at most five hours of sleep a night. We were on the road eighteen to twenty-three hours, so Heather and I slept in the RV to save us the time of driving to a hotel, as did most of our crew, once they realized they could get more sleep this way. (Charlie and his crew were willing to continue making the trade-off and slept in hotels fairly often.) That meant no showering, no laundry facilities, and most of the time in bed was miserable for both of us. Just imagine what it was like for Heather, to have her husband climb in next to her each night, sweaty, smelly, and desperately needing her touch to feel at all human. Even in my intense tiredness, I craved physical intimacy with her more than sleep. My sex drive was greater than I'd ever experienced, even in my late teens. (Viagra, move over! Just run until you feel like you're going to die, and your libido will kick into overdrive.) It was almost uncontrollable for me, as if Heather was my last shot at procreation, the object of an overpowering survival instinct. And when I finally did drop off, I tossed and turned and moaned, keeping her awake the better part of the night. Filthy and exhausted, even in my dreams I was restless and still running.

Somewhere in California, Charlie colorfully summed up one of my core racing strategies: "For an old fucker, he sure can move."

It's funny but true: I just keep putting one foot in front of the other, millions of times. I may not be the fastest runner, but I am one of the most obstinate. It's one of my trademarks, my stubbornness and single-mindedness.

Practically since the beginning of our run, I'd held steady out front, but at this early stage, my lead meant nothing, except that my running mate, a resolute competitor, didn't like being behind me even temporarily. We both knew we'd be trading places many times in the coming weeks, and that would work to our advantage. We'd feed off each other, both of us working to gain an edge. There'd be mind games and jockeying, with whoever was ahead running faster to keep the other guy from catching him, and whoever was behind pushing himself to gain the lead.

The psychological carrot and stick would help us both keep going with our race plan, a scheme I thought was nuts before we started. Charlie had announced to the press, our sponsors, and the film crew who'd signed on to make a documentary of the whole thing that we'd cover seventy miles every day and complete the entire 3,063-mile route in just forty-four days, two days faster than Frank Giannino had done it in 1980. It was madness from the word go. Here we were, a forty-some hotshot and the old guy nearing sixty, attempting to break a record set by a man half my age by outdistancing him every day of the run.

Experience told me that a better strategy would have been to start with fewer miles per day and then ramp up after our bodies had settled in. That's how Frank had done it. His race plan: Average sixty miles a day from San Francisco to Fort Collins, Colorado, then increase to an average of seventy miles a day. He'd run 2.5 miles at a ten-to-twelve-minute-

per-mile pace, walk some, run 2.5 miles again, and repeat up to twenty miles, then break for breakfast; run/walk another twenty miles and break an hour for lunch; then run as many miles as possible into the night. It didn't work out exactly as planned, though. Frank's progress across California was slower than expected due to traffic and the crew (his family) going out of the way to reach a KOA campground for a few comforts at night, such as showers. So they were averaging only about fifty miles a day until they established a new routine after Fort Collins: The crew would get up before sunrise, about three in the morning, and Frank would run twenty-five miles, then break for breakfast; he'd run another twenty-five miles before breaking for lunch; and then he'd go as far as possible by dark. They reached the seventy-mile goal almost every day and finished in 46 days, 8 hours, and 36 minutes.

That so-called slow start may have felt like a hindrance—falling short of his initial goal—but my gut said that it may have been the smartest way to begin. Then again, when I'd asked Frank for his opinion of running seventy miles a day out the gate, he'd said he thought it was possible. In fact, this was the first time he'd considered that his record might fall. He was impressed by our reputations, he'd said, and he'd encouraged me, much to his credit.

Like Frank, I believed it was possible to achieve—I'd approached running one hundred miles per day in multiday events in the past, such as when I'd run across Ohio and Colorado years ago—but I knew I'd suffer more now, as I didn't have the speed of my youth. Instead of averaging five or six miles per hour, I'd likely average four or five miles per hour, and this meant I'd have to stay out on the road longer to meet the seventy-mile-per-day goal. There was just no denying it: This was an improbable, punishing pace, something we should have made a private goal, but once Charlie had made a public declaration, I felt we had to do what he'd said we would. So I intended to go for it and hold his feet to the fire, too: seventy miles a day, come what may.

Numerous books have been written about how to run. Let my experience in the early days of this journey be a lesson in how *not* to do it: Go farther than your known breakdown point, deprive yourself of rest and recovery time, don't bathe, and wear the same dirty clothes day in and day out. Torture yourself. Hate it. Pray for something, someone else, to make it stop.

True, every runner wants to quit sometimes. By any definition, becoming a successful athlete requires conquering those psychological barriers, whether you're sucking air during your first jog or gutting it out in the final four miles of a marathon, axiomatically the toughest. When you push beyond the marathon, new obstacles arise, and the necessary mental toughness comes from raising your pain threshold. All endurance sports are about continuing when it feels as if you have nothing left, when everything aches, when you feel *done*—but you're not. You have to get beyond the numbers that, like certain birthdays for some people, just seem intrinsically daunting: fifty miles, one hundred miles, one thousand miles, two thousand miles, and random points in between. At such distances, the sport becomes every bit as much mental as physical. More so.

These high mile markers feel like rites of passage, similar to altitude records in mountain climbing. Yet there's a difference: In mountaineering, Everest is the pinnacle—you can't get any higher than that. But with ultrarunning, there's no limit.

The next mileage hurdle is daunting, no matter what the distance and the difference from your last accomplishment. Whether you're increasing from a 5K to a 10K, or a half-marathon to a marathon, or from the marathon to an ultrarun, there's a similar rush of exhilaration in breaking the barrier; it's a badge of honor. But after the line is crossed, there's a breakdown or depression, sort of like going from a sugar high to a depletion of energy in both body and soul. Writer and runner Haruki Murakami has described this effect, known as "runner's blues," although

he admits it would be better called "runner's whites." It feels like an opaque, viscous film, a malaise that slows you down and saps whatever enthusiasm you once had for the sport. I expect these dips and know how to deal with them, have experience with running through them, and can even relate them to my personal life and the feelings I had as Jean dealt with her cancer. There was elation as she went into remission (a milestone), but then came a feeling of defeat and a guilt-ridden acknowledgment that death was just waiting on her, not dismissed. The realities of a short time to live or a long way to go don't signal you to stop moving forward. It means you have to dig deep and keep on going. After the self-congratulation and the inevitable crash, the focus must return along with the relentless forward movement—there can be nothing else.

There are equally predictable, analogous physiological factors. Those last four miles of a marathon are especially hard because the body typically switches from burning carbohydrates to burning fat as an additional source of energy somewhere between eighteen and twenty-two miles. This conversion is called "bonking" or "hitting the wall" when it results in a depletion of glycogen stores in the liver and muscle. You can feel especially tired and find yourself dragging to the finish if you don't attend to it, eat some simple sugars, and maybe even walk for a bit. Marathoners avoid bonking by doing long slow distance (LSD) training to teach the body how to switch over to burning fat from carbs without inducing severe hypoglycemia. The more you train the body to make this switch, the more efficient it becomes at the conversion. The mental aspect gets fine-tuned by LSD training, too, building confidence that's crucial especially during this phase: You come to accept this conversion as necessary, and no longer let it catch you off guard.

For me, the transition from carb burning to fat burning is barely noticeable except for a slight dip in energy, a little tug of fatigue. Once I'm in fat-burning mode, though, I always feel as if I'm walking a tightrope—if I don't pay close attention to the need for calories, I can quickly slip into a tailspin. During the run across America, I bonked only once, and it was because I was alone on the road without food or drink for too long, but that was quickly remedied with a handful of Snickers bars, and I was on the fly again within twenty minutes. The fact that this happened only once is a testament to the discipline and expertise of my crew. Plus, I know my body. One of the greatest benefits of reaching the breakdown point over and over again is precise knowledge of exactly what your body can take, what it needs, and how to react accordingly. The same is true for mental strength—you become intimately familiar with your breaking points and learn how to do whatever's necessary to deal with them.

A few years before I began the transcon, I was asked to counsel potential Navy SEAL recruits and give them some pointers on getting through their infamous training camp. The whole point of Hell Week is to demonstrate absolutely that the human body can endure more than the mind commonly believes it can, and the people who participate are put to a harsh test: Trainees are exposed to the elements—cold, rain, mud, sand, and more—and allowed a total of about four hours of sleep during the entire training week. They perform 132 hours of physical labor while an instructor constantly reminds them that they can drop out anytime, echoing that voice in their heads that says, *I don't have to do this. I can stop.* About 70 percent of the trainees give up, signifying surrender by ringing a shiny brass bell hung prominently on the training grounds. When they do that, they publicly declare they're done. For good.

The key battle: Shut that voice up. Don't ring the bell.

To give the trainees some clear principles, I put together the "Ten Commandments of Endurance," based on my own experiences of grappling with that voice. A friend of mine likes to call this list "Marshall Law."

1. Expect a journey and a battle.
2. Focus on the present and set intermediate goals.
3. Don't dwell on the negative.

4. Transcend the physical.
5. Accept your fate.
6. Have confidence that you will succeed.
7. Know that there will be an end.
8. Suffering is okay.
9. Be kind to yourself.
10. Quitting is not an option.

All ten of these commandments were in play as I was enduring my own version of Hell Week in the desert along California Highway 88. Sure, I would think about stopping all the time, but I kept a lid on it. I never allowed myself to actually *consider* stopping, but instead let the thought enter my mind and then drift away, like a child fantasizing about living on the moon. *Yep, that would be nice, but* . . . Decades of training and confidence-building helped me surrender and accept the suffering. After years and years of thinking about it, I believe that such suffering offers a unique gift, allowing me to profoundly appreciate living, to pay attention to the little things, like the comfort of sitting in a chair or enjoying a meal on a plate with a fork and a spoon. These simple pleasures become infused with quiet joy, and the deeper things in life—love, compassion, connection—become supremely meaningful in the present moment.

Still, I asked myself, over and over again, why promote this madness in my life? Is it about me or about those who surround me, supporting me and loving me? As I headed down the road, there was plenty of time to contemplate this, and I hoped that I'd discover the true answer before land's end.

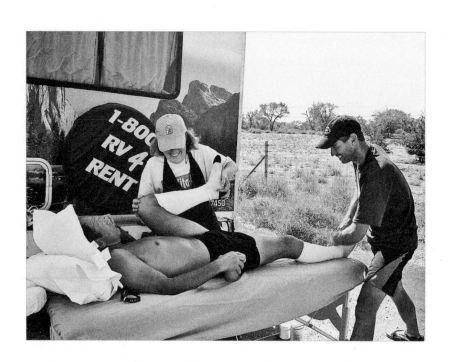

5.

Running Machine

Days 3–12

We'd come up out of the desert, but only for as long as we'd be in the Sierra Nevada mountain range. In cross section, the shape of the Sierras evokes a trapdoor, an apt metaphor for us as we began our ascent. Who knew what waited for us on the other side? The first two days had been predictably grueling—we didn't stop for anything but sleep and the occasional massage; we even ate on the go—but we had no idea how long we could continue at this pace, how long our bodies would allow it or how long we could hang on mentally. I'd been through extreme tests before and lost it, falling into a hallucinatory fog or having my body overcome my mind's ability to keep going. In 2003, I'd been nailed on are ankle by a rattler during a Primal Quest adventure race, which left me flat on my back and experiencing some entertaining hallucinations. (After a few hours, I recovered and continued with my team without telling anyone what had happened.) There had been a few other occasions when the physical simply overpowered the mental, usually due to injury or extreme fatigue and the delirium that accompanies it. It had happened only rarely, but it did happen, and I felt it could happen again, anytime.

For the moment, though, I felt "refreshed," if you can call it that. As we came into Jackson, California, elevation 1,240 feet, the increasing altitude suited me despite the taxing climb. We would continue up, reaching our peak at just over 8,500 feet. (You can equate each thousand feet of altitude gain with running about one more mile on the flat, so on the day we went up the Sierras, I effectively ran about eighty miles.) Ground and air temperatures were still hot, measuring into the eighties even at higher altitudes, so I needed electrolytes to help me retain water and reduce cramping. By this time, I was also depending on my LEKI trekking poles to move at a fairly brisk pace, averaging about four miles per hour, swinging them beside me and planting them a little ahead of each foot before it struck the ground. You use them similar to cross-country skiing poles as an aid for stability and engaging arm strength to help propel you forward, which also unloads weight from your quadriceps and hamstrings, and allows you to roll your hips, using different muscle groups to keep you moving while the ones you usually recruit for running can rest a bit. Charlie had overtaken me during my lunch break at about five thousand feet, and now he was way out front—I thought I wouldn't see him again until we got to New York, as he seemed to be moving well.

However, I caught Charlie at a higher elevation, around eight thousand feet, and he unceremoniously dropped his shorts to reveal some angry red welts between his butt cheeks. He seemed intent on showing me what was slowing him down and insisted I take a good look. I'd experienced that painful chafing (and seen worse) in the past, so I felt for him, but to be honest, I didn't really want to be inspecting his bare ass on this lonely stretch over the Sierra Nevadas. Or anywhere, I suppose. I averted my eyes and tried to sympathize.

"Man, that looks bad . . . um, real bad, Charlie." What I said to myself

was less charitable. *That's it? If that's all you've got, my gawd, just shut up and run.*

By day four, he could have skipped down the road stark naked and stopped to do a jig in front of me, and I probably wouldn't have reacted. On the third night, I'd finished my seventy miles again, then taken Ambien to help me sleep, and I'd spent the night with my legs up in the air, propped against the wall in an effort to drain some of the lactic acid, but that hadn't helped much.

After letting me sink into four hours of drug-induced doze, Heather had roused me to get going again, and I'd gone out that fourth morning, groggy and tired, my legs swollen, my calf muscles tight, and generally feeling like an old man with creaky joints and aching bones. I'd become increasingly sore, and I knew that my body was undergoing a tough transformation: slowly, painfully morphing into a running machine. It would probably take another week or more of this torture before I'd settle in and the aches and pains would subside some.

My predictions were proving dead-on. This was, bar none, the toughest thing I'd ever attempted. Even a hard day of climbing Mount Everest didn't compare with these seventy-mile days.

That was true even considering the worst conditions on the great mountain, which Tibetans call Chomolungma ("saint mother"): the sudden storms, the jagged crevasses and roaring glacial streams, the cutting winds up to 125 miles per hour, temps dipping to forty below, and oxygen deprivation. In high-altitude mountaineering, there's a saying about getting overzealous and doing too much under these extreme conditions, "Don't let your brain go to your feet," and by necessity, our pace on Everest was slow. So often, I found myself feeling as if I ought to be doing something more, but the altitude dictated plenty of downtime. As I ran across California, I never once read a newspaper or even sat in a chair, but at base camp, I'd sat and listened to a short-wave radio, tinkered with the generator to make sure it was in good shape (my experience with farm machinery got me the job as camp mechanic), shot the breeze and played card games with some of the other people on the expedition. Nearly every day during the couple of months in Tibet, I'd written about my thoughts and experiences there. I'd been fortunate not to suffer from most of the common effects of altitude (headaches, nausea, double vision, hallucinations), so my impulse was always to push harder, but it was tempered by the knowledge that reaching the summit of the tallest mountain on earth required that I slowly acclimatize, expending just enough energy, but not too much, at increasing altitudes. Pushing yourself too hard at such heights becomes idiocy: Muscles waste away with what I'd consider moderate use at nineteen thousand feet and above. Keeping weight on becomes a concern as you ascend; at common elevations, you'd need to run about fifty miles to burn a pound of fat, but in the "death zone" over twenty-five thousand feet, your body feeds off muscle even when you're sleeping—it's the fuel of choice at extreme altitude. When I came down off Everest, I'd lost fifteen pounds, most of it muscle; my spare tire still circled my midsection, though. Heather called me "the crooked man" because my hips canted to the left, no doubt because I'd lost core muscle strength.

Running, I felt isolated, alone. On Everest, I'd been constantly surrounded by people, some of them highly entertaining. Our Russian guide, Alex Abramov, was a real character and a confidence-inspiring leader. He stands about six feet, with hunched shoulders, and you'd never guess by looking at him that he's a world-class climber. In the sport of mountaineering, though, appearances don't mean anything; so much of success in climbing depends on weather, adaptability to altitude, genetics, experience, common sense, and luck. People you'd never expect will do extraordinary things, and ones who are "buffed out" can have the hardest of times, or fail.

The Russians had brought copious amounts of their favorite bever-

ages, rum and vodka, and they were generous with them at dinnertime, toasting round after round until everyone was shit-faced. They'd also brought a fifty-five-gallon drum of cabbage to make borscht, and loved to snack on salted fish and smoked pig fat cut into strips and eaten off the knife (like I'm accustomed to carving off a piece of cheese) or dropped into a vat, of fat and fried: full of calories and flavor. The team had spared no expense with the equipment and tents, making for quite a comfortable experience, save the harsh winds and temperatures, the trouble sleeping, and the suffocatingly thin air as we got closer to the top.

So we were in capable hands with Alex, and he had a great sense of adventure and an even better sense of humor. He's renowned for his skill and for being a bit of a wild card. One morning, I asked him over breakfast about something crazy I'd heard he'd done: made an expedition with a Land Rover to the top of Mount Elbrus. All true, he told me. They'd set a world record for vehicular-assisted mountain climb (18,510 feet), and then took off to sun themselves at the Russian Riviera, along the Black Sea. A few months later when they returned to fetch the Rover from the top of the mountain, he said, it was colder and dangerously icy, so he and the climbers went to get some chains and left the driver up top with the Rover. Impatient and foolhardy, Alex's driver decided he'd handle it alone. Of course, the descent got out of control, and he had to bail out—just in time, too, before the vehicle started tumbling down the mountain and crashed into some rocks, knocking a tire loose that shot down toward the climbers bringing the chains, nearly killing them all. But the driver and the team survived, and the Rover remains "parked" there on Elbrus.

No matter what you wanted, it seemed Alex could make it happen. While we were at advanced base camp one night, I overheard him talking to the cook about some meat Alex had ordered, but it hadn't arrived by porter yet. I couldn't see either of them, so I was picturing Alex glaring and growling at the cook, his bushy eyebrows knitted and his teeth bared. A guy who could survive a hurtling tire on Elbrus wasn't going to be denied his meat.

"What you think, we vegetarians?!"

Then he calmly got on the radio and called down to base camp, several thousand feet lower on the mountain, and menaced the cook there: "If you no bring meat up tomorrow, I come down there and *kill* you."

Of course, he was joking, and with his accent it sounded like something out of *The Rocky and Bullwinkle Show*. I must have laughed for five minutes afterward. But true to form, Alex came through: The next night we had meat on the table.

Just once that I can recall things didn't swing Alex's way. Before leaving Katmandu, I'd negotiated with the local dealer to buy our generator and come back with what I thought was a good price. Alex and I went to buy the thing, and he insisted on trying to get an even better deal—if Alex is any indication, Russians are *really* into dickering. He haggled, he argued, he pestered, and the dealer got so fed up with the intense bargaining, he didn't want to sell the generator to us at all. We finally settled on a price that was higher than the one I'd negotiated.

Yet Alex has my enduring respect. Russian climbers are considered the Michael Jordans of the sport, and he introduced me to the best of the best in his country, the Russian National Climbing Team—the best in the world, in my opinion. They had set up base camp a month earlier than us, and our group spent a lot of time socializing with the national team. They were setting a never-done-before North Face route *without* oxygen. They didn't use Sherpas but would do very heavy equipment carry-ins to their high camp at the base of Everest below the North Face, with half the group alternating weeks on and off, going up to set hardware and rope. Incidentally, the last three thousand feet of the North Face is vertical rock—unbelievably tough! These guys are hard-asses.

One of their new members was a man in his mid-twenties who had proven himself worthy prior to Everest, a real stud by anyone's account. I'd talk with him whenever he was in camp, and then one day he stumbled by me, looking dejected. When I asked what had happened, he

said that he'd gotten kicked off the team because, when he was up around twenty-seven thousand feet, he'd griped about his hands being cold. With stares icier than the glacial wall they were scaling, his teammates told him to climb down and go back to base camp. He was done. That's it: He was finished. The Russians don't stand for any whining, no matter how justified.

The team was successful, and three men made it to the top from the North Face and without the use of supplementary oxygen, completing what's possibly one of the hardest-core climbing feats in high-altitude mountaineering.

No doubt there's a Russian word for "macho," and they were defining it: to tough it out, never to complain, always to rely upon themselves first. But, sincerely, they would risk their lives for one another and anyone else on the mountain.

As I ran in the midday heat of the much smaller mountain range of the Sierra Nevadas, I thought about the cold and the camaraderie of my Everest adventure, and I wondered how this endeavor would ultimately stack up against it. So far, Everest was hands down the more pleasant experience.

Despondent, sitting on a prison bench with my head in my hands, I awaited the inevitable. It was coming soon, the ultimate punishment for an unexplained crime. The walls seemed to close in on me, the bars at the front of my cell making silent, steely condemnations. No escape.

A recurring nightmare had begun: Impending execution haunted my nights in the RV. Sometimes it was ambiguous like that, where I didn't know if I was headed for the electric chair or the gas chamber or lethal injection. Other times, I was standing in front of a firing squad. Regardless, just over two hundred miles along our route, a fear of death now dominated my dreams, torturing me in my sleep. My best guess was that my subconscious mind was trying to send a message: *You're killing yourself.*

The wry, sad look Heather gave me when I confessed this to her told me she and my subconscious were in agreement.

When we came down out of the mountains and reentered the arid, inhospitable desert dotted with sagebrush, I did my best to rest under the occasional shade tree and to stay out of the sun whenever there was a chance, but relief was rare. Although my crew was doing a great job of keeping me supplied with electrolytes and fluids, the heat was problematic. I was slowing down and feeling demoralized as we crossed the state line into Nevada.

> # Welcome to Nevada!
> ## "The Silver State"
>
> Arrival date: 9/16/08 (Day 4)
> Arrival time: 9:45 a.m.
> Miles covered: 230.5
> Miles to go: 2,832.7

Given all that, the sight of Carson City, the state capital just thirty miles across the border, was a relief. We'd find freshly cooked food there for dinner—at this point, I was living for the occasional milk shake or root beer float, and fried chicken or pork tacos, anything that didn't come in a sealed wrapper from a convenience store—and I liked imagining the people of the town, both in the present and the past. It is named after the frontier hero "Kit" Carson, and its downtown evinces the American Old West, but the historic trading post is now updated, more sophisticated than it must have been back in the 1860s when gold and silver miners, ranchers, millers, and gamblers first made their homes there. Thinking about all this as we entered the area, it was one of the few times that day when I dwelled on anything other than taking the next breath, the next step, and then the next, and the next, and the next on this road that seemed to push out to eternity, straight as an arrow.

The capitol dome loomed above the city, and it seemed hours before I finally passed the structure at the center of town, squared off in a post-and-lintel construction to support its six-sided cupola. Funny, if it weren't for the arches that held it high and the shine on its silver surface, that dome could have topped any one of the silver-and-brown-planked barns I'd passed along the road earlier that day. Once we were into the city, I got a close look at the capitol, as well as the massive buildings that lined the road where I ran, slightly north and midway through town. The traditional brick construction had been popular in the late 1800s, and it must have been enormously challenging to build, given that buildings were erected manually. At one point, I passed a modern casino, a stark contrast to the old structures, and its neon signs lit the way as I turned to head east. As always, I was relieved when we moved more directly toward New York, pointed straight to my goal just as a steeple on one huge church I saw pointed to the heavens.

As I ran into and through Carson City, I was feeling all right, comforted by being in a place where people live and work and lead normal lives. I ate with gusto, crunching my tacos and spooning a root beer float into my mouth while on the move. Later, leaving the area might have been a letdown—I always felt low just after a lift—except that a group of middle school kids who were playing soccer in a park had come out to cheer me on, and they cheered me up as I headed out of town. The documentary film crew had alerted the teams that we were on our way from San Francisco to New York, and they'd enthusiastically run out to the path alongside the park.

As I passed through, everyone chanted my name, "Marshall! Marshall! Marshall!" They ran with me for a couple of blocks, kicking up a big ruckus.

Who cares if it was contrived? Or that it was so quick that they were gone and I was on my own again in a matter of minutes? That small celebration gave me a big charge and kept me going. We exchanged plenty of high fives, and for a brief time, I forgot how tired I was.

Giving me yet another boost, some clouds rolled in to shelter me from the heat, and within thirty minutes of the lower temperature, I was feeling damn good and wanted to increase my lead. When I picked up the pace, my crew announced that I was running eight- to ten-minute miles, as good as or better than I'd run on day one—and it felt great to go faster. What a treat to let out my stride! I ran at this pace for another three hours. Game on!

When darkness dropped across the high desert, I could see little except what was directly ahead and illuminated by a headlamp I carried in my hand. Once again, fatigue took hold, I slowed down, and I resigned myself to running in this tunnel of light, blackness all around me. A passing truck's tailwind ripped my light away from me and sent it sailing out onto the highway, where the semi's wheels crushed it to bits. It snapped me out of my stupor, both frightening me and striking me as funny: Now I really was in the dark.

Dr. Paul fetched me a replacement, and the crew seemed to drift in and out as they stopped for me every mile, offering food and fluids. I moved through the night in a daze.

The next afternoon, I found out that Charlie was laid up in Fallon, Nevada, which I'd passed through earlier. I felt bad for him and worried

that I'd had a hand in his demise. My stubbornness in sticking to that seventy-mile-a-day promise was surely screwing us both into the ground. We'd both been having major trouble with our Achilles tendons, and the heat from the pavement radiated up through the soles of our shoes and climbed our legs like a forest fire licking tree trunks. I'd cut a 3/4-inch notch in the back of my shoe and recommended that Charlie do the same to accommodate his inflamed tendons, but I didn't have any remedies for the hot pavement except to keep pressing forward. Whenever Charlie didn't make his mileage for the day, I'd just put my head down and pull out farther in front of him, driving both of us on. In turn, he'd been pushing me along from the rear, and that combined with my competitive nature had certainly helped keep me focused.

What would I do if I had to go it alone? The idea terrified me.

The night ended with a spectacular display of stars, interrupted only by a few trucks that struggled up Sand Springs Pass beside me, breaking the quiet and the darkness. The elevation gain wasn't much, maybe a thousand feet; still, it took a lot of energy to get over it. When I ran down the other side of the pass, I was thirty-nine miles beyond Fallon, but my mind was back there with Charlie, fretting over the prospect of his injuries keeping him from going any farther.

Now the doubt that had been with me from the beginning began to overtake me, as I felt I was rapidly reaching the point of diminishing returns.

How could I keep this up?

Surely my support team was wondering the same thing, not only about me but also about themselves. They were putting in long hours of their own. Roger, Kathleen, and Heather had each logged about nineteen hours on duty that day alone. Heather's role had transformed into full-time crew member as soon as Jesse's energy had flagged; now he was also back in Fallon, sick with bronchitis. Dr. Paul was in Fallon, too, to treat Charlie and to work with his crew to ensure that they were taking care of him properly.

Every day, Roger was driving the RV, cooking, shopping, cleaning, running laundry, and doing other errands. Before we got going each morning, he'd create a daily planner for me, a crucial mental aid that gave me some sense of where I was headed, what I could expect, and for how long. Otherwise, I felt completely out of touch, just a pair of legs moving through the desert, a shadow flickering across the sand. Sometimes, he also pitched in to help the team with directly supporting me on the road. Heather was constantly torn between being there for me and completing any other tasks she had, like coordinating the crew schedule, doing the shopping with Roger for all the food and my supplies, desperately searching small-town stores for decent socks for me (I hadn't packed enough), working with the production crew to ensure that I was running through especially scenic areas during "magic hour" (that time of day when the light is just right for gorgeous cinematography), and trying to work within tight budget constraints. Kathleen was constantly on duty, bringing me food, fluids, and electrolyte tablets, giving me massages, stretching me, helping Roger with cooking breakfast and cleaning the RV, consulting with Dr. Paul about my condition and possible ways to help, and generally trying to keep the peace. This race was tough on me, but it was no holiday for them, either. It was far more than any of us had bargained for.

For me, life had become incredibly simple, as it consisted of running a mile to reach the crew van, getting a few mouthfuls of food as I slowed for a minute or two, picking up the pace again until the next crew stop, and doing it all over again and again. I drank constantly, relieved myself when necessary. At the end of the day, I slept, and in the morning, I got up to run some more. That simplicity was beautiful, clearing my mind, putting me in touch with primitive instincts. It made me realize how perfectly humans were built to hunt and gather, and it was easy for me to imagine that I was no different from the ancients who'd inhabited the area, simply surviving and not thinking about the next step. My crew took care of everything, so all I had to do was take care of myself by

obliging them. Nothing else mattered, and there was no reason to care about anything but breathing and running . . . down the road, up the hills, concentrating on forward movement. Paradoxically, I took comfort in it, a sublime effort that involved nothing more than running.

Yet the distances were taking their toll. The tendons in my upper and lower legs had begun to throb constantly, as if someone had cracked them both with a hammer. My muscles were so tight that they felt like guitar strings strung over the bridge of my aching bones. My Achilles tendon was giving me no relief, and my bones and joints hurt from the incessant pounding. I'd felt something like all this before—long adventure races would leave me with throbbing knees and aching legs—but this was different. The pavement was unyielding and unforgiving. Everything hurt now, even my arms and head from holding them upright. Surely, something would have to give.

Most of the time now, I was running in a trance, my mind focused far from the stress on my body and instead lingering on thoughts of my family, how much I missed Heather, how much I wanted to be with her. Whenever I saw my wife, it was usually for just a minute or two during a crew stop, when she'd bring me food or some other thing I needed, and we talked almost exclusively about the run: what I needed next, where we were headed, who was crewing, how it was going. I longed for the leisure to genuinely connect with her, and I spent a fair amount of time mooning, wishing for a cup of coffee and quiet conversation on our back deck at home. Occasionally, I'd be pulled out of my daydreams by something strange or beautiful in the immediate environment.

Outside Middlegate, for example, I saw a tree with something dangling from it—lots of somethings. It looked like one of the "sausage trees" I'd seen in Africa, huge kigelias hung with tubelike fruit. But when I was close enough, I could see that this was completely different: an old cottonwood festooned with thousands of shoes. Still, it sent me into a reverie, vivid memories carrying me away to a safari on the Serengeti Plain and then to the climbs up Kilimanjaro with Heather and Roger. I couldn't help thinking, too, about how much Heather's dad, Rory, would have delighted in this tree: quirky yet somehow artful, expansive and strange and right there in the middle of . . . nothing.

These "shoe trees" bloom on various roadsides of America. Some individual, in a fit of whimsy or irritation or rebellion, tosses a pair of shoes into a tree until the laces catch over a branch. Others follow suit, and soon enough, you have a tree laden with footwear. In keeping with tradition, Roger attempted to pitch a pair of my worn-out shoes into the tree and failed, the bright blue Pearl Izumis falling through the branches and into a massive pile at the base. Later, though, I was thrilled to hear that someone from Charlie's crew had come by with the camera guys and recognized my road-worn shoes by their color—especially easy to spot with the toe box cut out—retrieved them from the pile, and pitched them high into the tree, where I expect they still hang. I liked that we were all working together; this echoed the spirit of the run. Indeed, that tree was something to behold, out in the middle of nowhere, not another tree in sight, a testament to all the feet that had passed that way before mine.

Middlegate itself seemed emblematic. On the door to the little café/bar/motel there, a sign reads: MIDDLEGATE: HALFWAY BETWEEN HERE AND THERE. Boy, that's about right: halfway between heaven and hell, no man's land. Congratulations, traveler! You've reached nowhere.

Yet one of the great things about being "nowhere" is that you're able to see the incredible beauty of the stars undiminished by city glare. In the desert after dark, the Milky Way provided a stunning shimmer of light. And the flashers of the van, always just a mile ahead, pulled me along like a tractor beam. As my night of running came to an end, I could see the "Starship" parked a ways up the road, where Roger had found a good camping place and left the RV's parking lights on to guide me in. That night, like many others in the desert, it looked as if a path of stars led to our traveling home, where I would find solace and a place to rest in Heather's arms.

9,000'
7,000'
5,000'
3,000'
1,000'

———

The next day, as I ran down the main street of Austin, Nevada, two shop owners came out to see what was happening, which wasn't much, just the van passing through and me plodding along. One emerged from a gas station, a transplant from Mexico, I think, not saying a word but steadily looking at me from across the street. The other was a sun-baked woman wearing a flower-print working dress and standing near a store that sold snacks. She looked as if she had done this many times before over her fifty-something years. She calmly swiped a single wave, keeping an expressionless face as if my presence was an everyday occurrence and she fully expected me to be there.

We'd climbed our way from the desert floor into this town, set among undulating hills that rise gently to the horizon and sometimes break away to steep pitches. The area reminded me of many of the bluffs I've seen in Wyoming, and I was starting to notice pines and vegetation that marked an increase in altitude and available water. The brick Catholic church on the hill was in such good condition that it looked as if it had been built yesterday, with its new steel green roof and steeple, topped with the traditional cross. Yet it was the last one standing of the first four Catholic churches built in Nevada, back in 1866. We passed the international café, constructed of barn lumber, its second story set with oversized windows and spilling onto a covered porch held up by rickety posts. On top of the whole thing: a three-foot-diameter star. The signs on the main-street stores and antique shops looked as old as the buildings. It seemed a wonder to me that it had all remained standing, giving a glimpse of how things used to look back in the wild west: simple wooden and brick construction, squared-off buildings with the occasional brick church, one with a steeple that looked like a silver bullet piercing the sky.

Heading out of Austin and then off Scott's Pass, I was going downhill, both figuratively and literally. Now wearing a brace off and on to alleviate some of the unrelenting pain in my right knee, I stopped a long time for dinner at the RV and did something new: slept for an hour and a half in the middle of the day. Kathleen massaged my tired muscles, we iced my inflamed joints, and I headed back out, still sleepy. For the most part, the road was vacant and lonely, so I was especially relieved and glad to get some good news: Charlie was on the move again, about seventy miles behind me.

That night, my seventh on the road since we'd left San Francisco, I broke. At 3:45 in the morning, after running for almost twenty-one hours and now standing ten miles short of our goal, I told my crew I had to stop. Today, we'd have to be satisfied with sixty miles instead of seventy. I wanted to sleep and asked to be driven to a hotel in Eureka for a few hours' rest and a shower (my second of the run).

Getting up at seven and still feeling exhausted the next morning, I admitted to myself that this wasn't the last time I'd fall short of seventy miles. I couldn't keep it up and neither could my crew. We'd already lost Jesse to illness; he'd gone home the day before, and the remaining crew was feeling the strain of his absence.

Running all night on day eight sealed it. After sixty-two miles, I was stumbling around and babbling incoherently at 5:30 in the morning when Heather did something she'd never done before: She came out on the road, took me by the collar, and dragged me off the course for some sleep. This was just the kind of thing she'd known would happen, the reason she'd argued with me so strongly the year before we began. But now she was all tenderness as she took me to bed, an angel in the darkness. She took care of me while I slept, icing my legs. In less than five hours, she helped me wake up again and get back up on my feet for another day on the road, still tired but with a bit more of my wits about me.

Day nine, near Ely, Nevada: Word had it that Charlie was mounting a comeback and closing in on me. In my near-delirium, I couldn't give it much thought, though I was glad to hear he was running sound again. Despite the expert attentions of my crew, without whom I surely would have been roadkill, my days had become incredibly solitary, and it was heartening to know Charlie would be with me the rest of the way.

This is a great place for a prison, I thought to myself as we passed the turnoff to the state penitentiary. *If someone escaped, they'd have to run an awfully long way to get anywhere.*

No kidding. Those were the sorts of uplifting thoughts that kept me company.

At about seven o'clock that evening, I crawled into the RV for a nap. This was a horrible stop for both Heather and me, as she knew that I was in agony with every step, frustrated with my slowing pace. There was no way I was going to regain a daily distance of seventy-plus miles, much less do it in just fifteen hours as I had back in San Francisco.

So Heather consoled me, telling me everything was going to be okay, assuring me how proud she was of me, reminding me of how many miles we'd already come. She urged me to rest—that was the only thing to do now. I closed my eyes until eleven, getting maybe three hours of down-time, and then was off again, running in the dark, leaving Heather to her thoughts. I know now that she'd wanted to beg me to stop, that she'd been heartbroken to see me suffer, that she and the rest of the crew had been exhausted, too, but she'd kept her own counsel.

It was an unspoken code. She wouldn't tell me to quit, even if she wanted to yell it at me with all her being. She knew how hard I'd fought for this opportunity, how I'd given it endless hours of training and men-tal preparation during a year that gave me many excuses to stop. She knew that I wanted to (that I had to) finish this run across America, no matter what. So, unless my life was in immediate danger, she would bite her tongue and, out of love, support me. She knew that my mind was set and my integrity would be compromised if I settled for anything less than finishing.

Yet, despite her support and that of my crew, I covered just shy of forty-three miles that day, the ninth of the run, and had to stop at three in the morning. Dr. Paul ordered that I not go all night anymore. He said, emphatically, that I had to get more sleep. I couldn't disagree.

It continued to be hot, like most of the days before. And like most of the days to come, I imagined. I was moving slowly, dipping to about 3.5 miles per hour, around a seventeen-minute-mile pace, a shuffle barely faster than most people walk. We crossed into Utah close to midnight on day ten, and I went another 11.3 miles into the state, a bit faster now, finishing up my sixty for the day doing about 4.15 miles per hour.

Welcome to Utah!
"The Beehive State"

Arrival date: 9/22/08 (Day 10)
Arrival time: 11:36 p.m.
Miles covered: 633.3
Miles to go: 2,429.7

When I stopped a little after two in the morning, Roger drove us back to Border Town, where we stayed at what Heather called a dive—and she was right, but it was a palace to me, because I had a shower and fresh

sheets for the night. Heather was putting me to bed, gently guiding me from the bathroom to the bedroom, and trying in vain to explain to me what time I'd be getting up in the morning. We'd lost an hour when we'd crossed over into the new time zone, and I just couldn't get my head around the math and the mechanics of my watch. Physically, I was still able to move, but mentally, I was cooked. Heather gave up trying to help me understand and just allowed me to feel certain in my confusion, taking me by the hand and tucking me into bed like she would a child. She stayed up, as always, to ice my legs while I slept.

On day ten, I'd gone sixty miles, but I went only a little more than fifty on day eleven. Several days before, I'd acknowledged that my body had started morphing into a running machine, and now I had to acknowledge that the machinery was breaking down. My joints, bones, muscles, and soft tissue all hurt. I couldn't take a step without being reminded of the 650 miles that had already passed under my feet.

SEEING AMERICA, ONE MILE AT A TIME

"The Loneliest Road"
U.S. Highway 50 Across Nevada

Our route from San Francisco to New York City would stick pretty close to the old Lincoln Highway, "the backbone of America" and the first transcontinental road built for travel by car in the United States. Constructed in the early 1900s, at a time when there were no decent roads, and the ones we did have were disconnected and seemed to go nowhere, it created not only the longest roadway in America, but also a single, uninterrupted, coast-to-coast highway.

When the road was being planned all those years ago, the designers included one stretch that was well established and frequently traveled, dating back before the Pony Express. Today, that roadway across Nevada covers the entire state from Douglas County through Carson City, on to Fallon, Austin, and Eureka, and leading into Utah through Ely. As I ran it, the distance totaled about four hundred miles.

The road mostly follows a wagon route originally used in 1859 by Captain James H. Simpson of the U.S. Army Corps of Topographical Engineers. Leading an expedition from Utah to Carson Valley, Nevada, he'd sought the most direct line from east to west, blazing a trail that would get wagons across the state faster than the old, circuitous emigrant path from Elko to Reno. He figured that this new way cut more than two hundred eighty miles from the trip.

According to Simpson, the Pony Express started using his new route soon after he'd established it because of the abundant water and stock feed, ideal for the fleet of horse-riding mail carriers. Although the Pony Express enjoyed its glory days for less than two years (the telegraph and mail going by stagecoach replaced it), during that time, it helped entrench Simpson's route for swift travel across Nevada. The riders, renowned for their endurance and speed, helped weave the lore of the Great American West.

That way was all but abandoned for a while after the Central Pacific Railroad was laid in 1869. Rail traffic moved north, and the old Simpson trail became a quiet, less traveled route through the mountains and valleys of the Silver State.

When the Lincoln Highway project reclaimed, renovated, and revitalized much of Simpson's route, it suddenly became

the way to go for a taste of western adventure, fraught with perils (like poor paving) and lined with historical sites for the brave travelers who dared to drive it. Want to prove your "American rugged individualism"? This was the place to test your mettle.

Today, the desolate areas along the road, where the only company you'll find are the minerals and rocks that drew people to this place long ago, earned it the moniker "The Loneliest Road in America."

Was it the loneliest one for me? In some ways, yes. The daily mileage I logged across Nevada was chewing me up. But there were bright spots. Friends who drove to the middle of nowhere for a visit and brought me ice cream. The kids who came out from the soccer field to cheer me on. The incredible beauty of the desert, both by day and under the starlit night sky. And the inexplicable solitude that left me time to ponder my singular existence and discover how utterly frail, vulnerable, and dependent I was . . . but *not* alone.

On day twelve, we reached the end of the road, both literally and figuratively. Since day three, we'd been following Highway 50 from Carson Pass, and we were about to turn off it onto Highway 6 to take us through most of Utah and on to Colorado. As we came to my final miles on Highway 50, also known as "the loneliest road in America," I was no longer able to put any weight on my right foot. That morning, nearly two weeks into our transcontinental crossing, I covered just shy of thirteen miles before creeping into our RV for Dr. Paul to check me out. We iced the insanely sore arch, which felt like hundreds of needles jabbing, jabbing, jabbing.

While we were tending to that, Charlie passed me for the first time since he'd been ahead of me briefly on the third day, but I knew he was suffering, too. Both of us were dealing with acute knee pain, extreme muscle fatigue, and various other problems. We were essentially in the same boat, and now I had something else going on with my foot.

Charlie stopped to check on me and encourage me, and he reminded me of something I'd told him: "Never take yourself off the course, even if you're reduced to a crawl," meaning that you keep going until it's so bad someone else has to stop you. Then Charlie left to continuing running.

After a brief examination, Dr. Paul ordered that I be driven to a hotel in the next town, Delta, Utah. I'd have to elevate my foot and ice it, get a massage, and rest. Only then would he take a second look. He'd already guessed at the problem but held his cards close. He'd come by later to check on my condition and see if he was right.

Diagnosis: plantar fasciitis, an intensely painful swelling on the sole of my foot.

Treatment: eighty milligrams of Kenalog, an anti-inflammatory drug.

So that evening, he injected the Kenalog in my gluteus maximus, and my job was simply to wait to see if it would work. Although he never told me so, Dr. Paul estimated that my chances of being able to continue were only 30 percent. He did let me know that recovery was uncertain, and that I should prepare myself for the possibility that I'd be finished.

The folks at the Rancher Motel café cooked up a big plate of spaghetti for me, and despite my medical issues, I thought I was in heaven. This was going to be the longest break I'd had since we'd left San Francisco, and here I was, freshly bathed, laid up in a big bed with clean sheets, my wife nearby, and a delicious, freshly prepared meal to eat. There was also some cake—leftovers from Charlie's birthday celebration, I think—and the whole scene made me feel grateful indeed.

Heather and I didn't talk about it then, but we both harbored secret hopes that the doctor would say that I was done, that I shouldn't run another step, that I'd given it my all but now it was over. It's good we didn't share that with each other, because it could have turned into a

bell-ringing moment for me. The voice that tells me to stop could have gotten so loud that I wouldn't be able to ignore it any longer. We simply couldn't allow those thoughts to be spoken.

That night, I called a meeting of my remaining crew and two others who'd arrived to help. I explained my slim chances of recovery and the possibility that all of us were finished with this run, but I encouraged them, saying, "Don't ever count me out!"

I'd been down before and repeatedly come back from the dead in circumstances that seemed a lot more difficult than our situation in Delta. We'd know in the morning if this really was the end of the road for us, or if adventure yet called, and we still had new territory to explore.

PART II
Heartland

Bid me run, and I will strive with things impossible.

—William Shakespeare, *Julius Caesar*

6.

Coming Home

Days 13–24

All three of my kids did some of their growing up in a baby jogger. First Elaine, as I ran to deal with my stress. Then Taylor, who was born in 1983, just two months after I completed my first ultramarathon in Wyoming. And then Alexandra, who made her debut into this world as I was getting ready for my first Badwater crossing in 1990. By the time each of them reached two years old, they knew the routine: Daddy would grab the contraption, they'd climb in, and off we'd go onto the streets of Fort Morgan, where I'd train every morning. In our small Colorado town, there weren't a lot of other runners, and none were as constant about it as I was, so we were a curiosity. Everyone knew our family, and they looked out for us on the roads.

My youngest, Ali, proved to be the most lively companion, always finagling to get out of the jogger because what she really wanted to do was push it. (I still wonder if people thought I was making her do that.) The best way to get her to stay put was promising a ride through Dairy Queen, which she thought was the best part of any trip. We'd roll up to the drive-through window, place our order, and then trot off, Ali giggling with delight, her lap full of treats.

When the kids were little, it was easy to keep them close, to take them along, to include them in my routine, and I loved their company. Later, though, there were many times when I was distant or, as they say, "emotionally unavailable," ill-equipped for some of the demands of family life. Brought up in a home where men didn't talk about feelings, wounded by Jean's death, and then married less than a year after that to Danette, I was unskilled in dealing with the conflicts that arose. Whenever Danette and I argued heatedly and I felt that I'd reached my limits with her, I'd cut her off. It was as if I'd slam down the receiver in the middle of a phone conversation.

"That's it. I gotta go."

It was unfair. Constantly compared with Jean—I did it both consciously and unconsciously—and watching me deal with our problems as I had with Jean's illness, Danette bore the brunt of my alienation. If it got uncomfortable when things weren't going well, if I craved the comfort of familiarity, if I needed escape, I always had the road. No matter where I was, I could grab my shoes and head out the door. Putting literal distance between me and any trouble at home gave me a sense of control over the situation: Once again, running offered a way to deal with my problems or bypass them, think things over and calm down or ignore them altogether. At the time, it seemed like the perfect way to handle any issue, but now it's obvious that this contributed to the demise of my relationship with Danette. Leaving in the middle of a fight served only to make her more angry, so we were in a cycle of arguing, rehashing, and me repeatedly leaving to blow off some steam, which would trigger the cycle all over again. For a guy who prides himself on continuing even when it's painful, on going the distance despite obstacles, on staying the course no matter what, I'm embarrassed to admit my failure in this particular test of my emotional endurance.

With the kids, it wasn't so dramatic, but as in any other home where the parents aren't getting along, they sensed what was happening. They could read our body language and probably overheard some of our arguments. We tried to keep our disagreements away from them, but I know we didn't completely insulate them. There were times, too, when one or the other of our kids tried to use our growing disaffection to manipulate us, to pit us against each other to get what they wanted, just as most children in this situation do. It was trying, all of it.

Yet I don't believe I ever intentionally cut them off or disregarded them the way I did with Danette. My love for them runs deep, and their best interests have always been paramount. However, I do, still, have intense feelings of inadequacy as a father. The times when I fell short, when I wasn't up to the task of parenting, all remain vivid in my mind: The conversations where I couldn't come up with the words to say, or said too much. The long days of work and training when I wasn't there for them. The weekends spent in competition, a mental and physical escape from daily life. When Danette and I divorced, Elaine was almost thirteen, Taylor was nine, and Ali was two, and it was no small thing in any of our lives, as it split the family into two households.

Soon after the divorce, they watched me marry again, this time to a fellow ultrarunner. My relationship with Willette was largely about my attempting to recapture some of what I'd felt with Jean, as I'd thought that a marriage with someone who shared my passion for running would translate to one with greater intimacy and connection. But ultimately, both of us were disappointed. Even when Willette and I set a record together at Badwater one year for the fastest husband-and-wife crossing, it was deeply unsatisfying, as we'd fought most of the way, arguing as we ran, each of us wrapped up in our own "stuff," too self-centered to celebrate the kind of union I'd hoped for. Although the marriage was short-lived, it must have affected the children and given them more evidence of how Dad didn't have much figured out when it came to women. I still worry about the example I set, yet I'm proud of who my children have become despite whatever mistakes I made. All are independent, strong-willed, unique expressions of the best of me and their mothers—and their own people, besides.

So, when I heard that all three of them, grown adults (Elaine, thirty; Taylor, twenty-five; and Ali, eighteen), were coming out to support me for part of the run through Colorado that fall of 2008, I was excited and also apprehensive. This would be our first time all together during one of my extreme events.

Waking up in that hotel room in Delta, Utah, the morning after Dr. Paul had injected me with the anti-inflammatory drug for my plantar fasciitis, I was ready to give the foot a try, having rested most of the day before and slept amazingly well until about six in the morning. By seven, we were back at the stake-out point, and I'd pulled on a pair of black Crocs to give my arch a nice rubberized surface and provide cushioning under my heel as it struck the pavement.

Running wasn't an option yet. Gingerly, I stepped forward, hoping for the best.

After about an hour of going slowly but increasingly faster, I changed into my running shoes and grabbed my LEKI trekking poles. By putting downward pressure on the poles and pushing off slightly, I'd propel myself forward with a bit of weight unloaded from my feet. The pain had subsided significantly, and I promised Heather that if my foot really started to hurt, we'd stop. (That wasn't entirely honest, as the damn thing still really hurt. I should have said that we'd stop if it became unbearable to walk.)

But we didn't have to stop. That day, we headed up a valley of pasture-land dotted with cattle, and houses on small acreages flanking either side of the road. This meant that we'd come out of the true desert and were ap-

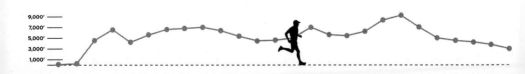

proaching an agricultural area. There was more moisture in the air, the temperatures were lower, and the smells of livestock and farming reminded me of my parents' place in Colorado. It drew me forward to think that we'd reach my old stomping grounds within the week, and then my children would be there to meet me.

EL JALISCIENSE (THE JALISCAN)

Making It in America

Sometime in 2004, Maria Gutierrez started cooking tortas and selling them to the local dairy and chicken farm workers to help her family make ends meet. Her husband, Jesus, was a cattleman himself, working three hundred head and growing hay on about forty acres of their ranch near Delta, Utah. Soon after she began her small enterprise, it became obvious that Maria's tortas could be the foundation of a successful venture, and Jesus was ready to capitalize on his wife's cooking to make a better life for his family.

A better life was the reason they'd come with their two baby daughters to the United States from Jalisco, Mexico, in the first place, back in 1985. With the help of relatives, they'd settled in the Cherry Valley in California, where Jesus worked as a foreman at a chicken factory/farm. Years later, when the plant closed, he moved the family east to Utah, where the beautiful green valleys and the low land prices had caught his eye. An ad in the *Thrifty Nickel* prompted him to look into a parcel of a hundred acres for $185,000. But it had a checkered past: It was part of the old Topaz Camp, where more than eight thousand Japanese-American internees were held in the early 1940s. Maybe it was the history of questionable treatment of immigrant families that made him decide to buy elsewhere. Ultimately, he purchased his cattle ranch for about $325,000 and then struggled to turn a good profit from the sale of beef and hay.

But Maria's tortas were selling like hotcakes—or, rather, delicious Mexican sandwiches. So Jesus and Maria purchased a catering truck from a cousin who lived in Oregon, and they also bought a small piece of land in the city of Delta, on which they could build a restaurant. By then, in late 2007, Jesus had the restaurant designed in his mind already, and they began permitting for construction. Meanwhile, they outfitted the catering truck to handle Maria's tortas, plus tacos, burritos, and other inexpensive but delicious foods they could continue to sell to the local community. They used their families' home recipes—authentic Jaliscan *barbacoa* (shredded beef), *carnitas* (fried pork), *mole* (sauce), salsa, and more—and tested their dishes on friends and family. If everyone loved it, they served it to customers at a fair price.

Jesus downsized the cattle operation and focused on bringing their food to the people in Delta, a community of just over three thousand people, of whom about 10 percent are Hispanic or Latino. For anyone in love with the flavors of Mexico, Jesus and Maria satisfied their cravings.

When we met Jesus as I ran through Delta, it was at their "taco wagon," and I ate one of the Gutierrez's pork burritos as I speed walked down Highway 50, exclaiming about how good it was. At that time, they were doing a brisk business, parked on the street in front of where the restaurant would rise, and groundwork was under way—we spotted some of

the bricks outlining the footprint—you could see what the place might become, and Jesus was eager to have it finished. He was risking it all to make the business go, as he'd decided to start this venture at a time when loans were scarce and he wasn't the best candidate for one anyway, given that the previous few years' tax returns from the cattle business hadn't shown much income. So, with no loan, he'd sold his water rights and maxed out his credit cards.

When I talked with Jesus, I mentioned that I was a "used cow dealer" myself, that a lot of my employees at the rendering plant were Hispanic, and that I'd found the people who'd come to Colorado from Mexico to be excellent workers. I was grateful to have them on board with me, I said, but Jesus stopped me and insisted that the people who emigrated from other countries and found work here were most thankful. It was a priceless opportunity, the promise of a new life.

Since June 2009, El Jalisciense–Ricos Tacos has been open for business in their new building. Last I heard, the restaurant was doing well—Jesus said they were selling seventy to eighty breakfast burritos every morning—and they're considering opening a second location in a nearby town. They continue to cook beef from cattle raised on his own ranch, use a local family's sausage (sixty to seventy pounds a week!), and make sure customers get exactly what they want, when they want it. "Whatever you want, all of the time, we're available," they say. And that's about right: They recently installed a drive-through window, and on weekdays, they're open from 5:30 in the morning until 10:00 at night.

The work ethic and the commitment to the customer speak volumes about the Gutierrez family's character. You can bet that the next time I'm anywhere near Delta, I'll be stopping in and *sitting down* with a big plate of carnitas and chile verde.

No one told me much about how Charlie was doing, but I knew he had to be at least thirty miles in front of me by then, September 25, just one day shy of two weeks since the start of our run across America. We'd traded places, and it was my turn to bring up the rear, but I was glad just to be back in the hunt. It wasn't so bad being behind: Out front, constantly being chased, I'd run scared of being caught, but in back, I could focus on reeling Charlie in. (Either way, it beat running beside him, as I could go at my own pace and make it a game of cat and mouse to keep me moving as fast as possible.) At the end of my first day out there with a bum foot, I stopped at about 12:45 p.m., having walked the entire fifty-one miles. When I stepped into the RV, Roger was waiting at the door, and we high-fived in celebration.

"I'm back."

We both grinned as I made my way to the rear of the RV and my bed, and I thought to myself, *Yeah, I'm back. Now what have I gotten myself into?*

In the days that followed, I felt as if I was coming alive again. We instituted a new ritual: When I finished the first marathon each day, I'd stop for a nap in the RV. This turned out to be a great way to ensure that I'd cover maximum miles and not reach that point of diminishing returns; it definitely made a dent in the sleep deprivation. (Another brainwave: I could take showers in the RV! Why didn't I allow myself to do this before . . . who knows? Now I wouldn't have to go to bed grimy anymore, even though most nights we didn't want to waste time driving to a hotel.) After leaving Delta, I consistently put in more than sixty miles

a day, and my foot actually seemed to be recovering on the fly. Amazing what small comforts can do.

As we reached the western edge of the Rockies, and the Wasatch mountain range came into view, I felt more and more confident and even happy with my progress, getting closer and closer to my home state. The uphill climbs were welcome, too. They seemed to stretch the arches in my feet so that my running form began smoothing out. We were dealing with my plantar fasciitis by icing it regularly, and that was successfully keeping the worst of the pain at bay. Meanwhile, people from the peach and apple orchards along the side of the road occasionally brought me some of their harvest, and their kindness warmed my heart. Think of it! Some fella runs by, and they take a few minutes out of their day to pluck some ripe fruit from their trees to give him a taste of sweetness. They had no clue what I'd been through, no reason to feel anything at all for me, yet they were just friendly that way. They also had no idea how much that meant, a simple gesture to a stranger. God, I was grateful.

At the same time, I was becoming even more dependent upon Heather and would feel disjointed without her, if she had to leave to do errands or miss an RV stop because she had some other business to attend to. Around Provo, Utah, Heather took her first day "off," heading into town to a Super 8 motel, where she stayed up most of the night paying our bills and attending to other personal matters, and then getting up the next morning to shop for my shoes, clothes, and socks. Her absence was completely disorienting to me. Every night before, she had undressed me, laid out my clothes for the morning, made sure I had my medication, and then crawled in next to me, waking up every couple of hours to ice my leg and foot. The rest of the time, she was there for me, my source of joy whenever I'd see her, a constant inspiration. Her devotion was unbelievable, and I could only imagine the sacrifices she was making to be with me and ensure that I was being taken care of. If I needed something, anything, I'd tell her and she'd handle it, down to the smallest detail.

"Make sure they put a straw in my cup, and don't give me too much ice or the drink gets too watery."

"Keep the food in the Coleman thermos warm, for God's sake."

"Don't do side roads if the slope of the hills exceeds a six percent grade or if a road winds around aimlessly without cutting the distance."

"Stop *every* mile, on the mile, or I get off track. Tell them not to push it."

"I need clean clothes."

"Keep my Sirius radios charged—I need to have the other one ready to go when the one I'm carrying loses power."

"Where's my popcorn?"

"Think ahead. Tell everyone to *think ahead*. Tell them to consider what I might be feeling out here. Wouldn't you be hot, cold, wet, hungry, *whatever* out here? Just think!"

They weren't unreasonable requests, and I made them politely, but they were also fairly frequent. Heather would listen and then relay whatever I needed. Early on, she'd seen herself as the "runners' advocate" and considered her job that of messenger, buffer, liaison, and consoler. She'd become much more than that, but still I complained only to her, and she always presented my needs as clear instructions to the crew.

Virtually no one but my wife understood how fragile and needy I was. With my world shrunk to the breakdown lane, a white line and the road's shoulder outlining my existence, my loneliness was intense. The smallest things made all the difference to me, and I craved connection. How different this was from the days when I'd run away from the women in my life! Now, I motivated myself forward with the notion that Heather was waiting for me. I knew that I'd come to a state of mind where I wouldn't be able to go on without her, and to lose her would be to lose myself.

The beautiful morning we arrived in Colorado, I'd been feeling small, insignificant, but in my proper proportion and place in the universe.

Although several people were with me as I approached the state line, they all held back when I walked up to the Colorado border sign, and then came Heather, we embraced, and the two of us hung on each other, both crying as we set foot on familiar ground. We'd covered the first thousand miles together and found ourselves, home again, in each other's arms.

> # Welcome to Colorado!
> ## "The Centennial State"
>
> Arrival date: 9/29/08 (Day 17)
> Arrival time: 6:00 p.m.
> Miles covered: 984.0
> Miles to go: 2,079.2

It got hot later in the day, over eighty degrees, but I was feeling all right. I'd been picking up the pace, as the altitude and hills were familiar, and my Achilles tendon and arch felt better than they had in a long time. The heat persisted into the next day, even at six thousand feet in elevation, and then out of nowhere, I found relief. Running down a back road, I crossed paths with a trucker, who saw me running alone and pulled over his big rig, stopping for a chat. Gerald Herst introduced himself as he walked toward me.

With the look of a trickster, he good-naturedly commanded me to bend over. Though it was a strange thing for him to say, and possibly more strange for me to hear, the guy seemed harmless enough, so I obliged and then felt a rush of cold on my back as Gerald splashed a big jug of water on me. Soaked, I came up howling with laughter, shaking like a dog shedding water, and told him that it was a great surprise. Thanks a lot! We stood there and talked a while longer, and another athlete rode up on a bike. (Strange how this hot, dusty, barren old road led to our meeting.) Brent Bardo told us he was cycling across the country, covering about the same amount of miles each day that I was.

So Gerald told Brent he should bend over, too.

"Go on," I encouraged him, slapping him on the back and laughing.

Gerald dumped yet another jug of water on Brent, and we all cracked up. In about twenty minutes, the three of us said so long, Gerald returned to his truck, Brent climbed onto his bike, and I started hoofing it. Leaving them, I felt human, connected, appreciative of their company and the circumstances that had brought us together.

Charlie wasn't faring so well. He'd broken down in Utah, a couple of days before, stopped by acute tendonitis, the same injury I'd had during the Badwater Quad when I'd run with those ice bags on my legs. Holy hell. Dr. Paul would take Charlie for an MRI soon, and would be determining his prospects for continuing based on the results. Soon after he'd stopped, I'd called Charlie to reassure him as he'd done with me, letting him know that the road and I would be out there waiting for him as soon as he was ready to continue.

When I awoke from my nap on September 30, eighteen days after we'd started, Charlie was at my RV door, crestfallen. Devastated by the prognosis for his injuries, he told me he was dropping out. *Oh, Lord.* This would have been my worst nightmare, and now it had happened to Charlie, a relentless competitor who'd invested nearly a year into making this race happen, and now he wouldn't be crossing the finish line. He wanted to know if I'd keep going, and I told him that I would, of course. I'd champion our cause. So we discussed the arrangements to be made with the sponsors. Now they'd need to know more about me; since Charlie had downplayed my part in the whole thing, some of the sponsors had no idea that anyone else was running. And I'd have to talk to reporters from time to time, now that I'd be attempting to complete the course

without him. The documentary crew might be spending more time with me, too. Fine, I said. You take care of yourself, Charlie.

Frank Giannino's story about his first attempt, how his running partner had dropped out and it had destroyed both their friendship and his chances of setting the record, haunted me as Charlie left. Later, when I was running again, I felt confused and alone in the middle of nowhere, memories of other losses in my life mixing with my new self-doubt and worry. *What am I supposed to do now? How will I do this by myself? Will I have to drop out, too? Is all this worth it?*

Charlie, too, had to be feeling despondent, lost, and broken-hearted as I ran on without him. Probably worse than I was, but in some hidden corner of my mind, I envied him. No way did I wish to be in his shoes. Still, I did allow myself to fantasize, for a moment, about stopping. That was a mistake, as it just made me more dejected to be out there alone.

But there was a silver lining, a big one: Now I'd have Charlie's support, along with his crew's help, going forward. Both crews would get more rest once we combined them. All of us would draw much-needed energy from one another when we closed ranks. Besides, I felt physically strong, like I might be able to pull this off.

The day after Charlie dropped out of the race, conditions were the best we'd seen to date. Near Steamboat Springs, day temperatures were tolerable, and the willows and aspens were in full color. Brilliant yellow and red leaves cast a glow on the horizon as the clouds above reflected them. Nature painted a warm panorama in front, around, above, and behind me. For the first time, I turned off the pavement and onto something like a trail—sweet relief! The old dirt road cushioned my footfalls, and gave my legs a respite from all the pounding. The rocks, ruts, and mud welcomed my feet. That night, reaching 10,476 feet in elevation, I was in my element, home at last. I touched out at sixty-seven miles, having dipped down into an eight-minute-mile pace, a far cry from what I used to do in my prime, like my sub-seven pace during marathons and negative splits during ultradistances in my forties. But considering the more than one thousand miles that had passed beneath my feet, it seemed extraordinary.

Even the crew was having fun. A few friends had been to visit, and at Heather's request, some had come to help, too, so crew shifts had shortened a little. The line producer's assistant was also lending a hand, and we loved having her around whenever she came. Not only was she a great multitasker, she was also the one scouting the route and could help us stay on course. Soon, some people from Charlie's group would be integrated with ours, so we all expected the crew's stress level to drop.

If I continued to run well, we'd reach Fort Collins, close to where I grew up, just a couple of days later. On our way, approaching Cameron Pass, we had our first rain-and-snow storm—it crashed around us suddenly, with lightning flashing and thunder booming nearby. Drizzle and flakes scrubbed the air, and lightning split through the oxygen, producing that distinct smell of ozone. It was a familiar aroma, an old signal from my childhood that maybe we'd get a break—if enough moisture fell, we'd get to shut down the irrigation pumps and let nature take care of the watering. Now, nearing home again, I was eager to see friends and, most of all, my children. Elaine would arrive first, coming from Washington, D.C., where she was a legislative fellow with the U.S. House of Representatives' Science and Technology Committee. That's right, "baby" Elaine is brilliant, a physicist and Wellesley College alumna, just as her mother had hoped. And she was going to take time off to come see her old man trudge across Colorado, from west to east, a new endeavor, a new direction. Previously, whenever I'd run across the state, it had been north-south, or south-north. Now I'd be able to say that I'd crisscrossed it.

At about ten in the morning, Elaine drove up and yelled, "Hey, Dad!" We embraced and then looked each other up and down, scanning for signs of stress, checking to see if everything was okay. We were both satisfied with what we saw, I think. My daughter's face told me she was

at ease, happy to be with her father. She looked beautiful to me, standing there on the side of the road with the green-golden trees behind her. As I peered at her through my sunglasses, she looked back at me through her own clear lenses, her hazel eyes so much like Jean's. She glanced at the support brace on my knee (something I'd been wearing on and off for a while), and took in the jury-rigging of my shoes, the toe boxes cut out to make room for my swollen feet, and the tongues hanging like an old dog's, as the sides could no longer be laced tightly enough to close over them. Though my skin was now darkened and chapped by so many days in the sun, I still looked all right to her. At least that's what she said.

"You look good, Dad."

We continued down Poudre Canyon as the crew leapfrogged the van ahead of us, and Heather took Elaine's car to Fort Collins to shop and call my mother to wish her a happy birthday. While Elaine and I walked, we caught each other up, fell back into our easy way of chatting and discussing, even though our views on so many things, from politics to parenting, lay at opposite ends of the spectrum.

Walking with my daughter, my heart settled, my mind calmed, and my mood lifted.

"How could you even think about doing this?"

A few years earlier, Elaine had been dead set against me climbing Mount Everest, and she'd been completely unambiguous with me about her feelings: It was selfish. Reckless. Simply the wrong thing to do when my youngest, Ali, was a teenager and depended on me. "You've been away from the family enough, Dad. Even when you were home, you were often far away. Dad! The death rate on Everest is ten percent. One in every ten people who reach the summit of Everest *don't come home.*"

She was right, and I still question my decision to go. My rationalizations: a wealth of experience with extreme sports, including the Raid Gauloises in Nepal, when I'd reached more than seventeen thousand feet and dropped to a frighteningly low oxygen saturation of 70 percent at altitude, which blurred my vision and left me barely able to move. Right after that brush with blindness and paralysis, I'd thought maybe Everest was out of the question, but later, after I summited Denali, Aconcagua, and Kilimanjaro with no ill effects from altitude, I came to believe that it was still worth trying. Many of the people who'd died on the Great Mountain, I believed, had been ignorant of or ignored their limits, but I'd learned not to push too hard at altitude. Through years of ultrarunning and adventure racing, I'd learned how to take care of myself, including hydration, electrolytes, and nutrition. I knew my own limits well enough to pull the plug if things got out of hand.

When the time came to summit, I was okay: As I climbed to the top, I felt well within myself, talking, gathering rocks, taking pictures, checking off everything on my Everest summit to-do list, and even helping Alex with a few things on his. He'd remembered to take a plastic troll and place it on the top but had forgotten to take a rock in its place—something he'd promised to do. So I supplied him with one. On my mental checklist: Take photos of Pemba Sherpa and another climber who'd summited with me, have someone take a full-body picture of me, take a picture of myself close up without the oxygen mask on, take a surround video from the summit, gather rocks from the top, and leave a card that Heather had made with a prayer on one side and pictures of her and the kids on the other, with the caption, "We love you. Get to the top . . . then come home to us." I'd called Heather on the satellite phone to tell her that I'd made it, and afterward, she remarked that I'd sounded surprisingly compos mentis.

Still, there were moments completely out of my control, including my nearly fatal fall into a glacial stream when I was on my own one day. By wrapping my arms around a large boulder, I was able, eventually, to pull myself to shore and safety. *Holy crap! I almost just became the first person to drown on Everest!* Shaking more from fear than from the cold, for the

next few miles, I climbed briskly, generating enough body heat to survive as I made my way up to advanced base camp and the warmth of my tent.

So I remain unresolved about the wisdom of my decision to go. In hindsight, I can say it was a good experience, an important one, and I returned to my family alive. That doesn't change the fact that Elaine was right, too. No matter how I spin it or justify it, the bottom line is that I chose to risk it, and I didn't put my family first. I prioritized my own dreams, and I didn't let anyone else's concerns sway me. Bring me to tears, yes, but I went anyway.

No doubt Elaine believed this run across America was ill-advised, too, but I think she was assured, at least, that it wouldn't kill me.

One of my closest friends, Mark Macy, and I have talked often about how our athletic careers affect our families. He's an ultrarunner, one of the all-stars of the Alaskan hundred-mile Iditafoot, and my teammate during all but one of the nine Eco-Challenges. We've spent countless hours and miles together in locations like British Columbia, Australia, Patagonia, Morocco, Borneo, Fiji, and New Zealand, most of the time cussing and laughing our way through some pretty hairy situations.

We agree that we're two selfish sons of bitches.

Still, Mace has done a better job with balancing the needs of his family and his own aspirations than I have. I continue to learn from him, including how positive relationships and great athletic achievement can actually complement one another, building courage, confidence, and perseverance for both. Even though he's a couple years younger than I am, he's a mentor to me, showing me how a man can both honor his family and follow his dreams, how he can be emotionally open and still a fierce competitor in the field—a temperance and temperament I have yet to master. His wife and children *always* come first. Whenever we entertain the idea of doing anything together, he thinks about how it will affect Pam and their three kids before he signs on. Would he have gone up Everest if he'd had the chance? I don't know. Maybe. But I know he would have consulted the family about the decision, not just announced it, like I've made a habit of doing.

In the evening after Elaine's arrival, I stopped at the RV to find a whole party of folks who'd just arrived, including Mace and two of his kids, and Theresa, the friend who'd introduced Heather and me years ago. Standing there with so many people to support me, I couldn't believe my good fortune: Heather and Elaine would crew together that day, and Mace said he and his kids would be going out to run with me as soon as I was ready. It was like a big reunion, and we joked and laughed, talking about everything but running, and before we knew it, it was time to get going again.

Leaving the RV on a high, I set out with Mace, his son, and one of his daughters to pace me, and we ended the night at the intersection of Colorado Highway 14 and Interstate 25, a major north-south highway. Well over a decade ago, I'd run the length of the state on I-25; everything around me was familiar that night, and I reveled in it. We staked out my finish and then drove to a nearby Super 8 for rest. In the van on the way to the hotel, I thought about how, for the next three days, we'd be on routes I'd driven many times back when I was behind the wheel of the rendering truck even before Elaine was born. Tomorrow, Taylor and Ali would join us. I'd be surrounded by the land and the people I love most.

The Colorado landscape features rugged beauty; it's a hardy and magnificent place. The mountains jut into the sky, rising from the plains that flow endlessly, undulating toward the horizon. Exquisite wildflowers—blue and red columbine, white prickly poppy, yellow alpine avens—defy the harsh, wind-driven winters and come back to bloom again each year in the warmer months. Our lower-lying agricultural fields, wedged beyond the rocky hillsides, remind me of Australia's Queensland, where Mace and I once climbed up the rugged Mount Bartle Frere for an Eco-

Challenge adventure race. We'd jumar, using mechanical devices with "gripping cams" that lock on to and slide up a rope, to help us ascend underneath a five-hundred-foot waterfall into a thick, leech-infested jungle (not that we have *those* in Colorado), and then drop thousands of feet into massive sugarcane fields that looked like corn stalks from home, as harvesters mowed through the fields in the dead of night. In a sleep-deprived state, Mace and I had thought they looked like alien spaceships hovering overhead.

Many of the traits I most admire about my home state and the untamed environments of adventure racing reflect the values I've tried to pass on to my children, and I thought about this as Mace and I ran on the asphalt of Highway 14, talking a lot but staying silent every now and then. *Strength. Resilience. Discipline. Follow-through. Responsibility. Honesty.* Perhaps most intently, *independence* and *self-reliance.* Both native to and cultivated in me, these things grew even more important in my life after Jean's death. The kids learned to not be clingy, to have strength and rely upon themselves and their own good judgment, and this has been a double-edged sword: Surely they've developed strong wills and stubbornness, but in fostering their independence, we sacrificed some interdependence, some connectedness, some closeness.

Like most parents, I can say I succeeded some of the time, and . . . well, I'm just waiting to see how a few things turn out before I decide to put certain events and actions in the win or loss column. Some of what I admire about my kids came naturally to them, like Ali's big heart or Taylor's ability to stay with something until it's finished. When he was just four and weighed maybe forty pounds, I brought a cord of wood to the house and started to stack it outside. Of course, Taylor wanted to "help." So I humored him: He'd wrestle with a piece of wood and throw it on the stack in the time it took me to get a few armfuls from the truck. Soon, though, a Broncos game started, and I told him to c'mon. Take a break. Let's go in and watch this on TV together, and then we'll go back out and finish.

Nope, he wanted to stay outside and stack.

Suit yourself, kiddo.

I figured he'd get bored and come inside in a few minutes.

An hour later, I went out to check on him, expecting that he'd wandered off to collect bugs or something, but there he was, finishing the job, having stacked nearly an entire cord of wood by himself. Holy cow, some of those split logs were as big as he was! We high fived, and I congratulated him heartily, man to man.

You'd think Taylor and I would have had an easy time of it, father and son, clearly a lot alike from the very beginning. But it wasn't easy, not for him or me, in part *because* we're so alike. Taylor, too, has always seemed determined to learn things in his own time, in his own way, by trial and error. Like me, he's learned from his failures just as much as his successes. That's brought him some hard knocks and a few false starts, but I think he's on the other side of that now, and I'm proud of him for having persevered.

Despite the fact that I love him so much and Taylor can be hilarious—he's got a sharp, irreverent sense of humor—our relationship has always been something like a bull elk with his offspring: serious, territorial, somewhat adversarial. So I was curious to see how it would be to have him with me and his sisters for this part of the run.

Around nine o'clock in the morning, we approached Ault, a little Colorado town about ten miles north of where I was born in Greeley. There, we met up with everyone: Taylor and Ali had arrived, and my mom, sister, and brother were with them, too, along with my aunt, nieces and nephew, some friends, a few local reporters, and representatives from the United Way. Such a homecoming!

Never had so much family come out to see me go. Here were three generations of the Ulrich clan all gathered, Mom the matriarch of the bunch at eighty-five years old. There was something overwhelming about it, to see her there with all my children, both my siblings, and Heather, along with some of my dearest friends. I couldn't help missing Dad, yet

the scene felt right, just as it should be. Everyone there was happy, proud, and loving. I was at peace, if just for a few minutes, as we stood near a farmstead that resembled the eighty acres where Mom and Dad had raised our family.

After the intense loneliness of the last three weeks, this was something else. Friends continued to show up, come with me for a while or stop and talk by the side of the road, and I was hungry for the distraction. Everyone's company was uplifting, deeply satisfying social nourishment, feeding my heart and my soul.

Because of this, I was running faster than I should have, juiced on the excitement. Later that night, after the visitors were gone, I was still high from all the human contact. Maybe it wasn't just that, though, because I found out later that Taylor and one of our new crew, an upbeat college kid from Texas whom Charlie had brought, had been having a lot of fun working together and even spiked some of my drinks with shots of beer. Reportedly, I'd picked up the pace again.

For the next couple of days, my kids stayed on, nicknaming themselves the MKC, "Marshall Kid Crew." It was comforting to watch them fall into old family patterns, poke fun, get on each other's nerves, and also pitch in together. As usual, Elaine would play "mother" and peacekeeper, trying to appease the bickering between Taylor and Ali, who tend to butt heads. (Ali usually appreciates this refereeing; Taylor, not so much, as he doesn't care for being told what to do/how to behave by anyone, including his big sister.) Family dynamics aside, they got the job done, and they were a delight to have around: There was Ali mixing drinks and fixing food in the van's "kitchen" (the backseat), Taylor taking the driver's seat (our "wheelman"), and Elaine acting as "the gimp," a name we gave to the person running food and drink out to me. They were a godsend, all acting like my kids but also keenly aware that their job was to support me instead of the other way around. It was a welcome role reversal to feel their care for me. They made my world, as small as it was, big with their love.

We were coming into the Great Plains, the expansive western prairie on the eastern side of the Rockies that reaches into the heartland of America. I'd be running the territory of the old bison hunters, among them the tribes of Blackfoot, Cheyenne, and Comanche, and later, Buffalo Bill and others of his ilk. We'd be in the Great Plains for the next six hundred miles, probably ten days, until we reached the Nebraska–Iowa border.

Having my children with me just as this run was becoming tolerable, even fun sometimes, made me wonder if their presence was making everything better or if the contrast helped me appreciate them even more than usual. They'd arrived right as we'd left the dry heat and harsh conditions that had persisted through California, Nevada, and Utah, which seemed fitting. Each of the kids, too, had taken me through a kind of parenting desert, the years when they'd been typical teenagers, resenting authority, thinking I couldn't relate to their young lives, believing I was too strict, or too stupid, or just plain wrong. Like most kids, they'd been right, up to a point. And, like most kids, they'd seen my actions only through the prism of their inexperience and justifiably self-centered youth. But now, they were showing me how mature they'd become. I treasured every minute with the MKC, looked forward to hearing Taylor joshing with his sisters and the crew, Ali tending to business and finding ways to be useful, and Elaine trying to set a good example. It felt like being at home, and took me back to having them all within reach, where I could overhear them laughing and crying together, but mostly championing each other's causes.

On the morning of day twenty-three, we expected to pass through Sterling, Colorado, but as soon as I woke up, I knew something was wrong. The plantar fasciitis was a familiar, now manageable pain, yet this was something new, excruciating and distinct. Elaine and Heather were on

duty in the crew van, and they noticed how slowly I was going, especially compared with the few days before, so we switched out my shoes and Dr. Paul stretched me. Then he focused his attention on the foot, breaking up some old adhesions, making me wince and producing loud, popping noises. About two hours into the morning's run, I stopped for a fifteen-minute nap and to rest the foot again.

Soon after that, Ali and Taylor joined Elaine, and the MKC took over the crew van, although Heather and Dr. Paul stayed close. Both of them were concerned when I told them that I wanted to keep moving.

"Okay, Marsh," Dr. Paul had agreed. "You go ahead and let me know when you've had enough."

Within twenty minutes, Heather and Dr. Paul drove up in a car (the crew van was still a half-mile off), and I admitted that things weren't going well. At the rate I was moving, it made no sense to keep on. They picked me up and drove me forward to the Sterling emergency room, and everyone else headed to a hotel.

Because the MRI was scheduled for the next morning, I thought I should try to get a few miles in before then, but Heather insisted that if there was a fracture, running on it could cause permanent damage, and if it was another soft-tissue injury, ice and rest made a lot more sense than going out and beating up my foot, only to gain very little distance. In other words, she was trying to reason with me; she and Dr. Paul had made a secret pact to stick together and convince me. Quickly, it was obvious that she was right. We went to the hotel, too, for rest, ice, and a good meal. Who knew what tomorrow would bring?

It had been days since we'd heard anything about Charlie, but we did know that he'd set out to ride the course on a mountain bike. NEHST would continue filming his progress, and now he'd help them interview folks. Fair enough, I thought; this would allow Charlie to stay in the game to some extent—I understood his inability to give that up—but I also wondered what had happened to our gentleman's agreement about helping the other guy if one of us dropped out. Heather and I both had a hard time seeing how Charlie's new plan fit in with an attempt to break the transcontinental running record, or a documentary called *Running America,* but that wasn't our concern.

He should be catching up to me any minute, I thought, as he was now able to travel three or four times faster than I could, and with me laid up overnight, his progress would be even more accelerated. My drive to stay ahead of him was thwarted by both my injury and his newly acquired speed, and I chafed under the realization that, even if I could still run, he'd always be ahead of me.

In the hotel, though, all of that seemed unimportant as I savored the time with family and the luxury of eating while sitting down. Propped up in a comfortable bed, my meal on a real, honest-to-God plate, and surrounded by family and friends, I felt like a king holding court.

Most everyone would be going home that night, so we took our time saying our good-byes. Our visit together had been so unusual, something like a breakthrough. I felt that my family really *saw* me, that even if they didn't understand what I was doing, they supported me in it unconditionally. Even my brother, Steve, who'd long ago written off running (and me, to some extent—it seemed we were constantly disagreeing about something), had come out to see us in Ault. Heather confided, too, that when she'd called my mother on her birthday, Mom had told her, "I love you," which had brought Heather to tears. It was an unprecedented declaration, as Mom had never said that to Heather before and had even stopped saying it to me long ago. (Why? I'm not sure, maybe something to do with my stubbornness, or my own reserve. I think both of us had forgotten that staying connected was more important than anything else.) It signaled a significant change, and Heather and I held each other, crying with joy. At the time, I had a hard time taking it all in, but I felt incredibly grateful for every subtle and positive transformation.

Once everyone left the room, I showered and tucked in for the night while Heather got up every two hours to ice my injuries. When I awoke the next morning, I was pretty well rested, although Heather was now

fatigued from many, many days of interrupted, short sleep. In the waiting room at the hospital, I grabbed a newspaper, another simple pleasure to enjoy. This was the first thing I'd read, other than food wrappers, in three weeks. The October 6, 2008, morning headlines clued me in, for the first time, about how the U.S. presidential race was shaping up ("Palin Accuses Obama of 'Palling Around' with Terrorists"), and how serious the financial crisis had become ("Dow Jones Industrial Average in Freefall"). It made me glad I hadn't been paying any attention to the nasty politics or depressing national news, and my only indicators of what was happening in the "real world" had been the fluctuations I'd seen on the gas station price signs. This week, I'd noticed, you could fill up for about $3.50 a gallon, down about 10 cents from the week before and almost a buck and a half cheaper than it had been in California at the start of our run.

After a short time in the waiting room, a nurse came to prep me for the MRI, and the whole procedure was over quickly. The day before, I'd told Heather that if the doctors found soft tissue injuries, I'd be continuing. If they found a stress fracture, I insisted, I'd get a walking cast and still keep going. Either way, I wasn't stopping. But Dr. Paul and Heather had other ideas, which they'd discussed privately and didn't share with me: They simply wouldn't support me going forward with a broken bone, risking permanent damage that would prevent me from ever running or mountaineering again. Although they were able to look at the big picture, think ahead to the future, I was not: My world was this run, right now. They were doing their job, looking out for my long-term interests, and I was doing my job, focusing on finishing this race, no matter what. We'd know soon if our interests would collide.

The doctor reported that I had muscle strain and tendonitis, including micro tears in the muscles of my foot and a longitudinal tear within the tendon of the outside of my right foot. There was no evidence of a stress fracture.

Would the pain eventually abate if I continued running?

The doctor assured me that, no, it wouldn't. So I asked what he recommended for treatment, and he suggested the usual runner's remedy: rest, ice, and elevation, plus an anti-inflammatory, like ibuprofen, to help with the swelling.

Rest? The last three I could definitely do (sometimes), but how would I manage that first one and still run the remaining 1,700 miles?

After a long pause, I quipped my counteroffer: If I ran only forty miles a day, instead of sixty, would that constitute rest?

The look on his face was priceless. At first, he laughed, but then his smile collapsed as he recognized that although I thought I was being funny, I was also totally serious about the mileage. He must have thought I was nuts. Heather has remarked since that his reaction was a second dose of reality; we'd been so cocooned in our own world that not only were we unaware of our country's current events, but we'd forgotten how crazy our own situation sounded.

I'm running across the United States, see, and I've already come over thirteen hundred miles, you know, and even though Charlie dropped out (he's bicycling now), somebody's got to keep running to the finish, and I don't give up when I've said I'm going to do something. I've been dreaming of doing this for years, and so even though this is going to be incredibly painful to run on these injuries, I want to keep going, so can I just cut back to forty miles a day—would that be all right?

Yeah, I'm pretty sure he thought I was nuts.

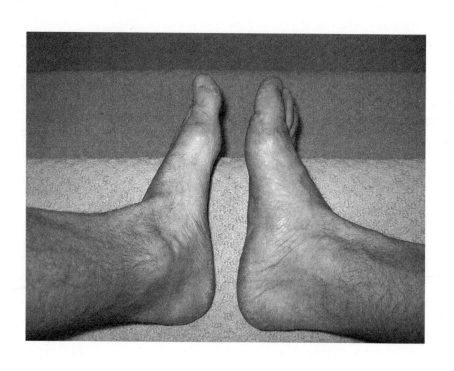

7.

This Is Not My Foot

Days 25–26

In 1928, when the bunioneers ran the first organized footrace across the United States, they'd been promised a winner's purse of $25,000, big money in those days—and no small sum for two months of work, even by today's standards. The race's founder, Charles C. Pyle, could be called the Depression-era Don King, the top sports promoter in his time. He'd dangled the money to lure big-name athletes, and offered decent, free food and lodging to all comers, which pulled another pool of men who hadn't yet claimed either fame or fortune, who either aspired to greatness, craved adventure, or needed a roof over their heads. They ran most of the way on Route 66, the Mother Road that stretched from Los Angeles to Chicago, most of which was still unpaved after two years under construction.

Good ol' Charley didn't exactly come through. Sure, a few days after the end of the race, he awarded the prize money to twenty-year-old Andy Payne, who came in first with an average pace of ten minutes per mile and completed the 3,400 miles from California to New York in 573 hours: he finished 84 stages, averaging forty miles per day.

But along the way, conditions were deplorable. Charley provided cold showers, scant food, and drafty quarters . . . some of the time. Men of means supplemented what they were given, but those who didn't have the money to buy extra food or other necessities made do with the meager provisions as best they could. It's possible that Charley (also nicknamed C. C. for "Cash and Carry") had always meant to skimp, but it's more likely that he just didn't understand what it would take to properly care for his runners as they raced across the country. Logistically, ultrarunning is like a cross between orienteering, camping, and a military march. Unless you've done it before, there's no way you can know what will be required, from how much food you'll need to where your runners will relieve themselves. Not only do you have to deal with the anticipated requirements to keep everyone on the move, but you also have to contend with the unanticipated, whatever special circumstances come up and demand that you forget your plans and wing it. From what I know of the Bunion Derbies, neither the expected nor the unexpected was handled very well.

The bunioneers' route (rough as it was) had been scouted, a race doc was on hand, and Charley had also hired a cobbler to fix runners' shoes when they fell apart, but their accommodations were nowhere near as fine as mine. What I had—occasional access to a toilet, a warm bed every night (even if it was most times in an RV that Heather and I shared with three other people), regular showers, clean clothes, gear and gizmos from sponsors to boost my performance and relieve my pain, Dr. Paul to "fix" me and Kathleen to massage me when I needed it, my wife to care for and comfort me, and about eight thousand to ten thousand calories a day—would have seemed like royal treatment to the men who ran in the Bunion Derby. Contrast these things with the bunioneers' sketchy lodgings, the nearly complete lack of facilities for personal hygiene, and the unappetizing fare. Sometimes they slept in barns, or on the floors in post offices and jails—and those were some of the better accommoda-

tions. More than a few of these men fueled their efforts with a single pot of beans every day. Then consider that the black men in the race were harangued, especially in the segregated South. In Texas, by law, blacks weren't allowed to share quarters with whites, so they bedded down wherever they could—but not in hotels, because none would take them in even if Charley had offered to pay.

One of the most promising athletes in the race, Edward "The Sheik" Gardner, was also one of only five African-Americans in the competition. In McLean, Texas, a white mob surrounded his tent and threatened to burn it. They also threatened to burn his trainer's car because George Curtis was black too, and when they heard a rumor that Eddie was going to push the pace through their town, they threatened violence if he finished the local stage ahead of a white man. But the harassment wasn't limited to Texas. The winner of the race, Andy Payne, later remarked that he thought Eddie could easily have won if he hadn't been slowed by onlookers. Indeed, in Andy's home state of Oklahoma, for an entire day Eddie was stalked by a farmer with a shotgun who threatened to shoot him if he pulled ahead of any white runners.

Though it was probably worst for the black bunioneers, all of the men suffered. Sure, a great deal of what they went through was self-inflicted or just part of the endeavor: Many hadn't trained for the event, many twisted their ankles and sustained injuries, and then there was the inevitable heat, wind, and cold that sapped their strength. Still, it's the small comforts that can make an effort like this bearable, and most of the bunioneers didn't have even the most basic amenities. Their story makes what I was doing seem plush by comparison, which provides a great example of how perspective—your mind-set and your relative experience—colors your perception and your ability to persevere.

People often ask me how I can endure what I do. How do I take the pain? It all comes down to focus, not a very sexy answer, but I think it's accurate.

Someone once dubbed me the "Zen master of extremes," referring to my exploits in Death Valley—the solo crossing and the Badwater Quad—which they imagined were possible only in some kind of meditative state. That's valid, but I think they also hit upon a deeper truth. My approach to the inevitable suffering of ultrarunning (and life) aligns with Zen's emphasis on experiential wisdom. This Buddhist prayer sums it up:

> *Let us rise up and be thankful,*
> *for if we didn't learn a lot today, at least we learned a little,*
> *and if we didn't learn a little, at least we didn't get sick,*
> *and if we got sick, at least we didn't die; so, let us be thankful.*

One way I deal with the pain is to embrace it, to realize that it also presents a gift: profound appreciation for whatever small thing comforts me, brings me pleasure, makes me laugh, satisfies my hunger, lightens my mood. *Yes, at least I didn't die.* In other words, if something hurts, I focus on what doesn't. The mind will naturally fixate on any irritation, but you can redirect it, make yourself look away or at least occupy yourself with something else for a while. For me, the most intense test of this came during the Badwater Quad, and what made it almost unbearable was that I allowed myself to focus on the misery of my tendonitis for more than two hundred miles. Thinking about my legs constantly, my only saving grace was that I had something else to consider: the charity that would benefit from the fund-raising associated with my effort, the Religious Teachers Filippini. More specifically, I pictured the war-widowed women and starving children who would receive food, water, and education because of the $70,000 I'd succeed in raising when I finished. I told myself that my suffering was no greater than theirs, that mine would end soon enough, that theirs could stretch on for years, that what I was enduring was nothing like the pain of losing your spouse, or your parent, or your child, and then having to struggle simply to survive. The contrast lent purpose to every agonizing step.

All pain is relative.

When I had my toenails removed back in the early nineties, I did it mainly to eliminate one of the inconveniences and irritations that had become routine in every adventure race or ultramarathon I undertook. Yes, I knew the procedure would involve cutting around the perimeters of the entire nail, practically to the bone, cauterizing the veins, and then applying acid to the nailbed to keep it from regenerating. The aftermath was supposed to be bad, but it seemed like it would be worth it: My toes were a mess from all the pounding against the front of my shoes, I'd become especially susceptible to "black toe," and I'd have to stop during every race to puncture blisters under my nails. It was a nuisance and a time waster. Besides, a couple of the nails were so misshapen that they kept poking holes in the tops of my shoes. In short, the temporary discomfort associated with the surgery would be considerably less than the problems I'd have if I let my toenails keep getting battered and blackened, falling off and growing back in all kinds of funky configurations.

I'd considered getting rid of them before, but one night when I was at a party with a surgeon friend, I'd had a few, and he said he'd do it cheap: He'd remove the toenails and perform a vasectomy at the same time, saving me some money by charging me for only one office visit. Always the penny-pincher, I laughed at him even while I was seriously considering his offer.

"Hey, I've got this fatty nodule on the back of my leg I've been thinking about having excised, too . . ."

He said he'd throw that in for free, so the next Wednesday, I went to the doctor's office and had all three outpatient procedures done, and then went back to the house. Danette was surprised—I hadn't told her what I was doing that day, and she couldn't believe I would just show up and announce it after the fact. *(Hi, honey, I'm home! I don't have those pesky toenails anymore, and I'm shooting blanks now. What's for dinner?)* But not too long before, she'd made some offhand remark about how I should get a vasectomy, so in my mind that meant we'd discussed it. Just goes to show you how in tune I was with the importance of communication.

The toes hurt a lot more than the testicles, for sure. Which brings me to the point of this story: Because my feet felt like someone had blowtorched them, I didn't even think about the tenderness in my undercarriage, and the incision on my leg could have been a mosquito bite. The whole thing was quite manageable, and in fact, I was back out running two days after the surgeries. All pain, from an itch to intense discomfort, is relative, and can be perceived as better or worse in comparison with something else, either your own experience or someone else's.

So, yes, I suppose I've become a so-called master of physical pain—bulling through it, finding something good in it, keeping my mouth shut about it unless talking means learning from it or laughing about it. I'm skilled at compartmentalizing pain, detaching and observing it without becoming its slave.

There is one man, however, who has taken this to another level. Undoubtedly the greatest ultrarunner alive, Yiannis Kouros stands unmatched, both in terms of his accomplishments and in his awareness of what happens when we run. At this writing, he holds 134 world records, and in his early fifties, he's still out there showing younger athletes how to get it done. He's also a musician and poet, as well as a student of literature, and he says that these pursuits inspire him when he's running.

When I had the chance to talk with Yiannis some time ago, I confessed that I'd once had a strange experience and wanted to know his thoughts about it. About thirty-five miles into the Badwater Ultramarathon one year, I saw the sun setting in front of me, and then had the oddest sensation, as if I was floating over my body and watching myself run. It was over in the blink of an eye, but when I regained normal consciousness, the sun was rising behind me and I was down the road fifty miles. It made me think of the Native Americans, the drifting spirits. I didn't want to make it sound too weird, but it *was* weird.

Yiannis was matter-of-fact. "Oh, that happens all the time to me."

Excellent! I wanted to know how I could make it happen again, too. Yiannis explained that this altered state is predictably accessible when you reach the limits of your physical capacity, your tolerance for pain, and your mental ability to carry on. It happens when you literally run out of anywhere else to be: The body is no longer habitable, and so the mind or the spirit or what have you slips out to another place, and the body moves down the road and beyond its pain on its own. For Yiannis, ultrarunning is about transcendence, transformation, new spiritual dimensions.

As for me, I've never been able to enter that intensely altered state again.

It's not that I've never reached into the void again, never been so wrung out that it would have been great to hover overhead instead of slogging it out in my body. Believe me, I've tried, but getting back to that state completely eludes me. I wonder if this experience is the enlightenment Buddhists strive to achieve. Is it the place where suffering ends? Nirvana?

I don't know. It's possible. I would have liked to find that place many times during the transcon, but it never happened; perhaps I've never achieved that escape again because I'm so intensely focused on moving forward, or because I'm usually blasting away the pain with loud music, or because my mental makeup is so stubborn and resolute that I prevent myself from slipping away. But I do have other ways of shifting my awareness, of dealing with the pain.

The morning after my MRI in Colorado, I sat on the edge of the bed and looked at my fat foot, so swollen it felt alien to me. There it was: The least pressure would stab my sole and shoot the agony up my leg into the pain sensors of my brain. It was as if someone had pounded sixpenny nails into the arch and side of my foot.

After we'd left the hospital the day before, Heather and I had attended a meeting with the documentary's director and line producer, as well as Charlie, his crew chief, and management personnel from the production company in New York, who participated by phone. Charlie was still encouraging everyone that the record was within reach for me, but I had my doubts. Once that was over with, starting around two in the afternoon, I walked and ran into the night, covering 32 miles. It had actually gone pretty well, but by morning the foot was so sensitive that I could hardly stand. We were already doing everything we could for it, so I was going to have to do something more, by myself, if I was going to keep on. We needed a mental trick; I'd have to pull a rabbit out of my shoe. What could I do?

Turning to Heather, I disowned my foot. Instead of embracing the pain, I rejected it completely.

"This foot doesn't belong to me anymore. It doesn't fit in with who I am, what I'm trying to do, or where I'm going. *This is not my foot.*"

If I wanted to keep running, I'd have to stop thinking about my foot altogether. I wouldn't be able to just gut it out as I had before, during the painful few hundred miles to the finish during the Badwater Quad. I still had over fifteen hundred miles to go, close to three weeks before we reached New York if I could keep a reasonable pace, and I knew that if I even acknowledged that the foot was still attached, that the pain had anything to do with me, it would end my run—I'd cry uncle at some point, and I wasn't willing to do that. So I decided to pretend that my foot, and the pain, weren't there. If I ever noticed that throbbing at the end of my leg, I'd dismiss it as "not my problem." I simply wasn't going to deal with it.

While I was handling my pain by ignoring it, Heather had her own struggles, which she had no choice but to confront head-on. The documentary production company was beginning to gripe about the budget: Why were we spending so much on food? Did we really need so many people to crew? How often did we plan to stay the night in a hotel from

here on out? Why did we leave the van running, wasting gas, at crew stops? She answered their questions evenly: Meal costs were high because we had to buy packaged food for portability and to be able to cook in the RV, and I was eating four times what any other person was eating; yes, we needed every hand we had, although we could perhaps move some people around—didn't Charlie need fewer crew now that he was cycling? We'd spend nights in a hotel only when we were within a ten-minute drive. We didn't turn the van on and off because it would kill the battery; this had already happened twice, causing a lot of unnecessary scurrying around, wasting time and energy to get it charged and the vehicle moving again.

Under normal circumstances, I bet Heather would have been inclined to see these questions merely as a reflection of their lack of experience with crewing for ultrarunners and the realities of keeping a team moving on the road, or as reasonable cost-watching measures, but these weren't normal circumstances. She was exhausted. She was also consumed with protecting my well-being. Her first and only priority was to see me safely to New York, and when anyone suggested that another concern was more important, it didn't sit well with her. To be blunt, it pissed her off. Still, she always tried to find a way to work with them, politely, even when she was steaming inside.

Have you ever heard of "Minnesota nice"? That's my wife. When the crew shuffle began, Heather made an effort to be accommodating. They wanted to send Kathleen home to save some money, because she was being paid more than some of the other crew. Heather knew that Kathleen needed a break; we had worked her incredibly hard. What's more, I could see and feel Kathleen's worry for me every time she touched me, not wanting to hurt me, feeling sorry for me and whatever pain I was enduring. She's a sympathetic soul, and wasn't able to keep up even the smallest pretense of bravado. I didn't want to ask her to fake it, but it was demoralizing for me to be so pitied. Given all the circumstances, Heather agreed to let her go. They'd wanted to send Roger home, too, but Heather dissuaded them; I'd already said no, he was too valuable, he wasn't burnt out, and he was an important part of my support system. Roger was also the only person on the road with whom Heather would voice her frustrations; purposefully, she didn't tell me about 99 percent of what was happening behind the scenes. So Charlie would keep Chuck Dale, his crew chief, and Jenny Longpre, another member of his crew, with him. We'd keep Brian Weinberg (the college kid who'd helped my son spike my drinks in Colorado), and continue to integrate Dave Pearson into our group. By now, Dr. Paul was no longer crewing but instead focusing entirely on being our race doc, overseeing Charlie's and my medical care. At one point, he remarked to me that the number of injuries that Charlie and I had sustained amounted to more than all the injuries he might see among the hundreds of runners at the invitational Western States hundred-miler and Badwater combined. Dr. Paul had his work cut out for him.

So now our crew consisted of Heather, Roger, Dave, and Brian. The next day, Kira Matukaitis, an ultrarunner some friends of ours had recommended, would join us, and we'd have a full crew again.

Right around the time we reached Nebraska, I asked Heather to make a sign for the crew van: DR. PAUL'S ROLLING REHAB CLINIC.

> # Welcome to Nebraska!
> ## "The Cornhusker State"
>
> Arrival date: 10/7/08 (Day 25)
> Arrival time: 8:45 p.m.
> Miles covered: 1,424.1
> Miles to go: 1,639.1

I was looking for distractions again, trying to make myself and other people laugh at our situation. The truth is that I was feeling pretty miserable. After my MRI, Dr. Paul and I had agreed that I would run fifty miles, no more, the following day. We both felt that pushing too hard might aggravate my injuries, might cause a blowout that would bring everything to a halt again. Fortunately, we were routed onto a dirt road, and the softer surface was a windfall for my sore foot.

Not that I was thinking about the foot. Anything but the foot. I was caught up in memories of my childhood, my adventures, raising my kids; in missing Heather, our home in Idaho Springs, and the MKC, who were now back in their own homes. The predictable post-high depression had set in now that my family was gone. The typical symptom: what psychologists call "rumination," my repetitive thoughts, questioning, sorting out, using the time alone as a way to review my life, my mistakes, my losses, my grief. This sadness, accompanied by busy mental processes, has been described as "exquisitely attentive to pain." It's interesting, isn't it, that at a time when I refused to succumb to the physical pain, my mind got to work on the emotional?

We were in the grain belt, America's breadbasket. Along Nebraska's Highway 6, corn lined the road, the tall stalks providing privacy for quick bathroom breaks but not giving much of a shield against the wind, which was my new bane. Early on, it had been the heat and the dryness; we'd had a taste of rain and snow; and now came the wind, pushing at me and slowing me down, which affected the number of miles I could cover in a day. Occasionally, the air currents would come from behind and urge me forward. At those times, I'd imagine that the tailwinds carried the spirits of the four men who'd died the year before, Ted's wisdom whispering in my ear, my dad's strength buffeting my body down the road, Rory's ebullience breathing new life into my steps, Chris's adventurous spirit infusing my forward motion.

Thinking about my goals and my ghosts, I was also reflecting on the people who'd crossed the country before me. Yes, there had been other contests, like the Bunion Derby. And other runners. Plus people who'd walked it and run it solo. Even before that, pioneers had moved across it with horses and wagons, on some of the very roads I was now traveling.

WALKING ACROSS AMERICA BEFORE THE BUNIONEERS: TWO BOLD WOMEN AND AN "OLD" MAN

Helga Estby (1860-1942)

In 1893, the United States was in a panic. Speculative investing in railroads had caused overbuilding, and iffy railroad financing had resulted in bank failures, sending the country into a serious economic depression. (Sound familiar? Just substitute railroads for houses, and we saw a repeat of the same dynamic while I was running across America in 2008.) According to some sources, unemployment rates peaked in 1894 at about 18 percent, and the credit crunch affected

people who'd never even been on a train, much less invested in the railroads.

Helga Estby was one of these people caught up in the domino effect of the depression, in jeopardy of losing her home and descending into poverty. Recently arrived from Norway, she'd married her husband Ole (also from Norway) in 1876, and they'd farmed and were raising eight children together in Spokane County, Washington. By 1896, they'd fallen on hard times; Ole had injured himself and couldn't work, and they couldn't pay their mortgage or back taxes.

That year, an anonymous sponsor offered $10,000 to any woman who could walk across America in seven months. It was a huge sum, comparable to about $200,000 today, and enough to save the family farm. So, desperate and defying the conventions of her time—women were supposed to be weak and in need of protection—Helga left home with her eldest daughter, eighteen-year-old Clara, and they became the first women to travel across the country without male company. In fact, they were the first people, men or women, to cross the United States on foot since the pioneers. Yet they were hardly "unprotected." The women were packing: They were savvy country folk who knew the dangers of back roads, stayed alert to any trouble, and carried a Smith & Wesson revolver.

They arrived in New York on Christmas Eve after more than a few misadventures and averting serious danger, having nearly lost their lives in the crossing. They'd left home with only five dollars (a stipulation of the sponsors) and worked to earn money as they went. They'd faced hardship, but they'd also had kindness from the ordinary people they met along the way; most wanted to help, and supported their effort. They'd also collected autographs from prominent politicians (another stipulation) who wished them well, including President-elect William McKinley. The sponsor balked and refused to pay the prize, however, when the women missed their deadline by a couple of weeks. Penniless, Helga and Clara returned to their family farm, partway by train (on a free ticket) and partway on foot, only to discover that two of Helga's children had died of diphtheria while she was gone.

The local Norwegian-American community, including her own family, disparaged Helga for having "deserted" her husband and children, but she felt convicted about what she had tried to do. Later, she became a suffragist, and this trailblazer, who embodied stamina and self-reliance, ultimately made strides to secure women's right to vote.

Edward Payson Weston (1839–1929)

"Weston the Pedestrian" set out in the spring of 1909 to walk from the east to the west coast, having already made a name for himself as a record breaker. His renown began nearly fifty years earlier, when he made a 453-mile trek from Boston to Washington, D.C., on a bet that he could arrive just ten days later and in time for Abraham Lincoln's inauguration in 1861. (According to a pamphlet Weston wrote, he "made no money-bets, but had wagered six half-pints of peanuts.") While the new president prepared to address the fears of a nation now facing civil war, Weston was making his way to the capitol, too, as people cheered and bands played along the way—

the event was sponsored and heavily publicized to defray costs—plus local eateries supplied plentiful food for free, and the townswomen gave him kisses to keep his spirits up. Perhaps distracted by all the fanfare, he arrived a day and a half late, missing Lincoln's oath of office, but the celebration surrounding Weston's arrival was so lavish that he was invited to meet the president at the inaugural ball, and Lincoln even offered to pay his way back home so he wouldn't have to return on foot. He declined; having failed the first time to arrive in ten days, as promised, he was determined to meet his goal on the return trip, which he succeeded in doing.

Years later, after the Civil War had come and gone, Weston gained greater notoriety by racking up records at a time when his sport became quite popular and the cash prizes plentiful. He cut a dashing figure; the dapper dresser smashed records and pleased crowds during walking matches staged in packed arenas. He walked one hundred miles in twenty-two hours nineteen minutes. He walked 127 miles in twenty-four hours. (Both are remarkable achievements; becoming a "Centurion," someone who walks more than one hundred miles in less than twenty-four hours, is extraordinary.) He walked five hundred miles in six days and was crowned the Champion Pedestrian of the World.

As Weston aged, he gained strength and speed. At sixty-eight, he improved his time on a Maine-to-Chicago trek, which he'd taken forty years earlier, by twenty-nine hours. And so, at age seventy-one, he decided to walk across America, and to do it in one hundred days.

Although he was well supported financially, Weston still had to deal with the unavoidable obstacles: In the Rockies, he had to crawl because the winds were so strong; in other places, rain and snow made the going plenty miserable. He also had to battle mosquitoes, which were coming to life in the spring thaw, as well as vagabonds who harassed him. Occasionally, he was separated from his crew:

> *Lost—One automobile, one chauffeur, and one trained nurse; incidentally several suits of underclothes, three pairs of boots, dozen pairs of socks, two dozen handkerchiefs, two white garabaldis, one oilskin coat, and one straw hat. All belong to Edward Payson Weston, en route from New York to San Francisco via a devious route, over sundry obstacles, chiefly clay mud, knee deep, and still becoming deeper. Last seen on Wednesday morning in Jamestown, N.Y. When last heard of it was jammed in a mud hole between Waterford and Cambridge Springs, Penn. Thursday night with a busted engine. Any one discovering this outfit will please notify it to get a move on.*
>
> (From an article by Edward Payson Weston, special to *The New York Times*, April 3, 1909)

This must have been completely unnerving, although he apparently kept a sense of humor about it. Weston arrived in San Francisco in 104 days, and is supposed to have said that this was the worst failure of his life.

So of course he tried again. Walking from Santa Monica to New York with a goal of completing the crossing in ninety days, he finished in seventy-six. He was seventy-two years old.

Once a day, my reveries would be interrupted by the sound of a kiddie horn coming at me from behind. Charlie had rigged his mountain bike with the thing and would honk, wave at me as he rode up, peddle alongside me for a few minutes, then honk again as he sped ahead. Annoying as hell. Okay, it was kind of funny, but it was also irksome. I'm sure that's exactly what he had in mind: Most of Charlie's antics were equally humorous and irritating, and he was clearly trying to diffuse his frustration at not being able to run and truly compete with me any longer. Zipping by me on his bike, he reminded me of a preschooler who has to beat his friends at everything, even if it's meaningless.

Yet now I knew that I wouldn't stop until I was done. Charlie could ride in circles for all I cared; I was headed straight for New York City. One of the things the crew and I would say to each other all the time now, as a kind of mantra, was that we'd keep on going until we ran out of land.

8.

States of Mind

Days 27–35

On October 9, as we arrived in the large town of McCook, Nebraska, a police escort joined us in front of the documentary production van, which was filming me and a couple of locals we'd just met, Mitch Farr and Blaine Budke, as we moved down East B Street. The attention-worthy scene: Mitch and Blaine on either side of me, riding low-slung custom motorcycles, all glistening chrome and badass paint jobs. The choppers' engines roared along, and I was amazed that Mitch and Blaine were able to go at my pace without tipping over, only about five miles per hour—fast enough for me but incredibly slow for them.

As I ran between them, the deep rumble of the engines was loud enough that I had to turn my head and yell at the easy riders to start a conversation, who quietly looked the part of leather-jacketed bikers. Blaine, who owned a hot tub company, suggested at one point that maybe I'd like to have a soak. We all laughed, knowing there was no way.

Riding along on his chopper with yellow ghost flames, Mitch offered, "If you stop long enough, I'll feed you a steak, too," as he owns a bar and grill in McCook. Again we laughed, but I told them both I wanted rain checks.

"The next time I see you, Heather and I will be on bikes, for sure! You guys have the right idea—riding definitely would beat running!"

They had it figured out: I wanted to see McCook and the surrounding area from the vantage of a soft seat, but still exposed to my surroundings with nothing between me and the environment. And I imagined that with my legs propped up on the foot pegs, everything would seem a damn sight more comfortable.

I'd never been escorted by choppers before, and I don't imagine they'd ever ridden alongside a runner, so we all made the most of it, joking, cutting up, and teasing one another, mostly about our age, for the couple of miles we were together. Getting to know them, I formed the opinion that the next time I came through, I could count on them for anything.

Meeting and running with Mitch and Blaine energized me and also provided some colorful film footage for the documentary (which, sadly, didn't make the final cut). The producers had arranged the whole thing during their dinner at The Looking Glass the night before, and I was grateful—jealous that they'd had Mitch's steaks, which they reported were delicious, but unreservedly grateful. Especially at this time, when I was still in a funk and doing everything I could to avoid thinking about my foot, having the opportunity to talk with a couple of guys, check out the detailing on their Big Dog and Texas choppers, hear about their local businesses, and kid around for a while was a highlight. Perks like this kept me going, put me in a better state of mind.

Ray Zahab is fond of saying that the challenge of ultrarunning is 90 percent mental, and the other 10 percent is all in our heads. He's got it right: Beyond the marathon, the primary test becomes entirely psychological. If you can run twenty-six miles, then your body can surely carry you even farther (barring calamitous injury), and the only question is whether your mind can go the distance, too. As you push the body beyond its limits, running hundreds of miles a week for weeks on end, the

physical challenges are predictable, with injuries and ailments nearly inevitable, and the mind can either help you or it can destroy you and diminish your chances of completing the task you've set for yourself. The difference involves certain skills and the ability to use the mind's tricks to your advantage.

Take hallucinations, for example. They're common during adventure races when a team goes beyond extreme fatigue, and they can range from mildly interesting to horrifying. During an Eco-Challenge in the northeastern United States, our group was sleeping about fifteen minutes a day for six days, and as we were paddling on the ocean near the beach in Newport, Rhode Island, all five of us started envisioning other people in the boats, some familiar to us and some not. I'd look at a teammate and see someone else instead. In my delusion, Alfred E. Newman from *Mad* magazine was aboard, for example. We also all started to think we were on a huge spillway, ready to plunge over the falls, because we could hear the waves crashing on the beach. The group paranoia got so intense that we paddled as hard as we could to reach the shore—and as we got closer, the sound of the waves grew louder, of course, making us even more frightened—which we could still recognize as our refuge, at least. By coming ashore there, we'd abandoned our original plan to go around the peninsula, so we wound up beaching our kayaks and portaging our boats through the city, right through downtown. We were lost for hours, struggling to find our way back to the beach on the other side of Newport, where the race finished. All of us walked away from that escapade with at most 20 percent of our faculties functioning; in fact, one of our teammates was hallucinating so badly that he didn't even recognize his significant other until after he'd slept for six hours. The race doctors had wondered if he'd ever regain thoughts of reality. We were all lucky that sleep brought him to his senses.

That was a dangerous situation, but there have been entertaining hallucinations, too: The wingless 747 that pulled up next to me during my solo crossing of Death Valley, people inside the plane waving at me and

cheering me on. Or the silver bikini–clad woman on roller skates who glided in front of me, her lithe figure swaying side to side for about ten minutes. I hung onto that one for while, as I've learned the art of perpetuating the illusions that suit me as well as the skill of putting the nightmarish ones out of my head.

Was the out-of-body experience about which I asked Yiannis another form of hallucination? It's possible that they're on some kind of continuum, that hallucination holds a glimmer of the transcendence I felt just one time, and that Yiannis experiences all the time, but no. To say it was like a grand hallucination would be like saying that the ceiling of the Sistine Chapel is a really nice doodle. Nonsense, not even close.

During the run across America, I didn't hallucinate, although that would have been okay by me. It's a compelling dichotomy: Running takes discipline and focus. What makes it tolerable, though, is letting the mind drift, checking out of "real life," where the legs keep moving as the world keeps turning, but the mind focuses elsewhere and notices, for example, the beauty of a bristlecone pine, bent and twisted by the wind.

A sports psychologist friend of mine, Dr. Murray Griffin, evaluated me in 2002, as he was interested in discovering what unique psychological traits athletes bring to their pursuits. My only off-the-charts mental skill, as it turns out, is my imagination. In fact, he says, what's most remarkable about my psychological profile is how "normal" it is. He observed:

> When Marshall's concentrating on running, or concentrating on blotting out pain or discomfort, he can ignore all around him. He clearly can get himself into an almost Zenlike meditative state where he detaches himself from his immediate environment. When he's in this place, if you stood in front of him he'd flip round you without breaking his stride. When he gets locked on and goes to "that place," he is in what psychologists call a *flow state*, but unlike others he can keep it up for hours. That one piece of psychological abnormality that

we found is relevant here. Marshall scores high (off the scale) on ability to fantasize, and he is clearly able to use this to detach himself from the collateral damage of the race.

Yes, I am great at fantasizing! The apple doesn't fall far from the tree. My aunt once told me a story about my father, how he'd come home from school with all the buttons ripped off his shirt. Seems his first-grade teacher was so frustrated with him that she'd grabbed him and popped them all off trying to get him to pay attention. Ultimately, he repeated that grade. My own mother used to tell me, all the time, to get my head out of the clouds, as I was a daydreamer. But she didn't fully discourage me: Mom, like my dad's mother, understood that her boy was bound for some version of greatness. Notably, my grandmother didn't say much about the button incident, either to Dad or his teacher. She just sewed the buttons back on his shirt. Dad went on to be extremely successful in business, due in large part to him being such a visionary.

Whenever I run through wilderness areas, I see myself embedded in the landscape, one of the trees, part of the wildlife. I think about how long the rocks have rested in a place, the swelling and drying up of the rivers over eras of rainfall and drought, the lives of the land's first people or of those who eventually developed the area. In my mind's eye, I picture a small settlement, or hunters moving across the plains, or a railroad or granary or industrial plant being built. When I cross paths with an animal, it stokes my imagination. What does the coyote think of me as I run past it? Where does the rattlesnake sleep? What did the falcon have for breakfast? What are the last thoughts of prey? What would it be like to make my home in a grove of Aspen trees, burrow under the leaves on the ground, catch my food with my bare hands?

Not too long ago, Elaine sent me an essay by Annie Dillard, "Living Like Weasels," which hit me right between the eyes. It seems Ms. Dillard and I share a common train of thought, an appreciation for what nature can teach us about ourselves:

I don't think I can learn from a wild animal how to live in particular . . . but I might learn something of mindlessness, something of the purity of living in the physical senses and the dignity of living without bias or motive. . . . I would like to live as I should, as the weasel lives as he should. And I suspect that for me the way is like the weasel's: open to time and death painlessly, noticing everything, remembering nothing, choosing the given with a fierce and pointed will. . . . Down is a good place to go, where the mind is single. Down is out, out of your ever-loving mind and back to your careless senses. . . . We can live any way we want. . . . The thing is to stalk your calling in a certain skilled and supple way . . . yielding, not fighting . . . yielding at every moment to the perfect freedom of single necessity.

If you pursue it long enough, running can certainly teach you about mindlessness and, perhaps, give you a sense of being "open to time and death painlessly." It takes you down deep and shows you the beauty of pursuing a "single necessity." Even without intending to, by training the body to accept long distances, you train the mind what *not* to think about, such as how much long-distance running hurts and how slowly the time passes. Surrender—an acceptance of the fate you've chosen—provides you with the ability to endure more suffering, and the more times you do it, the higher the pain threshold rises and the more finely tuned your ability to endure becomes. Owning responsibility for what you're doing, whatever that may be, empowers.

Combating boredom requires more than flights of fancy, although they certainly help. Music helps, too, something I've been slow to adopt compared with most other runners. The bulky old players were cumbersome, and I always thought the music would ruin my concentration. Besides, I'd never had music during physical effort before, so I didn't know any better. Sometime in 2005, though, I finally put on a pair of

headphones with a sleek little mp3 player and discovered that, if I like a song, I can listen to it over and over again, sometimes playing it forty or fifty times, falling into a rhythm, waiting with anticipation for a few words or motivating phrases that I especially relate to, applauding when they come. It doesn't mess with my concentration, and has turned out to distract me in a good way. During the transcon, there were about a dozen tunes I gravitated to, among them "Say Hey" by Michael Franti and Spearhead, "The Underdog" by Spoon, "Sing the Changes" by The Paul McCartney Project/The Fireman, "Real Real Gone" by Van Morrison, "Money for Nothing" by Dire Straits, and especially "Just Us Kids" by James McMurtry. Hearing the same song over and over operated like white noise, having a calming effect and blotting out everything else, the music fusing with the motion and taking the edge off the physicality of running.

The most effective boredom-beater is something I call "time compression." The longer you're out there and the more experience you have with the repetition of running, time can speed up. Or, maybe more accurately, time becomes less and less relevant. The miles and the moments melt into one another; as the terrain passes underfoot, the time passes, too. The two become almost indistinguishable.

It's a way of playing mind games with yourself to your own advantage. For example, with a set distance, you can focus on how quickly you'll move as you cover it, and set intermediate goals. It's wise to pay attention to those split times but not to get too hung up on the clock. I do know people who are totally into splits and beat themselves up if they don't reach those smaller, intermediate goals, but I'm more of a run-by-the-seat-of-your-pants guy: if I'm not feeling well, I slow down, and if I'm feeling good, I always try to work hard effectively—I focus on what's happening right now and make the most of it. I've had my best races when I loosely paid attention to my time and was pleasantly surprised by the split and the finish times.

In races where the finish is based on duration (say, twenty-four hours)

instead of distance (as in a hundred-mile race), I take a slightly different approach. It's an ambiguous mind-set with the distance to be determined, but I can compare it to my old contests with Steve: *How many bales can I put up in an hour? How many miles can I run in twenty-four hours?* I've seen people who drop out once they meet a mileage goal in such a race, but for me, it's always about upping the ante and achieving a personal best. I go till the clock runs out.

In fact, it was during that first twenty-four-hour race in Buffalo, New York, the one where I wound up winning by running 122 miles in the allotted time, when I'd realized I had a talent for ultra-distances. I owe this, in part, to the advice of a gentleman I met during the race, who suggested that I slow my pace and take my time for the first fourteen to eighteen hours and then, he said, "Look around and you might be surprised to find that you're in the lead."

His words stayed with me. I thought about him often in the years that followed, especially when I was out there in the void, running. I found out after the race that he'd been diagnosed with cancer not long before we met, and he succumbed to the disease a couple of years later. To my chagrin, I can't remember his name, but his advice was emblazoned in my mind: *Pace yourself. Believe in yourself. Don't sell yourself short. You have to think that you can win.*

During my run across America, neither time nor distance could occupy my thoughts. I would run at my own pace; the distance was set and the time it would take to run that distance didn't matter; it was what it would be, and so I could (try to) relax and not think about how long it would take me each day to cover the miles. Sometimes I succeeded in letting this go; sometimes I didn't.

Gaius Julius Caesar. King Arthur. The Greek god Apollo. At one time or another, I imagined that I was one with each of them. At least twice a week for a year in preparation for the transcon, a friend helped me condition

my mind for the run this way. We'd discuss my fears, hopes, and goals. She'd tell me about how formidable a warrior Caesar was—ruthless, a master of leadership, beloved and admired by his men. She'd compare me to the heroes of the Greek classics, talk to me about myths and mystery and mastery, and say that when it came to running, I was operating on another plane: No one could touch me.

You are a lion, Marshall, and show no mercy in the contest. You are one king-sized son of a bitch.

As I listened, I could feel her brainwashing at work, toughening my mind, impassioning and emboldening me to run. Even when I couldn't buy into it, I just kept my mouth shut. As she talked, I would inevitably feel powerful, like there was nothing that could stop me. I became invincible. Even as my farm-boy humility fought it, some part of my spirit latched onto the grandiosity that she knew I needed to complete this task.

People think Apollo is the god of light and niceties, but he was actually a raging, ferocious god responsible for sending the plague through the Greeks and the Trojans. He was easy to anger, and when provoked he would come crashing down the mountain, spreading black death . . .

There's an older story, one of the lesser-known chapters of Homer's Iliad *(which is the story of the Trojan War) about one of the great warriors, Diomedes, who actually wounded several of the gods, including Aphrodite, goddess of beauty, and Ares, god of war. Who knew a god could be wounded, even by such a warrior? Their veins run with ichor, not blood. To taste it is to die . . .*

Remember the wizard Merlyn turned King Arthur into a badger so he could learn a few things, finish his education. Hear this, from The Once and Future King:

> If you are feeling desperate, a badger is a good thing to be. A relation of the bears, otters and weasels, you are the nearest thing to a bear now left in England, and your skin is so thick that it makes no difference who bites you. So far as your own

bite is concerned, there is something about the formation of your jaw, which makes it almost impossible to be dislocated—and so, however much the thing you are biting twists about, there is no reason why you should ever let go.

And listen, when Arthur meets a badger (himself in the same form), the animal tells him, "I can only teach you two things—to dig, and love your home." Yes, badgers dig, dig, dig, going deep, down six or eight feet into the earth. They are relentless, noble creatures.

The stories she told me stayed with me. When we faced difficulties with logistics or other issues during the early stages of getting the run's start date secured, did I style myself after Julius Caesar to move the battle plan forward? No, but I drew something from the legacy of his strength. When I came up with plantar fasciitis and tendonitis, did I imagine myself an injured god? No, of course not, but the story was there somewhere in my mind, making me believe on some level that I was still invincible. And when Charlie angered me to the point of rage, did I rain down black death like Apollo? Or poison him with the ichor of my blood? I suppose I did, a little. But only once, and I'm getting ahead of myself now. Many emotional ups and downs had to happen before I completely lost it with him.

In McCook, the headwinds had come up again, and the hills had started to roll, both of which slowed me down, although I was pressing myself to maintain elite status. (Defining that status as sixty miles a day, a slightly adjusted "world-class" distance, was overly strict, but that's what I had in my head, nonetheless. Usually, this standard is set on a sheltered, flat track or field, not out in the elements, on the road, with unpredictable elevation changes and traffic. So I'd taken the usual number, one hundred kilometers/sixty-two miles, and done this calculation—*let's see,*

every thousand feet of altitude gain is equal to an extra mile—to come up with my goal of a minimum of sixty miles per day, cutting myself a whopping two miles a day in slack.) Having run over sixty miles the second day after my MRI and pretty much maintained that mileage since then, I was compensating, setting second-tier goals since I had to make my peace with not breaking Frank Giannino's overall world record. It was beyond my reach now: We'd figured that setting a new record would require covering seventy-seven miles a day from this point forward, nearly the same mileage that we'd done at the beginning of the race, before my injuries. Realistically, that wasn't going to happen.

Just as we were admitting that we'd have to lower our sights, I could smell the humidity in the air and knew rain was coming.

On day twenty-nine, near Hastings, the wet began and didn't let up for five days, which seemed apropos, as a new depression was setting in. The act of saying, out loud, that the record was gone made my defeat all too real. Sure, the new goal of sixty miles per day would keep me in the running for the grand masters and possibly the masters records, but I thought I wouldn't be able to maintain what I considered a world-class pace. The overcast weather suited my mood, and the rain fell like tears, slowly turning the dirt under my feet to sticky mud that threatened to tear my shoes off or, at the very least, weigh me down.

There were bright spots, though. My foot was actually improving, which baffled me. How was this possible? Perhaps it was because I was no longer running on radiant heat; day temperatures were pleasant, and the ground no longer sent fire up my legs. Perhaps it was because my body had become so efficient, with my metabolism revved up and certain systems shut down to preserve energy (my hair and nails had almost stopped growing), that healing was prioritized and sped up. Perhaps it was because I could, occasionally, get off the pavement and onto softer ground.

As the rain kept coming, some of the back roads became impassable for the van and RV, which meant that we had to either reroute or split up. On day thirty-one, we opted to go our separate ways, with me taking a direct route through a valley and saving four miles, and the vehicles following an alternate route and meeting me on the other side. For me, this turned out to be a wonderful solution: I had a good ol' time dashing through the mud, slipping and sliding over the uneven terrain. I covered only about two miles in an hour, but I enjoyed every minute. It reminded me of adventure racing, being on the loose and off-road. I'd started across the pastureland and then the trail had disappeared completely, but I just kept following a direct line eastward. When I reached a creek where a bridge was supposed to be, I wound up dropping down about thirty feet to reach the riverbed, hopping across, then scrambling back up the bank. Sure enough, someone had erected a bridge there, but it had long since fallen down. Built of old timbers and square-headed bolts with large cast-iron washers, the bridge looked to have been from the 1920s. Judging from the thirty-foot trees that grew on the old roadbed on the other side, and the erosion of the roadbed, it looked to me as if this bridge hadn't been used for forty or fifty years.

When I finally reached the crew again, I was in good spirits—better than I had been in some time—and Heather was glad to see it. While I animatedly talked to her about the bridge I'd found (I love old structures), I could see her eyes narrowing, but she just kept smiling, as I'm sure she was relieved to see me so excited about something. Only later did I find out that navigating had been the source of friction between her and Kate O'Neil, the producer in charge of the route, who'd kept insisting that, first, my crew *could* follow me on my way as planned and, second, if the roads were so bad that they really couldn't go with me, then it should be a simple thing to detour and find their way, as the area's roads were supposed to be laid out on a grid. But what Kate didn't know, and what Heather couldn't convince her of, was that out in the country, when it rains like this and roads get washed out, there's nothing easy

about navigating on the fly, and, besides, what you see on your sophisticated mapping software isn't always what you get in the real world. So
I'm sure Heather felt at least a little vindicated, not only because the old
bridge, supposedly still viable for crossing the creek, was down and had
been for a long time, but also because Kate's production group had gotten stuck in the mud for a couple of hours. Heather good-naturedly wrote
it all off as the ignorance of city folk and said nothing about it to Kate,
except, "Yes, it can be difficult to get through out here." We were lucky
that the obvious problems with our route had detoured our vehicles
elsewhere, and that our crew was skilled at dealing with bad road conditions, as the whole thing had turned out to be no inconvenience to me.
That bit of cross-country was probably the best fun I'd had yet, even if
I did wind up with about three pounds of mud on each foot.

We'd gotten into the routine of changing clothes and shoes fairly frequently, as the rain kept soaking through anything I had. No matter what
they say about waterproof, breathable rain gear, it doesn't work. Good
old fleece is the best as long as it isn't a complete downpour. So I made
another costume change and got back out on the road after my adventure, feeling a little better about things, but it didn't take long for my
mind to spiral back down into the vague malaise that had become my de-
fault mental state.

Two things were working on my psyche.

First, I simply could not get my head around the remaining effort,
about fourteen hundred miles and too many days to go. Now, I know I
shouldn't have even been trying to comprehend it: Thinking about how
much more I have to run is a bad idea in any long-distance endeavor,
and this was beyond anything I'd attempted before. But I couldn't help it,
especially at dusk, when whoever brought me the reflective gear would
arrive. Everyone hated that job, because I was predictably uncooperative
about putting it on. I'd start thinking about having another night on the
road, which meant I had hours to go before sleep, which meant that when

I woke up in the morning I'd be tired again, which meant that the first marathon of the day would be another period of "warming up" and "recovery" from the night before, which meant that . . . my mind would just take me out of the present moment and into a future I dreaded. Every day was like the next, so it made the current effort feel pointless, endless, empty.

And second, I was starting to feel helpless, even more dependent on Heather than ever before. Since I was out there on the road alone most of the time, I spent most of it missing her. Sure, I could distract myself with my usual tricks, remembering old Native American legends about the area, admiring a vintage 1950s 8N Ford tractor that reminded me of the one I'd driven as a boy, or just cranking up the music. But it seemed that my mind would always come back and settle in this unsettled place.

I was on a roller coaster of emotion.

Good thing Caleb Beasley caught up with me on a major road later on the same day that I'd gone cross-country, because I really needed another boost. He was someone who'd signed up on the Running America website to be a guest runner, and when he found me, I was delighted to have the company. As we ran, he told me that his wife and their newborn baby were in a car tailing our crew van, and Caleb said he'd be happy to introduce them when he was done running for the night. When we stopped, and his wife brought that little girl out into the darkness, my heart soared! She had the biggest, most beautiful eyes I've seen. As I held her, a wave of hope washed over me. *How precious life is! Oh, this little one has so much to learn, and has such a bright future with these two great parents loving and supporting her.*

> # Welcome to Iowa!
> ## "The Hawkeye State"
>
> Arrival date: 10/13/08 (Day 31)
> Arrival time: 10:53 p.m.
> Miles covered: 1,779.0
> Miles to go: 1,284.2

The rush from that encounter lasted for hours, throughout the rest of the night. It was a strange sensation, to feel so "up" yet melancholy at the same time. Holding that baby had put me in mind of my own children when they were that age, and all the old feelings of new fatherhood warmed me as I continued through the rain, running on Highway 2 and crossing the Missouri River. Not long after that, we arrived in Iowa, and early in the morning, just after 1 a.m., I finished my sixty miles for the day ahead of schedule. Although the weather was slowing me down, the exhilaration of seeing the newly born baby had allowed me to make up the time I'd lost, with very little perceived effort. It was fortunate that I'd had such a good night, because the next day would bring devastation.

A couple of days before, Heather had met with Charlie, Chuck, and Kate in Charlie's RV to discuss several crewing and production issues. There were budgetary constraints and the time-line slippage to cover, as we were behind schedule. They were also asking Heather to take a break, step back a bit, and let Chuck take up the slack. Someone had convinced Kate that Heather was overloaded, and supposedly there had been some complaints about my wife's demeanor: She was "too specific" in her in-

structions and requests; this didn't "empower" others, the mysterious "someone" had said. Charlie made some accusations that were both inaccurate and, frankly, insulting, but Heather kept her mouth shut, even when she was threatened with being sent home if she didn't shape up. (Surely these were empty threats, even if Kate actually believed this crap. Who would send a man's wife away from him when he needs her most?) She felt strange undercurrents in that meeting, as if there were some behind-the-scenes maneuvering, something she couldn't quite put her finger on, but she decided to let it go, not address any of it or mention it to me because it just felt like "drama." Instead, Heather would get back to work and let her dedication to me speak for itself. While the personal criticisms surely hurt, she set that aside and chose to go with the flow, even though she knew that at least one of the decisions in that meeting would prove to be agonizing for both of us. But she didn't know exactly when the hammer would drop.

On day thirty-two, after running with some local schoolkids and their teachers through Riverton, I took my post-marathon nap, visions of Mayberry-style towns dancing in my head. Everywhere we went these days, I expected to see Sherriff Andy, Aunt Bee, Opie, or Deputy Barney Fife . . . We passed barbershops with candy cane poles out front, ran down quaint streets lined with tidy sidewalks and ribbons of flowerbeds, noted the churches with round and square steeples—painted and precisely shingled, occasionally topped with rusted, corrugated tin roofs— admired the squared-off storefronts and brick buildings with their mortar perfectly pointed and maintained. It was Main Street, U.S.A., a throwback to the days some people call innocent. Certainly looked wholesome to me.

Shortly after I woke up and got back on my way, I saw the RV up ahead, which was odd so soon after I'd taken a break. When I got closer, I could see Kate there—also strange because she usually had a lot better

things to do than hang out at the Starship. As I approached, she informed me that they'd determined it was time to send Roger home.

Resigned, I told her that I wanted to tell Roger myself. I felt it would be wrong, somehow, to have anyone else break the news.

Heather and I had discussed this before, seen it coming, as production had been pushing to get rid of Roger since Sterling, Colorado. They had their reasons, some budgetary, some procedural—some legit, some complete bullshit—and we'd seen the writing on the wall. The most ludicrous reason to let him go: "All Roger does is drive the RV." Apparently, no one had noticed that he also prepared the daily planner and did most of the jobs no one else wanted: laundry, cooking, cleaning, and shopping. Although I'd insisted Heather negotiate to keep Roger when Kathleen was sent home, we'd known it was only a matter of time. Roger knew, too, and had told Heather to stop fighting for him; he could see it was a losing battle and it was eating her up. Still, we'd dreaded the possibility of losing our beloved neighbor, Heather's main support system, and an important part of my crew.

When I stepped into the RV and saw Roger there, I couldn't keep it together. I wept as I told him what was happening, already mourning the loss and regretting that this was where our time on the road together would end. When my legs gave out, Roger lifted me up and held me like he would a child, trying to soothe me. Here I was, telling him he was let go, and in turn he was comforting me, which shows what kind of man he is. After ten or fifteen minutes, once I'd finally regained my composure, Roger gathered up his things, taking no time at all, as he hadn't brought much with him, and he was gone.

Good-bye, my friend. Now what the hell are we supposed to do?

My feet dropped heavily onto the pavement outside the RV, and I pounded down the road, sobbing, my sadness masked by the rain. I wondered what was happening and could feel that I was being shielded from what was going on behind the scenes, and I wasn't sure if I really wanted to know what that was. Numb at first, I went faster and faster as my grief

turned to anger and indignation. *Had this really just happened? How could they not know how absurd and difficult this is, what I'm doing, and how important Roger is to Heather and me? How could they not understand that simple comforts like having one of my best friends here make this bearable? Am I just a running machine without emotional needs? No!*

It was painful, but a moment of clarity and resolve. I am not just a running machine. My relationships sustain me. Thank God I knew my wife was waiting for me that night in the RV. *When you're desperate, a badger is a good thing to be.* I'd just have to dig deeper, and go to the place I loved: Heather, home.

Although Roger's departure was a psychological blow, I was improving physically. The next day, I dipped down somewhere between eight- and ten-minute miles. My foot was still a mess, but it was the furthest thing from my mind; the road surface was good, and although my wife was still not crewing, I knew she was close by. They'd given me some cockamamie story about how tired she was—and I knew she was tired, but I also knew she wanted to be on duty. So she'd rest that day, but I was determined to talk Chuck into putting her back on the schedule soon, and I felt confident that he'd heed my wishes.

Things were definitely looking up. Just as I finished my first marathon of day thirty-five, I spotted a license plate on the side of the road near the RV. It wasn't anything special, but I thought I'd go take a look. What the . . . ? As I turned it over, I discovered it was a plate from Marshall County, Iowa, someplace far from where we were parked. It was out there on the road, nowhere near home, just like I was. A good omen! Smiling, I carried the beat-up, lucky plate back to the RV and put it just inside the door so it would be the first thing I'd see whenever I came inside. No substitute for Roger's smile, but it would do. And although I'm not particularly superstitious, I enjoy celebrating coincidences and anything auspicious. Growing up, we'd made a big fuss whenever a cow would

drop twin calves—not completely unheard-of, but rare just the same. It was like that, finding the license plate. You have to pick up good luck where you can find it.

Later that same day, I reached the two thousandth mile, and we celebrated with cigars and cake. Charlie joined us and seemed in good spirits. He was now on a mission, going out every so often to make speeches in local schools, talking with kids, telling them his story of running America, and motivating them to pursue their own dreams.

That night, as I was out in the rain again, I realized that the front of my right shin was developing tendonitis, the very injury that had put Charlie out of the race and that I knew all too well from the Badwater Quad. Crap! Was I going to have to disown my whole leg? I slowed my pace, running on the shoulder, distracted. In an instant, I caught the toe of my foot in a crack in the concrete and in an instant—*splat!*—down I went, flat on my face. All was silent around me. With no traffic and the crew van far off in the distance, I could hear myself breathing against the pavement.

Suddenly relaxed, I thought to myself, *It's comfortable here. I don't have to get up, ever, if I don't want to. It's just me and the road.*

So I lay there, and it felt good not having to get up ever again.

After a couple of minutes, I rose slowly, walked back a few steps, and looked at what had toppled me. It was pathetic, the state of mind I'd been reduced to because of such a tiny imperfection, less than half of an inch difference in elevation. I turned and started putting one foot in front of the other again, thinking that I had to be careful of little things like that, small imperfections in the road, or in myself.

9.

The 400-Mile Workweek

Days 35–38

"I almost got hit!"

Heather listened as I recounted the story, breathless and at breakneck speed. It was obvious I was scaring her, but I couldn't help myself—the adrenaline and my complete amazement that I was still alive drove me to tell her the details, not just once, but at least four times, after each mile as I ran up to the van again during the next few crew stops.

It was close to eleven p.m. the same day I'd belly-flopped on the pavement, but now I was running on the right side of the road, not facing traffic as would be safe (kids, don't try this at home), but instead taking a chance with my back to the cars because I was nursing that sore right foot and shin, and the camber of the road on the right was more forgiving. We'd doused my leg with some holy water from Lourdes that a friend had given us. Again, I'm not one to buy into ritual and things of that nature, but I'll take help wherever I can get it. Maybe it did some good, as I was moving down the road at a reasonable clip, wearing new Air-Drive headphones that allowed me to listen to music but also hear what was going on around me. It was reassuring when I heard a car begin to slow down, some fifty feet or so behind me—the headset was working perfectly—and I figured that the driver must have seen my reflective vest and flashing red lights. Even in the darkness, I felt safe.

The car was getting closer and starting to pass me on the my left when, suddenly, gravel was kicking up on my *right* as I heard the roar of a second engine, and out of the corner of my eye, I saw a vehicle accelerate—another car had come from behind the first one, and it was now attempting to pass on the shoulder, with me sandwiched between the two.

There was little time to react, as both cars were traveling at something like fifty miles per hour. Instinctively, I stepped slightly to the left on the white line, and within a split second, both sets of taillights surged ahead, leaving me shocked that I was still standing. How had neither car hit me? Panting, I touched my chest and hips to make sure I was still there, completely shocked at what had just happened; it was as if I had become invisible, invincible, lifted out of harm's way.

I muttered something like the Buddhist prayer: *At least I didn't die, so let me be thankful.* It came out as a four-letter word, but that's what I meant, anyway.

The driver who had passed on the shoulder sped off at a high rate of speed, but the other one stopped and turned around about a quarter of a mile ahead. Shaking uncontrollably, she came to check on me and was relieved to see me still on my feet, walking toward her. A young woman probably in her twenties, her eyes wide with disbelief, she gave me her view of what had just happened: Yes, the other car had zoomed by us both on the right, and she'd felt sure she'd find me lying dead or mortally wounded on the side of the road.

"You're really okay?"

Grateful that she'd come back to see about me, and impressed with her sense of compassion and her courage to do so, I consoled her and complimented her character. As she left, she was still shaking.

So was I, as I ran up to the crew van to explain what had just happened.

I was sure there had been some kind of divine intervention. Maybe it was my father, Elmer, or Heather's father, Rory, who'd looked out for me. Or perhaps God himself had lifted me out of harm's way. I couldn't help thinking about that holy water Heather had put on my shin, and the coincidence that this was the first time I'd worn those headphones. Who knows what had saved my life? Maybe all of it. Maybe none of it. Maybe I was just one lucky bastard. For whatever reason, I was spared, and I vowed to stay on the left side of the road from then on. I wasn't about to go all this way, cover all these miles, put my wife and crew through the wringer the way I had, only to get knocked off by a reckless driver and my own poor judgment.

The following morning, we started in the fog, running alongside the Mississippi River through Fort Madison, Iowa. I was excited and, despite my personal admonitions after my fall, distracted again. Not only was I watching the slow current of the Great River (translated from the Ojibwe *Misi-ziibi*) and marveling at how expansive this waterway is, but I knew we'd be crossing it soon. Yes! This was, so far, the most significant milestone for me, because I knew that once I'd made it to the other side of the Fort Madison Toll Bridge, I'd be in Niota, Illinois, setting foot for the first time in the eastern United States. This bridge was not just a fantastic work of engineering—the largest double-deck swing span bridge in the world—but also a potent symbol for me, the meeting of east and west, a balance point and, I hoped, a tipping point. The run thus far had been filled with contradictions, seemingly opposing forces, complementary opposites, the yin and yang of ultrarunning: hot and cold, dry and wet, dark and light, suffering and joy, grandiose plans and humbling circumstances, noble aspirations and petty indignities. Crossing the bridge would mean that I was considerably closer to the end than to the beginning.

Somebody handed me money to pay for my passage as I stepped onto the upper deck, but when I jogged across the solid steel floor of the bridge, I was too preoccupied to notice the tollbooth about a quarter of the way across. A hundred yards later, when I realized that I'd run right by it, I

turned around and headed back. The woman in the booth was waving at me, smiling, trying to tell me it was okay, I could just keep going, but I really wanted to pay the toll. She thought it was funny when I insisted on giving her my dollar, and we had a good laugh about it.

"We need to do the right thing, though, don't we?"

Already giddy, I felt happy to do what I knew so many other Americans had done. This place was steeped in history: Trains had traveled the lower deck's Santa Fe rail line since 1927, and the river had been a draw for settlement from Minnesota on down to Arkansas, served as an inspiration to blues musicians, and provided a literary metaphor for independence and adventure to the likes of Mark Twain. It felt fantastic, trotting across that enormous bridge, and then once we were across, we followed the river for another seven or eight miles.

Here again, once the elation of reaching this landmark passed, my mood sagged and I sank into another depression when I considered how far I had yet to go.

Damn! Now I have another thousand miles to run.

In training, I try to log about 120 miles a week to be in peak condition. At this stage of our trans-American crossing, I was putting in more than four hundred miles a week. To sustain this kind of effort, it takes the right amount of food and water, reliable gear, a few choice pieces of medical equipment, and key people to make sure all of it is available and ready as needed. It also requires a good deal of moral support and sufficient emotional resources to keep a runner in good mental health.

Everything hinges on the crew. They make sure that:

- **The runner always has fluid to drink, in hand.** Strangely, I consumed no water during the run across the United States, mainly because I needed all the energy I could get. Instead, I downed Muscle Milk (vanilla and chocolate), Red Bull, Star-

bucks DoubleShots and Frappucinos, Ensure, root beer floats, juice, soda, and O'Doul's . . . anything tasty and full of calories.

- **A proper balance of electrolytes is maintained.** We used Sustain tablets to help prevent heat fatigue and muscle cramps, with the amount depending on the temperature (more for higher heat). Not typically a sports supplement, Sustain is usually considered a first-aid supply, but I've been using it for years and have learned exactly how much I need. (You have to be careful with these, though, as they contain sodium and you don't want to overdo it.)

- **There's enough food and sufficient calories to keep running and avoid bonking.** Most meals I ate on the go, either ripping open a package of something or sipping a blended smoothie of some kind as I walked. (That's why I was so excited and grateful on the very rare occasions when I got to sit down with a hot meal and use a plate and utensils.) We had a terrific Vita-Mix blender, provided by the company, that would whip up just about anything into a drink. Most days, I ingested anywhere between eight thousand to ten thousand calories a day, a lot of it from a Muscle Milk/whole milk/coffee concoction, drinking about six ounces every hour (that's three hundred calories from the Muscle Milk, plus additional calories from whatever was mixed with it). In addition, grocery costs for my food alone were about $100 a day. What did I eat? A diet appropriate for the task: one higher in fat than would be advisable under normal circumstances, as I needed it to metabolize the rest of the food. Meals that were convenient to cook and portable. Not much in the way of vegetables, I have to admit. (Honestly, I would have had to eat a wheelbarrow of greens to get enough calories from them, and my leg and arm muscles would have been reduced to the size of string beans without the high amounts of protein I con-

sumed.) This meant a big breakfast of eggs, bacon or sausage, toasted banana bread, orange juice, and coffee; a lunch of "real food," like a grilled ham and cheese sandwich, tacos, or pizza; a dinner of more "real food," like fried chicken, lasagna, or pork chops; and a fifty-mile snack of popcorn and O'Doul's, along with some other hot food (soup, macaroni and cheese, some other single-serving frozen meal—anything that could be heated in the microwave). In between, it was one of my high-calorie drinks, along with snacks like granola mix, yogurt, deli salads, or cheese and crackers. I ate very little salty or sweet snacks, like chips or cookies, and almost no candy (except for the one time I bonked somewhere in Iowa).

- **Body temperature is maintained.** Early in the run, it was important to offset the heat, which meant the crew occasionally sprayed me with a cooling mist in addition to making sure that I had on lightweight clothes. Then, as it started to cool off in the heartland, we needed different material to keep me warm and dry(ish).

- **Medications and supplements are administered in the proper dosage and on time.** This included my prescription medications for hypothyroidism, high cholesterol, and exercise-induced asthma, as well as pain meds as needed. Mostly, Heather kept track of all that, giving me my pills and inhaler morning and evening; doling out the supplements with breakfast (a multivitamin, a probiotic, a squirt of liquid B in my orange juice); and handing me an Ambien at night. The crew also added powdered glucosamine either with my breakfast or whenever I had a smoothie, and I took Endurox R4 twice a day. The pain meds were ramped up the farther we went, though we used over-the-counter ibuprofen exclusively. After the second foot flare-up, the crew would give me a prescription-strength dosage every six hours.

- **The runner is protected from the elements as much as possible.** Although sunscreen would have been a good idea, it was sticky and irritating, so we dropped it early on, and by the time we left California, I was sporting an impressive tan. The lipshit, though, stayed with us the whole way, as I was prone to cracking and chapping and cold sores. Tubes of Neosporin and Carmex were always on hand. God only knows how many times the crew members asked one another, "Did you lip him?"

- **Regular stretching, massage, and physical therapy are provided.** In addition to the scheduled stretching that Dr. Paul provided on most days, Kathleen and, later, Kira would massage me whenever I needed it. Often, it would mean lying on the grass or on the shoulder of the road somewhere, having them work out the kinks and tightness of the last hour or so. On stops when we didn't include massage, I would sleep in the back bench seat of the van, a roll of paper towels for a pillow, while hooked up to one of the cold therapy devices provided by VQ OrthoCare. The company's representative, Robert Spieler, was usually within shouting distance, and he turned out to be one of our go-to pillars of support. Each of the devices provided a way to "ice," whether it was one of the cooler contraptions with a hose attached to sleeves/bags you could apply to the injury, a portable system that was basically a cooler and cast, or the simpler blue jelly packs we could freeze and roll onto and around my elbow or knee or what have you.

- **Any minor medical needs receive prompt attention.** This included blister care (though I didn't suffer too many of those, thanks to Sportslick skin lubricant, ENGO patches, and Injinji toe socks). Back in Utah and Colorado, the inside of my mouth got very sore from eating all the time, so at Dr.

Paul's direction, the crew would make me a mouth rinse of Mylanta and Orajel. Yum! Not really, but it worked.

- **The runner is as happy and content (and undistracted) as can be expected.** The crew made sure I had my music (mp3 player or satellite radio), sent friends out to see me when they knew it would lift my spirits, cheered me on, told me how great I looked, and didn't ask much of me except that I run. Little things, again, made a big difference. Kira once presented corn dogs as hors d'oeuvres for me, with "toothpicks" made out of a cut-up straw and a "serving tray" she'd made from a Triscuits box, just because she knew I'd think it was funny; Brian decided to call our fifty-mile snack "happy hour" and would bring out the popcorn and O'Doul's like a genial bartender; Heather always thought of ways to eliminate any extra effort, like removing the caps from the lipshit or opening any packaged food before handing it to me. Along with everything else she was doing for my morale, Heather kept all the behind-the-scenes stressors to herself. She was always smiling, complimenting, encouraging.

In addition to all these elements of direct support, the crew was responsible for preparing a daily planner that detailed the route, including terrain, towns, and major landmarks, expected weather, and plans for the night (RV or hotel); making entries as required by Guinness World Records in all log books; food shopping; ensuring that the crew van was fueled and filled with supplies—beverages, food, ice, clothing for the runner, medical and health/sanitary supplies, etc.; cleaning the crew van, keeping it usable, organized, and livable; monitoring the mechanical condition of the van; cooking and cleaning up; making sure the SPOT tracker (a personal GPS for monitoring my position) was turned on, working, and on my person while I was out running.

Ah, the SPOT tracker. That orange device started to get on my nerves,

I guess just because I'm an ornery, independent old cuss, and the idea that a little dot on a website was showing my exact location to whoever wanted to know it annoyed the hell out of me. Plus the thing kept falling off. Once, after I'd relieved myself in a cornfield and traveled a half-mile down the road, I looked down at my belt and saw that the tracker had gone missing. *Motherf...!* I realized it must still be back in the cornfield. Normally, I would have asked someone from the crew to go and get it, but I figured this one was far, far beyond the call of duty. There's no delicate way to put this: I'd defecated in that cornfield, and I didn't want anybody to have to go, literally, looking for my shit.

Indeed, I found it in the cornfield, right where it had dropped from my pack belt—and I'd accidentally defiled it, like some bear using scat to mark its territory. Disgusting, but it perfectly expressed my feelings, so I had to laugh. I picked up the thing and wiped it off the best I could using the dewy grass, then sheepishly asked Dr. Paul to give it a good once-over and return it to me when it was reasonably clean.

Crewing: The squeamish, faint of heart, self-centered, and glamour-seeking need not apply. It's a grind, plain and simple. Repetitive, demanding, detail-obsessed, often boring, sometimes distasteful. It takes a certain kind of person, someone who's really invested either in the runner or in the athletic accomplishment, to be an effective member of the crew.

Now that Roger was gone, and since Jesse and Kathleen had left some time ago, the remaining crew were doing their best to keep up with everything. Heather had been setting the crew schedule since the beginning, but in the last few days, Chuck had taken that over. Kira had learned how to stretch me whenever Dr. Paul wasn't with us. Without much fanfare, Roger had monitored food supplies, serviced the RV, cooked, and done the cleaning and laundry, but now those chores were backing up, although Heather, Brian, and Dr. Paul were pitching in. Roger's daily planner had been abandoned altogether, and I missed it. Not having a sense of where I was headed and what was expected set me on edge.

SEEING AMERICA, ONE MILE AT A TIME

A "Typical" Day on the Crew

No two days were the same for the crew, although many of their duties were routine. Long hours and repetitive tasks tended to make the days blur together, and the close quarters made for plenty of laughter and the occasional short temper. But the big perk was, as the crew mantra declared, they got to see America, one mile at a time.

Morning Drill: Often, whoever was on duty to crew in the morning would have slept in the RV with Heather and me (and other people) the night before. Cozy! Starting at about six a.m., someone prepared my breakfast; someone else massaged my foot and ankle; someone else checked that the van had been stocked the night before with food and clothes and anything else needed for the day. Two people would get into the crew van and drive me to the stakeout

point from the night before (if we weren't there already), and anyone else stayed behind to clean up the RV and make it ready for my nap later, prepare food, run errands, service the RV, and take care of anything unexpected. Some collaboration with the film crew facilitated route planning.

On Course: One person drove the van, pulling over onto the shoulder every mile and waiting there for me to run up from behind. This was the coveted job, as the driver controlled the music and any DVD they might be playing. The "wheel-man" also maintained the logbook, jotting down mileage and times, pace, injury updates, landmarks, people we'd meet, and any other thing of note. Another person did the "kitchen" job, preparing my food and drink, as well as serving as "the gimp" (our admittedly tasteless name for the job—thanks, *Pulp Fiction*), handling my gear and bringing me whatever I needed, including meds and lipshit. The gimp would walk with me for a short distance, check on me, see what I might need next, and then return to the van. In other words, drive, tend to the runner, repeat.

At the end of the "day," usually sometime between one or two in the morning, they'd stake out my finishing point and either drive me to a hotel or leave me at the RV.

TMI: Most of the time, the crew used the great outdoors as their bathroom. They reserved the RV toilet for me, which I used whenever I was there for a nap or the night, mostly because maintenance of the thing would have become a full-time job if we'd made it the public restroom, and even as it

was, we occasionally had a backup into the shower drain. To understate it, the crew put up with a lot. Gimps would scrunch in the backseat of the van between the two big coolers, one filled with food and the other with drink. I know their bodies got sore from sitting back there and climbing in and out of the vehicle. Rarely did they take time for themselves, although I hear that some showered more regularly than others, and therefore smelled better. Occasionally the crew ate a meal somewhere other than the RV or van. It was grueling, unrelenting, focused work. As Roger would say, "This train doesn't stop."

Crew Roster: Here's a full accounting of all the wonderful people who came out to help, in order of appearance. Heather Ulrich, Dr. Paul Langevin, Kathleen Kane, Jesse Riley, Roger Kaufhold, Dave Pearson, Brian Weinberg, George Velasco, Colleen Oshier, Becky Clements, Theresa Daus-Weber, Amira Soliman, Todd Holmes, Chuck Dale, Elaine Ulrich, Alexandra Ulrich, Taylor Ulrich, Kira Matukaitis, Rick Baraff, Jenny Longpre, Dave Thorpe, Alex Nement, Bob Becker, Cole Hanley, Kate O'Neil, Michael Mezzacupo, Tom Triumph, Mark Macy, Therese Triumph, Kathy Farrell.

We laughed our heads off. We missed our friends and family. We saw America. We watched Marshall accomplish something—daily—that is difficult even to wrap your head around. We met people from across the country, and saw towns and places and landscapes that many never get to experience. We cried. And we

argued at times. We made memories. I think we all came away changed.

—Kira Matukaitis

I've never been so tired, but I've never had such a unique experience. This adventure took me into the heart of America: I either drove very slowly or walked very briskly along a ribbon of highway that never ceased to introduce me to the beauty of city, ocean, vineyard, desert, mountain, evergreens, scrub bushes, a fall palette of glistening leaves, streams, rivers, sunrise, sunset, the first star, the Milky Way spilled out across the heavens from horizon to horizon, the waxing and waning moon. The quiet where I could find myself and God. And the people. One mile at a time, I met humanity.

—Kathleen Kane

There were many times when I thought it was over. There were several instances in which Marshall found himself doubting or having a hard time, not wanting to be alone out there. It's part of being human. It would have been *that* easy for him to quit, and we would all have understood. But he didn't. So I'd go out with him on these nights for as long as he wanted, until we were either laughing hysterically or so inspired that he finished extra mileage. He told me later that these conversations were pivotal to his success.

—Brian Weinberg

Silently, I would growl at no one in particular, *Why don't you try this: Go that way. Keep running for sixty miles. Who knows what you'll find? Heh, heh. Maybe there will be hills, or rain, or no shoulder to run on. We'll tell you when to stop, and then we'll tell you where to sleep. You don't need to know where anyone else will sleep, what they're doing, or if their needs are being met. Run. Just run. Go on, now—run thataway.*

It felt dehumanizing. Of course, I asked for details. Sometimes, Chuck, Dr. Paul, or Brian would give them to me. But it was frustrating not to be fully informed about our plans for the day, and it started to feel as if I was running to nowhere. Dammit, I missed Roger, and I missed the care he'd taken to let me know what was going on. Now that production had asked Heather to back off, and even taken her off the crew schedule a couple of days, she felt that she had even less authority (and, I came to find out, had never felt that she'd had much to start with) to ask questions and get answers.

But to be honest, all of that—the crewing details, who was doing what and how they were getting along and who was in charge—didn't occupy much real estate in my mind as we pushed through Illinois toward Indiana, rain still coming down, only four states left before we reached New York. As from the beginning, for me, it was all about the run. Run, then run some more. Breathe and step, no matter how difficult, how delusional, how drained. Stride after stride.

My focus was derailed, though, one afternoon when Charlie rode up, as usual, honking that ridiculous kiddie horn. Out of the blue, he asked, "What's up with you and needing clean laundry?"

"Why," I wondered aloud, "wouldn't I want clean clothes?"

He reminded me that when we'd done adventure races together, we'd never had clean laundry, and when he'd run the Sahara, they'd never had clean laundry. *Right,* I thought. *And the bunioneers didn't have clean laundry,*

and the pioneers didn't have clean laundry. I bet Alexander the fucking Great didn't have clean laundry, either.

What on earth was he getting at?

"Well," I pointed out, "I believe there are laundromats in all these towns we're passing through. Do you see a problem with us using them?"

The conversation went on, with me stating the obvious: Clean clothes and towels and sheets were preferable to dirty ones, and small comforts had come to mean an awful lot to me. They were the only comforts I had. Charlie then started suggesting, insinuation and accusation creeping into his tone, that maybe *I* didn't want clean laundry; perhaps *my wife* was behind what he implied was an unreasonable standard of cleanliness.

I sighed. "Don't even go there, Charlie." I told him that I wished for him what I had in Heather.

But he was on a roll. Agitated now, he told me that Running America was his baby. He'd gotten all the sponsors, he owned 25 percent of the project, and everyone out there was working for him. He was called "Mr. Atomic, the detonator," he said, because it was within his power to blow the whole thing up. Thirty-seven days into it, he could just make Running America go away, he assured me.

Still unclear about what he hoped to get out of this hostile exchange, I asked him about the documentary and its producers. He asserted, yes, they all worked for him, and some of them weren't doing a very good job, in his opinion. NEHST, he said, didn't have ultimate power—he could pull the plug on the project anytime, and he wanted us to stop interacting with Kate or anyone working on the documentary. It was his baby, and we weren't to touch it. Kate worked for him, he said, and he wanted her to focus exclusively on filming—nothing to do with the run was under her purview anymore. Now, everything dealing with my athletic endeavor would go through Chuck, Charlie's right-hand man.

I kept plodding, and Charlie kept pedaling. Was he actually threatening to kill Running America over laundry? It was all so overblown. And

this business of being cut off from the people in production? It was nutty, and sounded like an attempt to gain total control over my support system, to isolate me and make me dependent upon him and the people who reported to him. I couldn't believe that Kate and the rest of production were on board with all that.

"You know, Charlie, I'm going to have to get back to you on all this after I check with everyone to be sure that what you're telling me is true."

But, again, he didn't stop. He continued griping about the documentary crew, saying they'd gotten overly involved in the run. When I asked him about what the sponsors might say if he decided suddenly to halt production and stop all efforts on Running America, he gave me some blather about how he'd been blogging all this time and the sponsors had already gotten what they needed out of him and didn't care if we finished or not.

Now I knew for sure that he was full of shit.

Without breaking stride, I told him, "Listen, Charlie. It's very simple for me. I was hired to do this. Running America is a job I said I'd do, and I want to make it clear to you that no one and nothing is going to stand in my way of finishing it. That's it, Charlie, plain and simple. That's what I'm about."

Finally, he rode away. As he pulled out ahead of me and I lost sight of him, I had to wonder, *Was he really "the detonator"? Or was he just a frustrated guy on a bike, trying to get in the way of me accomplishing my goal?*

Either way, it was glaringly apparent that he wasn't my ally, and he wasn't going to let me focus only on running anymore.

10.

Competitive Spirit

Days 39–45

When Charlie and I met for the first time, he turned out to be a hero. It was eight years before we started running across America, during an Eco-Challenge in Sabah, Malaysian Borneo.

That event required a lot of trekking though thick jungles; days of paddling crude, outrigger-style boats; and entering the mountains' hot, humid caverns, where we'd jumar up the walls and have to wade through ankle-deep bat guano. My team, long ago named the Stray Dogs since we tended to pick up whoever was available and ready for a good adventure, included Mace, Adrian Crane, Maureen Monaghan, and me, and we felt our prospects were good, as all of us were accomplished athletes: Mace, Adrian, and I were ultrarunners of some distinction, and Mo was a champion bicyclist.

Minutes into the race, though, we went from being in the top twenty to dead last as a rogue wave in the South China Sea hit our outrigger from the side, immediately capsizing us. We'd been told that if the boat went over like this, there was little hope of righting it, and as we bobbed in the water, Mace and I joked that we'd be the first team ever to be done in less than an hour of racing. But the four of us gathered our wits, stood on one side of the craft, pulled on ropes we'd attached to the opposite side, and in a cooperative tug, heaved the craft upright. We'd done it! We all looked at each other in disbelief and then burst into laughter.

It would have been a simple thing to break out the radio and call it quits, and we considered it, mostly in jest. After a few wisecracks, we got over that and decided to press on.

We paddled to the first island and then had to split up. Since our mast had broken, Mo and Adrian stayed behind to fix the outrigger, while Mace and I went on the island swim and trek, and that's when we met up with Charlie and his teammate, who were also completing this portion of the race. Our map had sunk when the outrigger turned over, so Charlie agreed to share his with Mace and me. All right now! We were back in the game. The four of us spent the rest of the day and that night swimming and slopping through mud, generally having a great time, poking fun at our predicament when we got slightly off course. Once again, Mace and I didn't much care about losing our way, and we loved it that Charlie didn't, either. Some of the inexperienced teams had thought (wrongly) that because we were Eco-Challenge veterans, they should follow us. (One of the Stray Dogs' trademark navigational tactics is getting completely lost and laughing our asses off about it.) Using Charlie's map, we did eventually get our bearings and met back up with Mo and Adrian, and Charlie went his own way, rejoining his team.

With the mast fixed, Mace, Adrian, Mo, and I paddled from island to island. On one, we ascended up the belly of a hollow mountain, fires burning brightly on the floor of the cave. Ghostly shadows played across the walls as other men climbed hundred-foot rattan ladders to harvest swallows' nests for their aphrodisiac soup. Up we went, above them, into the bat caves. Gawd, what a stench! Later, we climbed up hills and over jagged, knife-edged cliffs and then, as morning broke, rappelled down a three-hundred-foot cliff into the thick jungle. I'd inadvertently left my

water bottle behind, so Mace shared his water with me until it was gone. A couple of hours later, Mace was in the worst condition I'd ever seen him in; he'd sacrificed his water and his well-being to help me continue. Reluctantly, he finally handed over his pack to the rest of the team so that he could continue, and we all staggered back to the outriggers, thoroughly exhausted. We thought we were really through this time.

But we encountered yet another team that had just withdrawn from the race. Word had gotten out that we'd lost much of our mandatory equipment, not just the map, when we'd capsized, so they generously provided us with everything we needed to finish, including water. Lucky for us, the race officials never heard any of this, or we would have been out of the race the minute the boat had capsized.

After just one more day, we did finish, and so did Charlie's group, not much behind us. We'd come back from all our travails to take twelfth place—thanks, in no small measure, to Charlie's good sportsmanship and the cooperation of his teammates.

This camaraderie and shared code of conduct is one reason I love these extreme sporting events so much. We help one another out with everything from blisters to heat exhaustion, share supplies, and cheer one another on, even as we do our best to take our friends down in competition. I arrived at the Pikes Peak Marathon one year without running shorts, at Everest without a climbing harness, and at many other events or checkpoints without some crucial piece of gear, and just by asking around, got what I needed to participate. Crews, too, check on each other, make sure everyone has what they need to support their racers and climbers. Heather has remarked that she's never met a more welcoming bunch of people. Occasionally, some completely self-centered prick will come along, but someone like this tends to be short-lived in the world of extreme sports. If you don't help others, it can be awfully lonely out there when you're the one who needs help.

Sure, we play mind games, indulge in some trash talking. That's all part of it. I can't tell you how many times I've heard that so-and-so,

who's in front of me during an ultradistance race, is doing great and is many miles ahead, when the poor runner actually is puking or ready to pass out and within my striking distance. As a competitor, you learn to take all reports about other runners with a grain of salt, and to implement your own disinformation campaigns. (The first time I got sucked in by the "looking great, miles ahead" routine, at 120 miles into my first Badwater race in 1990, it most certainly slowed me down: if I'd known he was only two miles in front of me, I would have poured it on.) Everyone knows that there's plenty of bullshit being tossed around during these events, and it's all part fun, part strategy. Before our transcon, I'd teased Charlie, "Better put on your dust mask," and we'd thought it would be funny if we kept up the taunting, made it a friendly battle with verbal jabs like they have in Big Time Wrestling. We loved the banter, and we kept it going, right up until that strange roadside confrontation about my laundry, after which all the friendliness seemed to disappear.

Generally, ultrarunning is a sport where people do more than just play fair; we encourage one another to excel, because it pushes the envelope of human endurance. We also hold one another accountable, sometimes through ribbing. I gave Charlie a hard time about being boastful (making big mileage claims) and about me being the "invisible man," which he'd laugh off, nervously. Sometimes I can be a real hard-ass about accountability, something my kids were never too fond of, and something that I've pushed too far once or twice with a fellow ultrarunner. But in the sport, we all know what's what: Although we're competitive, there's a mutual respect for one another and the suffering we all go through. A team must act as one, with a common goal in mind, and all teams are respected equally as a credit to them for taking on an almost insurmountable task.

This is why, when it came to Charlie's tomfoolery—everything from the pre-event business with the sponsors and the media, when he never

bothered to mention my name, down to that stupid horn—even though I'd felt like an old dog annoyed by a young pup at times, I never expected him to stoop as low as he did.

Everything came to a head on October 21, day thirty-nine of the run, after I settled down in the RV for my marathon nap. Where was Heather? Odd, I'd seen her just six miles ago in Watseka, where Dr. Paul was finally available to treat my back, which had been bothering me since the night before. Heather had answered my questions about what was upcoming for the rest of the day. She'd shown me a state map, brought me a chocolate milk shake, helped Kira and Jenny restock the van, and said she was scheduled to crew that afternoon. It didn't make sense that she wasn't where she'd said she'd be; the only other time she'd missed my marathon nap was back on day thirty-seven, when she'd attended that all-hands crew meeting. So far, this had been a good morning, running a couple of miles with my friend Jim Simone and some boys from his drug treatment program, which he operates south of Chicago. These were fifteen young men who'd earned the chance to come out with us for their good behavior, and the time we spent together was moving: To connect with each of them and hear about their troubles and their intention to make a better life for themselves was so raw, so honest, and it was fun, too. Later on, I'd picked up the pace with Robert from VQ OrthoCare (gotta love Robert, as he likes to run with me, seems to know a little bit about everything, and has a dry sense of humor). Once I was in the RV and had started to doze off, alone, I heard the RV door open, tentatively, and then caught the sound of Heather sniffling, carefully walking around and putting a few things into a shopping bag, trying not to disturb my rest.

I sat up. "Hey, what are you doing?"

Obviously shaken and upset, she told me that she'd been pulled from crewing permanently, that she wouldn't be allowed on the road or in the RV anymore, either, and she just needed to gather up a few items before going to a hotel, where she'd been told to spend the rest of the day.

Oh, for Pete's sake. This was insane! When I followed Heather out of

the RV and asked Kate what the hell was going on, she told me that Dave and Brian would be crewing for me that day, and that Heather would be waiting for me at the hotel.

Go on, now, run thataway.

Heather was sitting on the bumper of Kate's van, crying. Things had spun way, way out of control, and I felt completely confused. Since when does someone else get to decide when I see my wife?

Oh, this is not going to work.

Running this course was already something like torture. Watching Heather get into that van and ride away in tears took the whole thing right over the top. Was this what Charlie had been reduced to? Picking away at my support system, since he could no longer compete with me directly?

Yes, I blamed Charlie, Mr. Atomic, the detonator. There was no other explanation. Even though Heather hadn't filled me in on the details, I knew what he was doing. Before this race, I'd had dealings with him where he'd lost his temper and turned nasty. And just in the last month, I'd heard about how he'd yelled at people, tearing them down and then manipulating them into compliance. I suspected he'd poisoned the well against Roger, run a campaign fueled by gossip to send him home. And now he wanted to take out my wife? The minute he'd tried to pin that dumb laundry bit on Heather, I'd seen right through it. The man didn't have enough to do, his competitive drive had gone sideways, and he was messing in my business; he was losing control and he wanted it back—but now he'd done something incredibly stupid. *No one was going to separate me from Heather.*

As I ran forward, my stomach was in knots. I grew more and more angry, wanting to give it all up. *I have no business being out here anymore—it's all gone completely wrong.* But the minute these thoughts entered my head, I beat them back, realizing this could mean my complete defeat.

Instead, all I could think about from then on was getting to the hotel, and I ran faster and faster, wanting to reach Heather as quickly as possible. Around sunset, I crossed into Indiana, we stopped to snap a photo

at the state line, and then I took off again. The whole evening and early morning was like an impulsive sprint to get to her and to the bottom of it all. After I finished my sixty miles, I finally stopped running.

> # Welcome to Indiana!
> ## "The Hoosier State"
>
> Arrival date: 10/21/08 (Day 39)
> Arrival time: 6:47 p.m.
> Miles covered: 2,246.6
> Miles to go: 816.6

Around one-thirty in the morning, I put my key in the lock, opened the door to our hotel room in Remington, and closed it behind me. Heather and I were alone at last. She was calm now, having spent the better part of the day arranging her solution to our problem: She'd rented a car and would see me on the half-mile marks, she promised. The crew would take care of my physical needs every mile, and she'd be there to take care of my emotional needs between their stops.

But I wanted to know more about what was really going on. Why was this happening at all? Finally, Heather revealed more of the story: how Charlie had berated her during that meeting in his RV; how he'd scolded her for insisting that my crew attend to certain details, that they crew me in a certain way; how he'd clearly bent Kate's ear and convinced her that Heather was a troublemaker; how there'd been an argument about laundry, who should do it and how often (ah, now I understood why he'd brought it up with me); how they'd accused her of not getting along with other crew members. And on and on it went, petty complaint after petty complaint. Heather was completely befuddled—she'd never had this kind of trouble before although she'd crewed for me many times in the past. She wondered, was she losing her mind? All of it had been so crazy-making: Was she really so hard to work with? Was she such a horrible person? If it truly came down to that, she assured me, she could make herself scarce and I'd be the only person who'd interact with her.

In her frustration, Heather had told Kate that she quit but that she refused to be separated from me: She'd follow her plan with the rental car from there forward. They'd succeeded in breaking her spirit, demoralizing her, and getting her to question her sanity, she said, but there was no way she was going to leave me out there alone with that lot.

Turning Heather into a shadow crew was an option, but I wasn't having any of it. This had clearly gotten out of hand. Everyone had been out there on the road for more than a month, and was tired and probably homesick, but that was no excuse for this juvenile behavior, all the back-biting, complaining, blaming, and scapegoating. We were all professionals of one stripe or another and should have been focused on a common goal. Everyone knew a lot was resting on my shoulders—I wanted and needed to finish the run, not just for me, but for the sponsors and for the documentary, and I needed Heather to do it. What kind of shoddy production would this be if I didn't continue? Were they going to release a film called *Running America* that featured some guy on a bike who'd bullied an old dude's wife and forced him out of the race? What the hell?

It simply didn't make sense that NEHST was really in Charlie's camp. Maybe they didn't realize what he was doing by slowly tearing apart my key resources on the road; maybe even he didn't know what he was up to, and this was a purely subconscious sabotage. Maybe he just didn't understand that we weren't interested in being bit players in "The Charlie Show." Maybe he didn't expect me to fight back.

At about 2:30 in the morning, we called Kate to meet with us, and when she arrived, I laid it on the line: The crew van was rented in our name, we hadn't been reimbursed for it, and so, legally, it was our vehicle.

Heather would continue to use it, period. She and I would enlist the help of friends to come out and crew for us; we didn't want Charlie or anyone connected with him to assist me any further, with the exception of Brian, who'd already promised to stick with us to the finish, and who'd demonstrated his loyalty to Heather and me already. Perhaps Dave could stay, too, but we'd have to talk with him and see. It wasn't that the rest hadn't done a good job—they had—but we were going to extricate ourselves from any continued involvement with Charlie. I didn't want to put anyone in the middle of my rift with him, and I also understood that their friendship with him was important to them, as it should be. In sum, we were done with Charlie's mess, and were taking our future into our own hands. I was running to New York without any more contact with him.

We had no beef with production. In fact, we would welcome their presence filming the rest of the run. Isn't that why they were all here? Kate would have to talk with the powers that be in New York, she told us, but she also said that she'd like to think that they'd all stay on board with me. We could keep using the RV, too, unless word came down that it was no longer okay.

Notably, what Kate didn't say was, "Oh, no. Charlie's in charge and we do what he says."

Nope, no mention of him, his authority, or his detonation power. She's a smart woman, and I think she knew the score, but I wanted to be clear: This was no power play on my part; it was a decision made to ensure Heather's and my well-being while being mindful of the sponsors' needs—we were committed to making sure that the people and companies who'd supported us were given what they expected.

We left it at that, and we all turned in for the night. In the morning, we'd have some answers from New York and know whether we'd be continuing with or without the film crew.

The next day, we all acted as if nothing had occurred. Kate had asked that we hold off on notifying the crew of any changes, as she wanted to be able to give them the whole picture based on what she heard from

NEHST. Two days later and to my great frustration, Kate still hadn't informed the crew; perhaps she procrastinated because she felt caught in the middle, between me and Charlie, who had a financial interest in the film and was one of its producers and so had some authority over her. He had, at least, intimidated her. So I took the matter into my own hands. I figured I'd waited long enough, even laid off one day after only fourteen miles so that NEHST could take care of it and so I wouldn't have to run a lie. But they didn't take care of it. They did assure me that they supported our decision and were committed to seeing me finish the run, and on day forty-one, I decided to take action so we could all move forward.

It was important to me to be up front with everyone, to let them know that we'd be phasing out some people—that they'd done a good job, but it was time to make a change. So I told Charlie's crew chief, Chuck, what my plans were, and he remarked that he'd never been fired so nicely. Then, I believed, Chuck would talk with everyone else to tell them they'd continue until the new team was in place.

Although disappointed that I'd had to take care of this administrative task myself, I was glad to have the crisis resolved. Believing that everyone was in the loop, I could set out with a clear conscience. Dave and Jenny hopped in the crew van, and we set out to continue on. Finally, I could get back to running.

But we should have known Charlie would try to get in a few licks before it was really over. He was all manic-antics now, catching up with Dave and Jenny in the crew van and demanding they get out and abandon it idling by the side of the road, unattended, where Heather and Dr. Paul would find it later. (After that, we never got to see Dave again, so we lost our chance to ask him about staying on to crew, and I still wonder if Chuck ever told them, really, how grateful I was for how they'd performed up to that point and that the changes were because of what had happened with Charlie and nothing they'd done.) Then Charlie sought me out and brought Rick Baraff, the cameraman, to film his outburst,

when he made a point of pestering and provoking me. *What was this*, I wondered, *some low-brow reality TV show? Too bad I'm almost bald, or we could shoot some impressive hair-pulling scenes.* Not long after his first tirade finally ended, Charlie came back, riding up next to me on his bike *again*, now attempting to smooth things over. But when I wasn't having any of it, he started yelling, and that's when I finally lost my temper and gave him a verbal pounding.

Shouting and pouting at the same time, he announced, "Let the record show that I tried to make this right and you refused!"

I couldn't help thinking about Frank Giannino and his running mate, and their friendship that had died on the same road nearly thirty years before. Now, way beyond my tolerance for wasting any more time with him, I waved my hand in his direction, shooing him off. *Please, God, make him leave me alone to run in peace.* Charlie rode away in a huff, and I continued on, finishing out that crazy day with another sixty-two miles underfoot.

The temperature was dropping, hovering around forty degrees as we got closer to Ohio on day forty-two, October 24. The drizzling rain and overcast weather were making it more and more difficult to stay warm, and my muscles were tight. Dr. Paul's stretching helped, but I felt as if my legs stayed stiff even after I'd put in first marathon. The clothing we had wasn't right, either: If I wore a Gore-Tex jacket, it wouldn't breathe sufficiently and I'd sweat and soak myself from the inside. If I had a fleece jacket, it was raining hard enough that I'd get soaked from the outside. I spent a lot of time changing that day, and the van was draped with my wet clothes as the crew tried to dry things out as fast as they could.

With Chuck, Jenny, and Dave now prematurely out of the picture, Heather, Kira, Brian, and Dr. Paul had overtime crew duties. Amira stepped in, and Rick would occasionally help out when he wasn't filming.

(So much for keeping production at arm's length, which we never thought was all that important. Besides, we all loved having Rick around, as he always had everyone in stitches.) We'd lined up a number of people from the ultrarunning community to help, and we joked with one another that the cavalry was coming. My good friend Dave Thorpe was the first one scheduled to arrive, and he'd be there late that morning. An accomplished racewalker, Dave had helped crew and pace me at Badwater in the early nineties, back when I was setting course records and winning the race. In 1991, I set the fastest record by running 133 of the 135 miles to the Whitney portals, and in 1992, I didn't feel that I could run any faster, so Dave suggested I walk most of the steep uphills. That year, I power walked at least thirty miles of the course and was behind my record by about fifteen minutes at the 120-mile mark, but then Dave paced me up the portal road, keeping me focused. Fueled by the energy I'd reserved while I'd walked instead of run, I was able to kick it into gear at the end and break the record again by almost twenty minutes. Dave's probably one of the most positive people I've ever met, and I knew it would be great to see him again.

When the cavalry rode in, it came with coffee and doughnuts. Hello, Dave! What a welcome sight he was with his big smile and American flag baseball cap. He quickly sized up my wardrobe problems, took off for Fort Wayne, and then returned with some new clothes. It was like early Christmas for me, as everything he'd brought back was perfect: super lightweight Gore-Tex jacket, fleece, a wool stocking cap, wool socks, long underwear, a couple Capilene long-sleeved shirts. Dave toweled off my back and dried my feet, and then he helped me dress. It was such a simple gesture, but so appreciated. He cared about me. He understood what I was going through.

Crossing into Ohio, we met a state patrolman who stopped to check on us, and we took a picture together. For the most part, in all of the states

we'd gone through, officers had been excited to see us and were willing to help in any way they could. It always put me in a patriotic mood: *Isn't this what America is about? Having the freedom to go where we please and, if we abide by laws and common sense, having the support and protection of law enforcement? We're truly fortunate to be living in a country with such liberties.*

> # Welcome to Ohio!
> ## "The Buckeye State"
>
> Arrival date: 10/24/08 (Day 42)
> Arrival time: 9:15 p.m.
> Miles covered: 2,398.0
> Miles to go: 665.2

Not everyone in the Buckeye State was so happy to see me, though.

Passing a farmhouse late that night, I spotted a couple of hounds running toward me, and it seemed they had merely come out to greet me. No problem. It did give me pause, just for a moment, as earlier that evening I'd tangled with a German shepherd, the only dog among the dozens I'd met on the road who'd wanted a piece of me. I'd fended him off with a stick and chalked that encounter up as one more near miss. Here, where the hounds had come out to say hello, we were just outside Upper Sandusky, a small town with a population of about seven thousand and a rich history. It seemed a peaceful place, with lots of farmland surrounding it.

But then suddenly I heard a loud *bang!* About fifty feet away, bullets ripped through the field next to me, and I jumped straight up. A man had raised the garage door on the farmhouse and was standing there, backlit,

with a shotgun in his hand. Quickly turning off my headlamp to make myself less of a target, I threw my hands into the air.

"I'm on a county road! Why are you shooting at me?"

The van was parked a few hundred feet ahead, and Heather had heard the whole thing and come running.

"Get the fuck out of here!" the silhouette yelled back.

Heather tried, "We're just passing through!" She'd also reached up to turn off her headlamp and, when she'd been unable to work the switch, pulled it down around her neck and cupped her hand over the lens. (How did we even think to do these things? Survival instinct, I suppose. We'd certainly never been in this situation before.)

The man wasn't appeased. "I don't give a fuck what you're doing! Get your ass down the road!"

He still had his gun in his hand and Heather was pulling me toward the van and away from him. At this point, I knew she was right, but I was also angry and fed up with having my autonomy trampled. From the very beginning, we'd expected the physical challenges from the terrain, the weather, and even my own body, but we'd had no idea about these other extremes—the threat of being squashed between a couple of cars, the drama of dealing with Charlie, this bizarre incident in what I'd later refer to as the Buckshot State. I'd had enough.

"Heather, call 911, tell them I've been shot at, and give them our location," I instructed.

Just then, a sheriff's patrol car rolled by, and we flagged him down to tell him what had happened. Five or ten minutes later, he came back and explained that people in those parts had gotten mighty nervous lately because there had been three murders in their area, a double-homicide where the killer burned the house down and another death they weren't sure was related. Of course, I understood how that could put folks on edge, but that didn't give someone the right to shoot people who aren't even on their property and without any warning. Shoot first and ask questions later? Wasn't that just an expression?

The sheriff sized me up and then explained that folks in the country view things a little differently from how they do in the city.

"I'm a farm boy from Kersey, Colorado," I informed him. "Our 'country folks' don't shoot at other people for no reason."

He was still reluctant to do anything about the incident.

About that time, the county sheriff showed up, and we told him we wanted to press charges. "Well," he replied, "I'm not sure what I would charge him with."

Seriously? A man shoots at someone with no provocation, and you don't know the charges?

This was another one of those surreal exchanges where you can't figure out what the hell is really going on. What was it, though, that Mark Twain once said? "Truth is stranger than fiction." Damn straight. We'd sure learned that over the last few days. "Because fiction is obliged to stick to possibilities; truth isn't."

Ultimately, we drove to the sheriff's office and filled out a bunch of paperwork, and promised to come back to file a formal complaint in a few weeks' time, after I'd reached New York. It all made for another late night.

Meanwhile, my body was up to its old tricks. My feet still hurt, of course, and my left big toe had become infected. I'd even suffered some bouts of diarrhea, and I'd noticed that my muscles were beginning to shrink visibly. A few days after our encounter with the farmer, I felt and heard another loud *pop!* This time it was a blast from my own body, a noise coming from the side of my knee followed by excruciating pain. This was surely the end of the line for me. It was all I could do to walk like this, but when Dr. Paul examined me, he calmly informed me he could fix it. When he was done manipulating my leg, he advised that I ice and rest it, and all should be fine. So we did just that.

When I woke up from my nap, I realized my leg was nearly pain-free.

Whenever something went wrong, no matter how serious, it seemed that Dr. Paul's expertise could always help. Later, I found out that I'd dislocated my fibula, and Paul had "relocated" it. Indeed, it seemed as if luck was always on our side. We'd overcome a lot of obstacles, but there was always someone nearby to help and give us what we needed. It was almost miraculous that we'd made it this far! And though I'd enjoyed finding those talismans along the way, I believed that through dedication and caring, we were making our own luck. When I was injured, Paul was there; when I had reached my emotional limits, Heather was there; when it was wet and miserable, Dave was there; when it was dangerous and dark, Brian was there. I reflected on the wonderful response we'd gotten from our friends, who were coming to be part of the crew just when we needed them most. Funny, as trying as aspects of this run had been, when we really needed something, it was always provided.

Friends, teammates, and athletic colleagues had come through for me: Back in Nevada, Phil and Kari Marchant had paid me a surprise visit, bringing me ice cream in the hot desert. In Iowa, Heather's mom and sister had driven down from Minnesota, leaving loads of wonderful homemade food. In Colorado, other visitors had included Roger's family, longtime friends Gary Kliewer, Deb Sensensey, and even Bud and Penny Smith, who were watching our dogs. In Illinois, Dr. Bob Haugh had driven in from Kentucky and run with me thirty-four miles through the night. Near Indiana, Chris Frost and Steve and Barb Shepard came to visit and run with me. In Ohio, Jean's cousin Craig brought his wife and her piping-hot blueberry cobbler.

Now, Alex Nement was on his way from Cleveland and had recruited his friend, Cole Hanley to help, too. Bob Becker was coming from Florida to help us in Pennsylvania, and Tom and Therese Triumph would crew all the way from Pennsylvania to New York. Just as he had done from the beginning of the run, Frank Giannino would continue to call and check on me. I could talk to Ray anytime I needed him, and he would listen to me; no matter what was going on, he would always tell

me that I was going to let loose as I neared New York, that I was going to get through it and shine—this was my moment, he said, and it was exactly what I needed to hear. Elaine, Taylor, and Mace would meet us in Pennsylvania to crew, and Ali would be there in New York to see me, God willing, make it to the finish.

No matter how lonely I sometimes felt, never was I truly alone out there. All this adversity composed a simple refrain, one that applies to life as much as to running: *Keep going, one foot in front of the other, millions of times.* Face forward and take the next step. Don't flinch when the road gets rough, you fall down, you miss a turn, or the bridge you planned to cross has collapsed. Do what you say you'll do, and don't let anything or anyone stop you. Deal with the obstacles as they come. Move on. *Keep going, no matter what, one foot in front of the other, millions of times.*

PART III

Liberty

*All men should strive to learn before they die
what they are running from, and to, and why.*

—James Thurber

11.

Stop Crapping in Cornfields

Days 46–52

My wife understands adversity, perseverance, and the rewards of continuing even when you desperately want to give up. Heather had her own, deeply personal experiences with this long before we met. Trauma scarred her but it also shaped her character, tapped the depths of her strength, and made her acutely aware of how short and fragile life can be. Not too long after we started dating, she told me this story, something that had happened to her when she was a young volunteer with the Fish and Wildlife Service.

Having arrived just one week earlier on Adak, one of Alaska's Aleutian Islands, about halfway between Russia and the United States, she set out with three other people on a boat to visit a neighboring island and move a field camp. Just as they were about to start setting up the camp at the new location, headquarters radioed to tell them that a storm was on its way and that they should return home before conditions got too severe. So they got on board for what should have been a forty-five-minute trip back to Adak, but soon after leaving shore, her four-person crew was slammed by the storm and became disoriented at sea. Snow fell, ruining visibility, and high waves broke over the boat. They dropped into troughs so deep that all around and above them loomed dark, threatening water.

The radio stopped working. So did the radar and depth finder.

After four hours in whiteout conditions, the *Kittiwake* flipped over, stem to stern. With little room to breathe in the small air space created by the cabin of the capsized boat, and no one else out in that storm to hear them scream for help, three agonized souls tried to keep their heads up. The captain had already disappeared from sight, alive or dead in the icy waters outside the cabin, no one knew.

Not long after that, one of the women in the cabin perished, and her body floated away, toes down, through one of the broken windows. Heather and one other crewmate worked their way closer to the bow, on top of the steering column and farther into the upside-down hull, desperately trying to keep the battering waves from drowning them. The water had already ripped off some of their clothes, leaving them exposed and vulnerable, especially whenever the water crashed in. They couldn't feel their feet.

Six hours later, Heather's friend died, despite her efforts to keep him talking, alert, alive. And then he, too, slipped through the windows of the overturned Boston Whaler.

Only Heather remained in the boat.

After seventeen hours in the Bering Sea, after eating waterlogged Triscuits and sipping juice from a Dinty Moore beef stew can to try to get some energy to warm up, after holding back tears for fear of dehydration, after struggling just to stay awake, much less alive, after pleading with God, *Please, let someone find me today—I can't survive another night,* blessed relief came. A stranger's head appeared around the wall of the cabin: a hallucination? an angel? the real thing?

He smiled at her and said, "We have to stop meeting like this."

Heather was rescued from the wreckage that freezing cold January day, spared her ultimate demise, though she did endure the incredible emotional pain of watching two of her colleagues succumb to hypothermia, then drown, and the physical pain as medics thawed her frostbitten feet. (The captain, who'd made his way out of the boat when it flipped, had gotten to shore.) She was twenty-three. When we met years later, I sensed in her a deep appreciation for life, a seriousness and sensitivity underneath her infectious laugh. There was more to this woman than her Midwestern accent, that was for sure. And when we shared our personal tragedies with each another, I understood why I'd been so attracted to her, not just physically but on some other, deeper level. There were things she understood, having been through this kind of experience—things she understood about herself, about me, and about what's important in this life.

Her past also helped her sympathize with my ups and downs as I ran across America. Nothing I've ever done compares to the night she spent in the Bering Sea, but analogies can be made. Winston Churchill once advised, "If you're going through hell, keep going." If Heather had given up . . . I can't even go there. But she understands perseverance, and especially perseverance when it feels as if everything has been lost.

I needed her. As I neared Pennsylvania, the last big state of this run, I needed her more than ever.

Rain, sleet, and snow pelted me on day forty-six, October 28, as we left Canton, Ohio, and passed through Lisbon, East Palestine, and into Pennsylvania on various highways. That morning, I'd been dismayed; the map showed us that the next few days would include many hills, and maybe we'd have them all across the state. The route itself was discouraging, too. Except for the major interstates, the road structure looked like

spaghetti, meaning that although we'd be going generally in an easterly direction, we'd also travel north, south, and even double back, heading west sometimes. Of course, I wanted to know where I was headed, but the obstacles were daunting.

Now, the infected blister on my toe was improving (thanks to antibiotics), but my calf muscles had been shrinking, and my back was starting to be an issue, owing to my tight hamstrings. I was dealing with a touch of diarrhea (also thanks to antibiotics) and some attendant chafing. Yep, my butt cheeks were burning, and I had to laugh about it all sometimes; this was yet another pain in the ass. It seemed that everything that could happen would happen. That much was par for the course; I'd expected physical discomfort when I'd committed to doing this run. Ray had counseled me to be prepared to be injured, sick, and otherwise inconvenienced by my own body, and he'd been right. So my approach was to consider this period as a life compressed: We'd take one thing at a time, fix or heal the problem, and go on. We'd try to mitigate the bad stuff and focus on the good stuff.

The scenery near the Ohio–Pennsylvania border gave us all plenty to appreciate. Leaves were falling, but the colors were still brilliant on the trees and on the ground—the countryside was beautiful, the autumnal carpet dotted with snow, and it offered many views into our nation's past. Going through East Palestine, I spotted a restored log home, probably built in the 1820s, during the decade when James Monroe, John Quincy Adams, and Andrew Jackson were elected, and when Thomas Jefferson and John Adams both died, within hours of each other, on Independence Day. At the state line, I stopped to examine an old concrete marker, an obelisk about four feet high engraved PENNSYLVANIA, much more interesting than the modern sign that was erected a few feet away. This area played a key role in our nation's history: the Declaration of Independence, the Gettysburg Address, and the U.S. Constitution were written here.

Welcome to Pennsylvania!

"The Keystone State"

Arrival date: 10/28/08 (Day 46)
Arrival time: 8:52 p.m.
Miles covered: 2,634.0
Miles to go: 429.2

The quaint country roads with scant traffic, the picturesque landscape, and the throwback lifestyle were all as I'd imagined they'd be. Moving across the commonwealth, we passed Amish families in horse-drawn buggies (and I picked up a horseshoe for good luck); a one-room schoolhouse with a bell on top, girls dressed in ankle-length skirts and bonnets, boys wearing black pants and white shirts; a huge house with an expansive front porch and laundry strung from one end to the other. Signs of fall surrounded us, with cornstalks browned and tied together, pumpkins carved and lit at night, and Halloween crafts floating in the trees.

Crew tensions had disappeared, thank God. That previously constant anxiety was gone, and there was no sign of Charlie. Everyone was doing their jobs, working together respectfully, and Kate had begun taking shifts, too, as Kira, Alex, and Cole had gone home and we'd be short-handed for a few days until the second wave of friends and family arrived. Despite the few differences we'd had with Kate, on the whole our interactions with her and all the people from NEHST had been very positive. We were grateful to have Kate on board, along with her assistant, Amira Soliman, and Rick, when they weren't strictly on duty with production. It seemed they were nearly always working, though. I can hardly remember ever seeing Rick without his camera perched on his shoulder, or in his lap when he was in the van, and Amira always had her clipboard in hand and pens stuck in her thick, black hair, wrapped in a loose knot at the back of her head.

As I had done since leaving San Francisco, I continued to tell corny jokes to whoever was around, and especially to those behind the camera, hoping to make them laugh or at least groan, but they were too professional, or I wasn't funny enough. Either way, at least I could count on a smile.

Crossing the Allegheny River on day forty-seven: "Knock, knock!" *Who's there?* "Allegheny!" *Allegheny who?* "Y'all-a-gain-y weight if you eat too much!"

We passed a few coal strip mines, which seemed out of place in this bucolic setting. Meandering creeks decorated rolling hills, the curves occasionally contrasted by angular old barns and farmhouses. I enjoyed reading the natural signs around me, which revealed what to expect ahead, such as the way a creek would trickle downhill toward me and signal that I'd be going uphill for some time, or how a tree's branches, inclined to grow a certain way, indicated which direction the wind usually blew.

My crew was giving me signs, too. They'd surreptitiously picked up a few political yard placards and retooled them for our use, using the sturdy wire frames to post notes for me by the side of the road. I could only hope they'd selected an equal number of them from the opposing sides, and it amused me to know that the candidates were getting a little less promotion wherever we passed through.

As we were nearing the end of this transcontinental trip, we were also nearing the upcoming Election Day. This would be the year we'd elect our first African-American or our first woman to serve as either president or vice president, and while I'd been slogging it out across the country, another contest had been going on, holding the rapt attention of many

citizens. Although I'd seen a great deal of America during this adventure, there was also an America that I hadn't really seen at all: "Joe the plumber"? Never heard of him. I never watched the debates, saw the slogans, or heard any of the rumors. The political fracas wasn't part of my consciousness, except when I saw those repurposed campaign signs, which made me chuckle. I had no idea what was happening, and I didn't want to know. It's not that I didn't care about the outcome, just that I trusted the American people to make a good decision. This year, my job was to get across the nation; theirs was to choose our leaders.

There was an odd sort of synchronicity between what was happening in our country and what was happening in me. September and October 2008 were the most volatile and uncertain months in stock market history. People were losing their jobs and their homes, and they were being called upon to muster all their emotional reserves. Everyone was tightening their belts; our proud country had been humbled, and no one was sheltered from the economic environment, from the turmoil that had developed that fall and then come to a head right about the time we arrived in Pennsylvania.

Running through huge snowflakes, nearly every muscle in my body rebelling against the daily grind of my current reality, I desperately craved relief. *I just need to hang on for a few more days,* I'd tell myself. *Soon this will be over.* No doubt there were millions of other Americans who were telling themselves the exact same thing.

On November 1, I awoke in Pennsylvania at the Millheim Hotel after five hours of my usual strange, deep sleep. These days, anytime I'd wake up a little, to turn over or for any other reason, I was disoriented. *Am I at home, in Colorado? In the RV? What state is this? This bed feels nice. Is this a hotel? Ah, there's Heather.* And I'd drift off again to sleep. The nightmares had finally stopped, but I would replay the days' efforts in my dreams, and

Heather would nudge me, as my arms and legs moved in the bed, and tell me, "Marsh, honey, you're running in your sleep again. Rest, sweetheart."

We'd come to the pretty little hotel the night before, on Halloween, just before one in the morning. It had been built sometime in the 1800s and boasted a claw-foot tub in the bathroom shared by everyone on our floor. Who knows how long that tub had been there, or how many travelers before me had sunk into its warm waters? I do know that no one appreciated the deep soak more than I did that night. The heat eased my taut leg and back muscles, soothed my aching feet (the plantar fasciitis was acting up again), and took the persistent chill off my bones. I went to bed feeling grateful and relaxed.

At daybreak, though, I was confused and emotionally fragile, a condition that had been building slowly for a long time but had seemed to really be charging at me during the last couple of mornings. As I put my tender feet on the hard, cold, wooden floor, I felt unhinged, the pain in my soles shouting at me about the nearly five million times they'd already hit the ground in the last forty-nine days. I hobbled around for a minute or two looking for my socks, to no avail.

When I asked Heather for them, she responded sharply that she didn't know where they were, either. Immediately, I felt the tears come, and I put my head in my hands. My emotions were so raw, and the least little thing could set me off. Seeing my sad state, Heather came to me, held me in her arms, and whispered assurances.

"Ssssh, it will be okay. You will be okay. I'm sorry, Marshall. I didn't mean to snap at you. We're both just tired . . . We'll get through this. Sssssssssh, now. You're all right . . ." Over and over again, she stroked my head and helped me get it together.

My breakdown was over quickly, and I composed myself. I knew I had to put those thoughts of distance and pain aside, tuck them away until after we reached New York and they'd be moot—only then could I allow myself to "process" that emotion. Not now. Gotta run. Only a few hundred more miles to go.

Dealing with this kind of self-doubt wasn't foreign to me. I've had these thoughts before: entering active military service, going into college, seeing my children being born, other races in other places. *Am I man enough to rise to the occasion? Will I fail? How could I have ever thought I could do this?* It would be so much easier to just lie back and not take the steep and challenging high road.

In moments of questioning and self-pity, including the morning when errant socks had me at my wit's end, I've reminded myself that others have gone this way before me. My life, including my extreme adventures, I remember, is so much easier than those of the pioneers who set out on uncharted routes, in inhospitable climates, with wild animals and even hostile people to make it infinitely harder than anything I've ever experienced. My ancestors, most recently my parents, once struggled just to survive; for the most part, I've chosen my hardships and always had the option to make them stop. Even when I don't allow myself to seriously entertain the idea of quitting, it's still there, still a choice I could make if things get unbearable.

On rare occasions, I have thrown in the towel. In training for the trans-con, for example, that seventy-two-hour run broke me when I started questioning myself. The sometimes overwhelming desire to quit comes from the mind whispering *I can't* or *I'm not good enough, strong enough, smart enough.* Whatever. Enough. We can be our own worst enemies when it comes to those doubts and negative self-talk. Being around people with positive attitudes helps, but ultimately it has to come from within. In the darkest times, no amount of schmaltzy platitudes will get you through it. When it counts, when you have to pull through, what you need is grit. You wrestle that bear to the ground, chasing it out of your psyche. You remind yourself that it's easy to quit but hard to live with it afterward—it can turn into a virus that spreads and becomes an uncontrollable urge.

Knowing someone loved me and was keeping the faith with me—or for me—made it tolerable that morning in Pennsylvania. Heather and I knew what we had to do. She knew what to say to me, and what not to say.

She understood that one of the keys to not giving in has always been to suppress the whispers and never give them voice. I don't say "I want to stop" unless I *intend to stop* with that very next step. If I'm truly done, then okay, I'll say that I'm done, we're packing up. Taking a lesson from some hard-core Russian mountaineers, there's no complaining or else you really are finished. Just because your hands are cold doesn't mean you have to *say* they are.

So we found a pair of socks, I finished getting dressed, and we continued on.

KIDDING AROUND

Footloose

Of all the chance and arranged meetings I had while running, the ones that stand out the most for me are those with the kids, from a tiny baby to university students.

Early on, there were the two soccer teams, near Carson City in Nevada and then near Steamboat Springs in Colo-

rado, who lifted my spirits and enlivened my run with their cheering and jostling and nonstop banter.

Midway, I ran with two teenaged boys in Hastings, Nebraska, who told me that Kool-Aid had been invented there. I reminisced with them about how my mom had made me cherry and grape Kool-Aid as a kid, and enthused about how Heather and Roger were using the sugary mix to make me slushies on the road, one of my favorite treats. It also turned out that one boy's aunt worked for the United Way. Delightful! We were raising money for the Live United campaign to combat childhood obesity. How fitting was it that I'd be out there burning some calories with these energetic and healthy boys?

Just west of the Iowa border, I spent those magical minutes looking into the eyes of the Beasley baby. Such a light for me in the darkness of a long, long night.

The morning after we crossed the Mississippi River, on a particularly low start of the day for me, I noticed a farmstead right across from where we'd parked the RV at one point, with about a one-acre yard set up as a fall festival, "Rogers Pumpkin Patch." Little ones ran to and fro with painted faces, not a care in the world. They jumped in a bounce house, took wagon rides, petted the horses, navigated the corn maze. What a godsend they were; just when my heart was heaviest, during probably the most difficult emotional "crash" I'd experienced during this cross-country trek, they came along with their joyful play and laughter. I stood and watched them for a while, refreshing myself for the thirty-five more miles I had yet to complete that day.

And the kids kept coming: Jim Simone brought his boys

out from the drug treatment program south of Chicago; about a dozen Amish elementary school children playing in the yard of an old schoolhouse just across the Pennsylvania border shyly waved and smiled at me; and a huge group of college kids in Bloomsburg, Pennsylvania, made a big fuss over what I was doing.

East of Millheim, I met a fourteen-year-old entrepreneur, David Beiler, the proprietor of David's Awesome Cookies. He and his younger brother, Sam Jr., had grown a roadside business into a seasonal full-time "shop" selling their wares mostly to football fans headed to games at Penn State. Dave hopes to put himself through college with the profits, and I'd say he has a good chance: Since it first started, the kids have gained such a following that they (and their dad) had to upgrade the business from a stand to a health department–certified shed, complete with a commercial stove and large Hobart mixer. They can move one hundred dozen cookies in a day, and they offer nearly a dozen types. Sometimes, Dave breaks out his guitar and serenades the customers.

The Beilers have done it up right in the true spirit of American free enterprise: Who doesn't want to spend time and money in a place with warm hospitality, live music, and delicious chocolate chip cookies? All brought to you by a couple of kids.

Each of these encounters encouraged me when I really needed it. The cliché is true: Children are our future. But if we're paying attention, we see that they're also our present. Children's exuberance, their lightheartedness, and even their silliness can reconnect us with our best selves. I get a kick out of kids just being kids.

And evidently, they get a kick out of watching some of us grown-ups. A group of elementary school students in my hometown of Greeley, Colorado, decided to "race" us across the United States. Their P.E. teacher, Tracy Pugh, challenged his first- through fifth-graders to run laps on the playground and around the school, as well as on a makeshift 440-yard track, and log their miles; they'd "compete" as a team, using their cumulative, combined total miles to compare with what we were doing as we trudged along during our transcon. They learned the capital cities of the states we crossed (one of the children already knew about Carson City because his dad watches *Bonanza*, Mr. Pugh reported), talked about how to eat and drink when going such long distances, and debated whether—if they finished ahead of us—they might be awarded a world record.

In fact, the kids did win the race. They'd logged 3,078 miles by 1:30 p.m. on October 31, 2008, and reached their finish line well ahead of us. Believe me, if I could give the children at Jackson Elementary a record, I would.

In the Poconos, I slowed to a walk as a reporter interviewed me for his local paper. His questions struck me as shallow and irrelevant ("What kind of shoes are you wearing?"), and I was in a bit of a mood—impatient to be on the road, run on to New York, and get this whole damn thing done with. Not that I was impolite. I answered his questions reasonably well, I hope. Then he asked me something worthwhile.

"What's the first thing you want to do when you finish this run?"

If he expected me to say something refined, like how I wanted to pop the cork on a bottle of Dom Perignon, I'm afraid I disappointed him.

"Three things: I'd like to sit in a chair, take the time to have a meaningful conversation with someone—and I'd like to stop having to crap in cornfields."

Funny, he didn't really have any more questions for me after that.

On day fifty-one, I woke up in tears again. What sent me over the edge this morning was having spent the night in bed feeling Heather's warm, soft skin against mine. The prospect of getting up, leaving her, and going out for another day onto the cold, unforgiving highway left me sobbing. Once again, she pulled me close and soothed me, telling me everything would be all right.

God, when would this be over? We had, perhaps, only three more days to go, but nothing was a given. Anything could happen, even in these final miles. If we'd learned nothing else, the road had taught us that lesson quite thoroughly. I was losing faith. Would that be the thing that would keep me from the finish?

No, it wouldn't. My connection with Heather would hold me up. When it felt as if I had nothing left—no will to continue, no strength to take another step, no air to breathe—her touch and her words would motivate me to keep going. Years before, she had rescued me when I was drowning in my loneliness and taught me how to love again. And now, one more time, she would help me out of my despair so that I could recognize how much I had to be grateful for. The crew, the sponsors, my friends who had come when we called, bringing fresh smiles, clothes, and hot food. My family, including my children, who'd suffered years of having a father who was gone much of the time racing around the world, lost on some level, his heart and soul having taken a blow when Jean died.

Now it was time, finally, to let go of Jean. Years ago, I'd held on to her

body just after her death, cradling her in my arms and crying out her name, alone in that bedroom at her parents' house. It had been quite a while, I don't know how long, before I'd released her, willed myself up off the bed, wiped my tears, and gone to tell the family that Jean was gone.

Yes, it was time to let go. Completely, now. Time to rise. Time to go on, finish the race, and then stop running.

How could I not realize that the people who surrounded me today were reason enough to go on? How could I not embrace who and what I had become? How could I not finish? Life was unbelievably simple, and the beauty of it lay in every individual footstep, taken one at a time, over and over again.

When we got started for the day, we headed up Nescopeck Mountain and the hilly terrain. As expected, it was cold and, from all appearances, would stay that way. But now I didn't care much about the weather, as I was moving well and at a fairly good pace. Off in the distance, two huge cooling towers, probably from a power plant, lit up the dark with their pinpoints of light. Winding up and over a two-mile road on a hill, I'd loop around those towers. This epitomized the run—slow and sure—and it also reminded me of approaching the summits on Kilimanjaro, Aconcagua, or Everest. There, you coil around these gigantic mountains, just as I circled the towers here. It put me back in mind, again, of how great this nation is, and the immensity of change we've experienced, from buckboards and buggies to towers and skyscrapers.

Now I was yearning to see those skyscrapers, imagining that I'd catch a glimpse of New York City every time we crested a hill. Perhaps tonight? Surely the glow of the city would reach me . . .

In the afternoon, just after my marathon nap, the entire production crew gathered at the RV. Kevin Kerwin, Kate's husband and the documentary's director, interviewed me, which I can say I handled with more grace than when I'd talked with the reporter. It's to Kevin's credit, though, as his questions were better, and he gave me the opportunity to talk about how important Heather was to my ability to finish this run, about how I wasn't just some empty shell of a man moving down the road, but that I needed nurturing that could come only from her.

This was, I thought, the last I'd see of the documentary crew, as time had run out—their contracts had all expired, unfortunately. Kevin, Rick, and Kate would be there to get footage if I made it to the finish, but everyone else would go home. Dr. Paul, too, would be leaving the next day because he had professional obligations.

So I said good-bye to the production crew. Good-bye to Paul. Good-bye to my pride, while we were at it, as I was having trouble even walking because of back pain. I just kept telling myself, *Only a little farther.* At the end of the night, I was fairly chanting, *Not much longer, not much longer. Just one more mile.*

How often had I said that on this road? How many times had I pushed myself to go one more day, travel one more mile, take one more step? But isn't that the way of any endeavor, of any trial, of any life? Instead of wearing me out, those words propelled me forward.

Besides, the countdown was on. No longer did I feel as if I was on a treadmill, running with no end in sight, emptied of reason and purpose and passion. Now I knew—I could *feel it*—that every stride took me that much closer to the doors of New York City Hall, the end of the road.

When we ran through the town of Jim Thorpe, named after one of my childhood heroes, it felt as if everything was coming to a fitting close for me. My father had admired Jim's achievements, too, remarked about what a phenomenal and versatile athlete he was, to have played football, baseball, and basketball professionally and to have won Olympic gold in the 1912 pentathlon and decathlon. The champion's humble beginnings and his love and mastery of multiple sports impressed me as a kid, and I felt a certain kinship with him as an adult. I liked that he hadn't limited himself, or thought of himself as achieving success in only one sport.

Like Jim, my dad had been an incredibly versatile man, constantly willing to try new things. He'd been a doughnut maker, a butcher, a store owner, a dairy farmer, a pet food manufacturer, and later the president of the National Farmers Organization. He wasn't afraid to do anything, and was good at everything he did. No doubt he liked the challenge of jumping into a new profession every ten years or so, just to make life interesting. I wished Elmer could have been there to go through Jim Thorpe with me, and in a way he was. I no longer felt so alone. It was as if every person who had contributed to who I am accompanied me, anyone who had ever encouraged or challenged me, all those who had loved me, the children who'd followed our progress from their classrooms, the men and women who'd climbed with me, run with me, paddled with me, walked with me in any way—they had come with me. All of them were a part of me, and I was a part of them.

The crew was filling out again. Mace had come back, as had Elaine and Taylor, and my friend Tom had joined us. When Mace and I crossed over the Delaware River on day fifty-two, Taylor and Elaine met us at the end of the bridge. We were in New Jersey now! The second-to-last state, and the skinniest of them all. With a little over eighty miles to go, we were knocking down the miles. *My God, this might, just might, happen. We're going to run out of land soon.*

Not without one last wrinkle, of course. My back was in knots, and I was moving at a snail's pace. With Paul gone, we did our best to get over it: Tom stretched me, Robert used an electro-stimulation gizmo, and Heather brought me Chinese food. Bless them all! My back was recalcitrant, though. It had had enough these past two months, and it was ready for me to quit. But we kept going, moving slow as molasses.

> # Welcome to New Jersey!
> ## "The Garden State"
>
> Arrival date: 11/3/08 (Day 52)
> Arrival time: 1:30 p.m.
> Miles covered: 2,983.0
> Miles to go: 80.2

That night, our last of this long effort, we stayed at the Triumph house. (Seriously, that's Tom's last name, and we stayed at his family's place in Mountain Lakes, New Jersey.) It was the first time we'd been in someone's home since leaving our own nearly two months ago, and Heather said it was comforting to her, to be out of the RV and the hotels, as a guest in a place where people led normal lives.

Tom ran me a hot bath and then helped me into it, holding my arm and steadying me as I sank into the water, my back throbbing. As I slumped into the tub, I wondered if I'd have to crawl into New York City. I knew one thing, the grand masters record was mine—I had smashed the old time, and I could take up to twenty-eight hours to get to the finish, if I had to, to break the masters record, too. *Less than fifty miles to go.* For now, I felt like the luckiest person in the world. My dream was within reach. This would end tomorrow, I was sure. And tonight, as on so many nights before, there was an angel in my bed.

12.

Running Out

Final Day

For more than two decades, I'd been running. Sometimes I'd run away from things; sometimes I'd run toward them. This day, what drew me forward was the promise of reaching New York, our last leg on this long, long road.

If nothing too extraordinary occurred, I'd own this son of a bitch.

"This is going to be ugly, pathetic! I'm going to have to walk all the way to New York—this is not how I imagined it at all."

At 5:30 a.m. on what was supposed to be our final day, my back was killing me, and I was in pieces. Yet again, Heather soothed me.

Tom had gotten up before us, and he came upstairs to let us know that he'd already arranged for me to go to a chiropractor friend's house for an adjustment. Grateful, I followed Tom to his SUV. We slowly hoisted my body into the passenger seat, and I winced as he helped me sit down, my leg and back muscles in spasm, tensing and protesting. Like I said: *pathetic*.

On the way, I was thinking about what wonderful friends we have in Tom and his wife, Therese. Who finds a chiropractor to treat you in her home at six o'clock in the morning? Tom, that's who, because he has exceptional friends of his own. When we arrived, she immediately went to work, positioning me on her table and using a strange instrument, something with a small plunger that tapped my misaligned vertebrae back into place. Would this really work? I was accustomed to chiropractors bending me like a pretzel and then, without warning, snapping my back or twisting my head. This was a lot less jarring, and I wasn't sure I could even be contorted into the right position for a snap or a twist, but it seemed a rather gentle approach for such an intense problem. She was calm and confident, working her way along my spine with that little clicking device, and after about ten minutes, she had me turn over onto my back, measured my legs, and proclaimed that she was done.

That's it? That's going to get me to New York?

Rolling onto my side, I slowly slid my legs off the table and dangled my feet toward the floor. So far, so good. Carefully, I scooted off the table and put my feet down. *Ouch.* My feet hurt. *But wait a minute. If I'm noticing my feet instead of my back, that's an improvement.* This morning, I hadn't even thought about my feet until then. Now, moving across the room, I felt very little back pain. Walking down the stairs and out the front door: even less pain. We thanked the chiropractor and said good-bye, Tom helped me into his car, and we drove to his house. I helped myself out of it when we arrived.

"Holy shit, I think she cured me," I said under my breath. Then louder, with emphasis: "No kidding! I think she *cured* me."

I grinned at Mace, who was waiting anxiously to see how I was and to head out on the road with me.

"I don't want to jinx anything, but I'm telling you I think she cured me."

We grabbed our gear from Tom's house and headed back to the stake-

out point. I'd put on my long-sleeved Capilene shirt, one of my two favorites, which I'd been wearing every day since Dave Thorpe had bought
them for me back in Indiana, and which had been laundered for the first
time the night before. (Thank you, Therese!) Those shirts and the match-
ing long underwear had been indispensable the last six hundred miles,
as they were the only ones that really worked in the rain and cold, so I'd
refused to go without them long enough for them to be cleaned. In fact,
like that seemingly eccentric bunioneer all those years ago, I'd worn just
my long johns through most of Pennsylvania. To the brand's credit, they
hadn't gotten too terribly offensive—the fibers stayed relatively odor-
free, as Heather had hung them up to air out every night—but I appreciated what Therese had done. As everyone knows by now, I love clean
laundry.

In the van, I was so excited about being close to the finish and able
to take full strides that I laughed out loud. I actually stood a chance of
running into New York City. Who would have thought so just an hour
before?

This will be a good day, a very good day, indeed.

At about 7:45 in the morning, Mace and I headed east on Highway 46.
Running! I couldn't help grinning as I thought about how blessed I was,
not only to be moving again, but also to have all these friends along the
way who'd helped me, and to have Mace by my side right then. Nothing
ever felt too serious or insurmountable when we were together. Two of
his favorite sayings, when things get really tough, are "It's all just a test,"
and "Calm down, calm down, calm down," comforting words to hear
when things are in the toilet. Thank God he didn't have to say them
anymore today.

As we loped down the road, my friend Sister Mary Elizabeth Lloyd,
who lives in Morristown, New Jersey, appeared up ahead. I'd known she
might come out, but it was a real pleasure to see her, and I felt honored
that she'd take the time to stop by; her presence brought peace, joy, elation. She rambled along beside us for a while, her black habit flapping in

the cold air, and we talked about the long journey behind me and what lay ahead. I told her about the near miss with the two cars, and how we'd doused my leg with holy water right before it all happened. We chatted, as we always do, about her life's work, the women and children she serves. Over the years, I've raised money for her order of sisters, the Religious Teachers Filippini, whose motto is simply "Go and teach," but who are in constant motion, doing the real work of peace and justice. Sister Mary Beth has also gained some acclaim for being "The Running Nun," since she uses the sport, completing marathons and fifty-mile races, always wearing her habit, to raise awareness for their causes. We stayed together for about a mile, and then she went her own way. We wished her well, and Mace and I headed through a small town.

CROSS-TRAINING:
RELIGIOUS TEACHERS FILIPPINI

Running the length of the United States was grueling, to be sure. But the pain I endured was nothing compared with how some people suffer every day. According to the United Nations, in Ethiopia alone, 470,000 children are orphaned by AIDS every year, creating families led by children under the age of eighteen. Many of these minors, suddenly the heads of households with other children to clothe and feed, lack the skill needed to provide for themselves and the others in their care. All of them struggle to survive. Many don't.

These impoverished children need the basics: water, food, clothing, and shelter. They also need schooling and opportunities, when they're old enough, to learn a skill or trade so that they can improve their conditions. The Reli-

gious Teachers Filippini provide all of this and more to children in Addis Ababa, Ethiopia. Siblings are kept together, housed in a hostel, and given the essentials. Mature boys attend the Christian Brothers school in town, and mature girls stay with the sisters and learn to set up and run their own restaurants or sewing shops, or to embark on a career in business and technology, or to become nurses and teachers.

Heather and I have seen for ourselves the amazing work these sisters do both at home and in other parts of the world. We've traveled to Eritrea and visited the cities of Asmara and Tukul to tour the schools and women's empowerment programs that they have created there, and to the Muslim village of Hamelmalo, where the sisters built a clinic, in part with funds I'd raised for them with my Mount Everest summit and Badwater races. We feed each other: Remembering the women and children we met there, and at other mission sites, has kept me moving on many occasions, especially at Badwater. They provide perspective and give purpose to my steps, when what I'm doing helps raise money for their cause.

The sisters live their motto to "go and teach" by providing education and the basic necessities of life to children and women around the world. Their schools and programs are supported only through grants and donations, which are distributed to mission sites. They work to promote the dignity of people who might otherwise perish, who live in some of the poorest countries in the world and also here in the United States.

The traffic on the streets was getting heavier, so Elaine, Therese, and a friend of hers were scouting the road ahead, while Heather, Taylor, and Brian stayed close in the van. This was exciting! The increase in traffic told us we were getting closer to the Big Apple. But we were hardly all business. Spotting a toilet someone had left on the sidewalk to be picked up by sanitation workers, Mace and I stopped dead in our tracks and, like a pair of teenagers, had to play around with it. He sat down and posed as *The Thinker*, and Taylor snapped a photo while I stood by and laughed my head off.

On we went. It was warmer now, in the mid-sixties, and I was wearing shorts and my Capilene shirt. We had to dodge cars at intersections, and we ran around people, laughing at things that normally wouldn't be funny at all. Listening to Mace's commentary along the way was all the entertainment I needed to keep me in high spirits. I was floating on air.

Somewhere along the line, I'd gotten word that the production crew had decided to stay on without pay to see me finish. Now, how fantastic is that? This day was turning out to be better than good. Great things were lining up like cattle in a chute.

Around noon, I stopped to ice my foot and take a short nap. Ever since I'd first injured myself, we'd stopped multiple times a day for this routine of icing and rest. Today was no different, despite the intoxicating feeling of being near the finish, as the pain had crept up in intensity, as usual, and the swelling intensified. My foot injuries, I thought, had a silver lining: They reminded me that, no matter how tough or impervious I may imagine myself to be, I am imperfect, fragile, scared, and vulnerable, just like every other person on this planet. No matter how unique any of us wants to believe we are, all of us hurt, suffer, and feel sadness. Some of us are just better at covering it up.

We moved through small towns and seedy neighborhoods in New Jersey, crossing confusing intersections without missing a beat, mainly because the crew was on top of the route. Therese's friend, not a runner herself, jogged ahead of us to show us the way up a ramp that crossed

over a busy highway. Elaine, waiting at another intersection to point the way, grabbed my shirtsleeve just as I stepped out into the road and pulled me back, and *whoosh!* A car whizzed by right in front of me—another close call, and if Elaine and Mace hadn't been there with me, I would have walked right in front of the car. It felt safe with the people I loved around me; they were protecting me, had been protecting me for a long time.

As we approached Fort Lee and the George Washington Bridge, suddenly there was Rick with that big camera on his shoulder. New York City was still out of view, so it surprised me to see him there, but he guided us through a few tricky turns and up onto the bridge, running the whole way with that heavy HD video camera; that thing weighed about seven pounds, so it was as if he was running sprints with dumbbells, but Rick was in good shape and up to the challenge.

Mace stayed back to let me trot alone across this bridge over the wide Hudson River, and I savored the experience. Within minutes of setting foot on the trestles, I saw Manhattan for the first time, off in the distance. *Unbelievable!* The great buildings jutted up into the horizon, a postcard's skyline. Goose bumps broke out on my skin, and warmth flooded my entire body. It all seemed terribly far away, but when I considered how far I'd come, suddenly it felt as if I could reach out and lay my hand against the cool walls of the Empire State Building. *I'm here!* Rick sprinted ahead for a shot and filmed me as I passed him, then repeated the process many times. It reminded me of my footsteps all across the United States, one after the other, over and over again. Just a few more hours and who knew exactly how many more of those footsteps, and I could stop. I COULD STOP. So close to the end now, I was happy to be running, and gratitude swept over me, an amplified echo of my feelings atop many of the mountains I've climbed.

> # Welcome to New York!
> ## "The Empire State"
>
> Arrival date: 11/4/08 (Final Day)
> Arrival time: 4:29 p.m.
> Miles covered: 3,050.2
> Miles to go: 13.0

Inching ever closer to the skyscrapers ahead, I moved forward in amazement. Had I really come all the way from coast to coast, from "sea to shining sea"? Had we finally run out of land? It didn't seem possible to me now. I had been running for such a long time that it just didn't seem conceivable that it would *ever* end.

Down a corkscrewlike walkway, we came into Manhattan and Riverside Park. The crew greeted me, and it felt as if I'd just stepped onto another continent. The green grass, the trees' leaves exploding with color, and the sounds and smells of the city filled my senses. *I'm here, now, and life is good.*

Only thirteen miles to go.

A group of more than half a dozen runners joined me around Ninety-ninth Street. They seemed as elated as I was, and they ran with me along the path in the park, listening to some of the stories I had to tell. And yes, it was Election Day, November 4, 2008. We hadn't planned to finish on such a historic date, but it looked like that's what would happen.

A jog over to Seventy-ninth Street and onto Broadway would take us

into Times Square. Now, when I say "onto Broadway," I mean I ran down the middle lane of Broadway, behind a procession of vehicles with Kate leading the way. The producers had set this up, anticipating a great shot, and they got it. With the city all around me and the traffic parting like the Red Sea for Moses, I don't think my smile could have been any bigger or my steps any lighter, or my head held any higher. For me, this part of the run was the most exhilarating experience I've ever had in my life, even more than summiting Mount Everest, as this had been a longer, tougher journey, by far.

In Times Square, the election returns blared on the CNN jumbo screen. People were shouting and dancing and generally carrying on, as the first states were called for Barack Obama. A few onlookers had also heard about what we were up to, so I was cheered on, too.

"Right on!"

"You go, dude!"

"Holy shit! Look at that guy running down the middle of the road!"

Every now and then, people had rooted for me like this in some of the towns we'd passed through, all across the country. I'd talked to truckers, tree trimmers, college kids, shop owners, people from all walks of life.

"Ain't that the damnedest thing?!" Yes, yes it was.

At one light, a black Escalade pulled up beside me, and the driver leaned out the window, smoking a cigar.

"I heard what you're doing." He grinned at me.

I stepped closer to the car and asked him, "Can I have a puff?"

He handed it over, and I took a couple of draws, trying to blow smoke rings in the air while we waited for the light to change. We both laughed and we bumped fists as I handed back his cigar. The light turned green, and we took off together, him driving and me running, which struck us both as funny as hell.

It was fabulous. I felt no pain.

Before reaching Times Square, Tom had pointed out the tremendous

Chrysler Building towering in the east, lighting the upper regions of the sky. Our final destination, City Hall, was beyond, way downtown toward the tip of Manhattan.

"That's where we're headed! City Hall is right down there."

Only a few miles to go.

It was magnificent. I'd wave at people who were calling to me from the sidewalks and occasionally give a thumbs-up. My smile widened as we got closer and closer to City Hall, and I knew then that I was being rewarded for my struggle and my perseverance. These moments would be forever frozen in my mind.

When we arrived at the tall iron gates of City Hall, we had to stop for a security check with metal detectors. Heather, Elaine, and Taylor would accompany me the rest of the way to reach my younger daughter, Ali, along with other family members, friends, and the rest of the production crew, all waiting on the steps of City Hall. Mace and I would wear special T-shirts a friend had made for us, emblazoned with our accomplishment and honoring its inspiration:

TRANS CONTINENT RUN

USA 2008

MARSHALL ULRICH

WITH THE SPIRIT OF

TED CORBITT

Among the people on the steps of City Hall was Frank Giannino. Twenty-eight years earlier, he had made this very same journey and set a world record that would remain intact despite my best efforts. Frank and I are nearly the same age, and he'd been hoping I might be the one to outrun his time. Now at the end of my road, I was amazed at how fast he'd completed this course.

In the end, we broke the grand masters and masters records, the latter

by almost twelve hours and on a longer course. But Frank's finish remained the all-time best, the one to beat.

Not for me. I was done running.

Heather and I climbed, alone, to the top landing at New York City Hall. It was 7:10 p.m. We hugged, laughed, and cried all at the same time. I raised my arms to the sky and basked in the moment.

When I looked down, there in front of me was that small group of people who had made all this possible. Everyone was euphoric, and that feeling was starting to mushroom throughout the city, not because of what I'd done, but because of what the country had done. The future of our nation had been at stake, and the voters were in the process of choosing a candidate who represented positive change and social progress.

Hope. We were all living it, celebrating it, praying it would mean something different for our collective future.

When Heather and I walked back down the City Hall steps, Frank and I shook hands and hugged. I felt honored to be in his presence.

Later, Heather held me up as she had done so often in the last fifty-two days, and helped me off the grounds of City Hall. I looked in her eyes and remembered the many times she'd cupped my face in her hands, telling me, "You can do this. I have faith in you."

In that moment, at the end of this journey, I could think about only one thing: how lucky I was to have her by my side.

13.

Rest

Somewhere along a road in Indiana, I'd found a teddy bear with stuffing poking through its torn back and leg. Just as I'd done with the license plate and the horseshoe, I'd picked it up, taking a token of my run along that stretch, a mascot for the miles ahead. We'd perched him on the dashboard of the crew van along with the rest of my collection, and he'd accompanied us all the way to New York. Much later, after Heather and I returned to our home in Colorado, I'd given "Indy" a bath and repaired him with black thread, making a path of careful crisscross stitches through his pale pink fuzz.

Now, whenever I talk in front of a group about my run across the United States, I take Indy with me and show him to the crowd, noting that his little X's mark the spots of my own injuries. As we explore the meaning of this effort, the determination that secured the finish, the pain endured to get there, the kindness and encouragement that aided my every step, that small, soft toy serves as a reminder. This endeavor wasn't only about toughness and grit, but also about tenderness and grace. We found joy along the way, appreciated small comforts, turned to each other over and over again.

Heather and I required more of the same once the run was over: some tender care, some cosseting, some time to hold each other and enjoy a bit of ease before we could resume a sense of normalcy.

When we left City Hall, we stayed in Manhattan for several days, getting babied and catered to like we've rarely experienced. Everyone else went home, and we rested in the comfort of a friend's care, feeling rooted and safe. This was the same friend, my mentor and my muse, really, who'd introduced me to Ted Corbitt and sat with us in her living room as we talked about the history of ultrarunning, our admiration for the bunioneers, and our aspirations to finish a transcon ourselves. She was the one who'd called me with the news of Ted's death, and she was the one who'd admired Chris Douglass's work and mourned with us when he died so soon after we met him. She'd offered her money to finance the run; in the year leading up to it, she'd coached me and talked with me about myth, mystery, and the mastery of running, and her words had echoed in my mind all the way across the United States. She'd met us at the finish line with T-shirts honoring Ted's memory, and then she'd brought us home with her to begin the process of recovering from our ordeal. The only reason I haven't mentioned her by name is that she's an intensely private person who prefers to remain anonymous. Her interest has always been in the sheer athleticism of this event, and all the rest of it—the personal dramas and whatever notoriety might be gained— are of no consequence to her. It's one of the things I love about our friend, her dedication to running as an art form, an expression of who we are, boiling life down to its most basic stuff. Her love of the sport is pure, and we both have a commitment to honoring its past while looking to the future with dignity and grace.

When we left her home in early November, we drove the rented crew van back to Colorado in a state of disbelief, unable to imagine how we'd ever gotten across the United States. That's not to say we were impressed with ourselves; I mean, literally, that we couldn't get our minds around it. It was as if the 52½ days had disappeared from our memory banks, as if we'd stood in San Francisco one morning, and then *poof!* We'd magically appeared in New York City on Election Day.

It took a while for reality to dawn. In the first week at home, I felt the oddest sensation, or lack of sensation, related to time. Twenty-four hours seemed to stretch into forty-eight, time spooling out in a way that was disorienting at first. It felt so good to sleep that I spent about half my time in bed for nearly two months, sleeping upward of twelve hours a night. And I was constantly hungry, having become used to eating a few mouthfuls of food at least four times an hour, so I was snacking all day and then sitting at our table for three full meals, savoring every bite, chewing slowly, and eating until I was stuffed—I gained about fifteen pounds within a couple of weeks of coming home. It took longer, some months, before my body stopped hurting all the time. Not until close to a year later could I finally get back to my normal routine of running about sixty miles a week without feeling like hell, which it just now occurs to me is the same distance I covered nearly every day during the transcontinental run.

The first time I spoke publicly about this journey, a few months after we'd returned home, I hardly knew how to talk about it. There were parts of my experience that still made no sense to me, stuff I still needed to sort out. But I showed my photos and my mementos, and I told my surreal story. After that speech, to my chagrin, I cried during the airplane flight home. There was still a great deal that I didn't understand.

Now, though, it all just strikes me as the hardest thing I've ever done.

In April 2009, Heather and I returned to our route, driving this time. We retraced all 3,063 miles, still having a hard time comprehending the distance. We revisited the desert along Highway 50 from California to Utah, went up and over the Rocky Mountains in Colorado, traveled by seemingly infinite cornfields as we covered the expanse of the Midwest, crossed the great Mississippi River, and went on through the northeast to arrive, once again, in New York City. That car trip was about remembering and finding some semblance of closure. We both wrote journals in our hotel rooms at night, jotting down our memories of each day's route, reliving a lot of the emotions, including the highs and the lows. We stopped together to admire some of the sights we'd passed, often separately, during the run: the diverse natural landscapes, the small towns, the landmarks. We also stayed at places we'd wished we could have, ate in restaurants we should have, and checked out the chambers of commerce and local museums. We studied maps. We talked with people who'd seen the small commotion we'd caused the first time we'd come through—shop owners and townspeople, farmers and other local folks with an impressive knowledge of the history of their hometowns. We ate steak with Mitch and Blaine in McCook, Nebraska, and we spent some extended time with the Beiler family in Milheim, Pennsylvania.

It was surprising how vividly we could recall details—so many of them that there's a great deal that doesn't appear in the main narrative of this book. I've had to omit a lot, mostly because these details mean more to me than they would to almost anyone else. I don't mind so much that I didn't include the day I ran naked out of the RV, or the crazy Halloween costumes the crew wore to make me laugh hysterically in the middle of an interview with NPR. It does bug me, a little, to leave out some of the details of natural beauty and personal reflection, like the time I ran toward a solitary tree, its bare branches backlit by a full moon after a brilliant sunset. The gnarled old bristlecone pine reminded me of something I'd drawn for an art contest back in high school, a strange coincidence. It also kept me company out there and caused me to wonder what it had endured long before I ran by it. Many minutes—perhaps an hour or more?—passed as I contemplated the various traumas the environment had inflicted, shaping its growth, and the strength of such a tree to withstand them.

However, if I were to try to take you with me, give you an account of my every step, or every mile, or every hour, or even every day, you'd probably be incredibly bored. You'd also be inclined to think I was making a bunch of stuff up. As wild a story as I've told you here, there's more, again, that I haven't included because it's just too petty or too random and, ultimately, means nothing.

Sorting through these details, and also watching the film *Running America*, which captured many elements of the run I didn't know anything about at the time, has given me some new perspectives. What the country was enduring while I was running now evokes my sympathy: During the fall of 2008, the financial tailspin and the cantankerous electioneering put the nation into a strange state of uncertainty, which the documentary captured. It also elicited the fortitude of Americans and reinforced my own conviction that there are certain basics we'd all be wise to embrace again, an emphasis on values, morals, and ethics, which individuals should take the time to consider, to define for themselves, and then put into practice in some meaningful, if highly personal, way. As the mountaineer Lucien Devies once observed, we find ourselves when we've lost everything. That's when we recognize, appreciate, and embody the essentials.

In the aftermath of the run, Heather and I had plenty to address, some rebuilding to do in our own marriage. We'd spent two months intentionally *not* saying the most difficult things—the truth about my pain, our shared desire to quit, and her private anguish and resentment—and when it was over, we needed to start speaking the "unspeakable." I became even more aware of how emotionally torturous it had been for her not to ask me to stop, to end my pain simply by deciding not to finish. After all, in the previous year, we'd both watched men we loved suffer—men who'd had no choice in the matter: Heather had cared for Rory for months as he fought the cancer that attacked his back and then his brain, taking away his ability to walk, to sign his name, to talk with his family. And then we'd rushed to my father's side even as he struggled against the respirator tube down his throat. Both men died, so soon after Ted's passing, and then Chris was gone, too. It was a helluva thing to ask Heather to do, to come out and watch me suffer, too, to assist me in doing something that probably wouldn't kill me but that, Dr. Paul cautioned her, would age me in ways we wouldn't know until it was over, and would cause damage from which I'd never recover.

She admitted to me that two times, she'd almost broken: when I'd told her I felt like I was killing myself during that first week, and again when we'd waited to find out if I had a soft tissue injury or fracture, and I'd said that I'd continue regardless. On both occasions, she'd nearly given up and given in to her instincts to do whatever it took to get me to quit, whether that meant begging or demanding or threatening me. But she didn't break. Not once.

She put me first.

Talking about all of the most difficult aspects, we also realized how we'd set her up, in some way, to take a fall. By having Heather relay all my requests, we'd played a game of good cop/bad cop: I'd been able to remain gracious and grateful with everyone, and she'd been charged with making sure they gave me exactly what I needed, how I wanted to receive it, down to the smallest detail. To be honest, there's not much wrong with that plan, except that it gave someone something to complain about, and an opportunity to blame Heather for the fatigue or frustration or whatever other unpleasantness they were feeling. It's one of my few regrets: putting her into a position where she was misunderstood and then mistreated.

We both came out of the run somewhat traumatized but stronger, broken but healing. To repair and recover, it's good that we've talked about our hardships, mutual and individual. That was necessary. Throughout my relationship with Heather, I've been learning to be more open, to stop holding back on what I feel, to reveal it to her when I'm hurt or in pain—even when it will be hard for me to say and for her to hear. In our "real life," we attempt to tackle our issues head-on, to strengthen the bond between us through honest disclosure of our deepest selves, to honor a sacred trust that flourishes only with effective communication. Talking about the run in a way we couldn't have while it was under way has been a purging process, cleaning out the clutter that accumulated while we couldn't allow ourselves to voice all the intense emotions. In the end, what I know for sure is that, despite the difficulties we both faced, she gave it all she had, and so did I. Of that, we can both be proud.

Since completing this run, I've also learned more about what Charlie endured, how from day one he'd been battling illness and injury, pushing through his pain, but then ultimately gave up about a third of the way across America. This defeat surely influenced his behavior and contributed to his rancor. The passage of time has allowed me to get a greater sense of why things went south between us, why we couldn't be friends when it was all over. We could analyze his character and mine, pick apart every action and decision, dissect every conversation, speculate on every motive, but it all boils down to one, essential thing: *the miles.* The miles, ultimately, are what overcame Charlie, what made me feel so fragile, and what made everyone so tired and susceptible to drama.

To state the obvious, the absolutely greatest obstacle we encountered during this effort was, simply, the distance.

Yet it allowed us to amass some strange and surprising statistics: During the transcon, I lost only four pounds. I threw up only twice (after aspirating some food) and bonked only once. I drank no water, wore— and wore out—more than thirty pairs of shoes and dozens of pairs of socks, and ran the equivalent of 117 marathons in well under two months, completing two each day plus a 10K, running over 120 hours and 400 miles per week, ascending over 84,000 vertical feet. At the age of fifty-seven, I attempted to break a record set by a twenty-eight-year-old and finished the third-fastest crossing ever made on that route.

One thing's for sure: This beat me up and beat me down, enough where I've wanted to stop running for good. After all, this was the last thing on my tick list. Going forward, the distances I travel will likely be far shorter, more traditional ultrarunning lengths—one hundred miles or perhaps more—and the speed at which I will complete them will be much slower. I'll be taking my time, savoring each moment as the clock keeps ticking and my feet keep moving. I'm in no hurry now, and when I put myself to the test, it has to be for a reason. No more running aimlessly— in the past, I've sometimes used my athletic pursuits to run away, but I believe this accomplishment was more about running *through*. Things have changed. I once told a reporter that the reason we run extreme distances in harsh environments is that there's something in us—instinct? primal urge?—that wants to get out there, in the middle of nowhere, and think about something. My psychologist friend, Murray Griffin, suggests that it may be an evolutionary impulse, a drive to improve the species, to strengthen our stock. It's certainly a way of freeing ourselves, getting back to what I really believe people are supposed to be doing instead of relying so much on a bunch of material crap that only weakens us. We are built to walk and run, to cover great distances, for survival's sake. But now I think I may be able to satisfy that "something" in ways other than running. More Badwater races: yes, perhaps walking. More mountain guiding: yes, that's my favorite. Coaching people and helping them achieve their own goals? Absolutely. Anything else: Who knows? Really, there's nothing left to prove, and I don't feel the need to punish myself anymore. I've paid my dues.

This race may have answered many of my personal questions about my own psyche, but it's opened new ones. Before we began, my best explanation for why I had to attempt this crazy feat was "It's who I am." Then who am I if I'm not running extreme distances? If I'm not out there pounding and in pain, who am I becoming? What's next for me? It's confusing to contemplate, but it feels healthy to apply myself to finding some answers. The next few years will be about rediscovery of myself, reinvention, and deepening and strengthening my already strong marriage. It will also be about reconnecting with family, about exploring a new kind of relationship with my now adult children, about rebuilding bridges with my brother, spending more time with Mom, saying "I love you" more often, and not letting old differences keep us apart.

My focus is changing, my intensity shifting, and that's okay.

Each year brings more thought, building the strength to succeed and the courage to fail. Each year brings more depth of character, more maturity, a greater understanding of the man I've become as well as the child who once aspired to scale Mount Everest. There was a maturation process, too, from the first 10K to the marathon to the ultras, adventure races, and mountaineering. Each event built on the others both physically and mentally. I thought I knew a lot about running before I started the transcon, but after finishing it, I know that I learned more during this one run than in all the other years of running combined. Still, all those early years were necessary to get me to that period in time, September 13 to November 4, 2008. Before then, I hadn't yet amassed the wealth of experience or, more important, partnered with the woman who could carry me through it, letting me run to my own outer limits of endurance every day, all the way. It would have been impossible to do without her being invested in helping me succeed.

It started with baby steps, that first run out the door of my house, attempting to get my blood pressure down and find some way to deal with the unimaginable. After that, it took dedication, hard work, and some support along the way. It was nearly thirty years of running to get to the starting line in San Francisco. And as morbid as it may sound, I wanted to live every day as if it were my last. This popular quotation, widely attributed to the writer Jack London, sums it up:

> I would rather be ashes than dust! I would rather my sparks should burn out in a blaze than they should be stifled by dry rot. I would rather be a superb meteor, every atom of me in magnificent glow, than asleep and permanent as a planet. The proper function of man is to live, not to exist. I shall not waste my days trying to prolong them. I shall use my time.

I love to think about how Icarus was cautioned not to soar too high or his wings would melt—yet how else would he feel the warmth of the sun? Icarus flying close to the ground is like running in Death Valley during the winter: *Why do the easy, expected thing?* It takes guts to follow your dreams. Courage. Many people, even those who love you, don't understand how compelling that can be, and will try to keep you in the "safety zone." But fuck that. Half the fun is venturing into the unknown, taking on the difficult task that yields new knowledge, doing more and testing your limits.

Often when I'm addressing audiences, it's the eighty- and ninety-year-olds who really "get" my message, who come up to me afterward and say, "Bravo! Good for you." Why is that? Because they have seen and survived the world, and now their eyes are open. They probably took on great challenges or championed the causes of those who did, and with their long lives mostly behind them, they understand better than anyone else that our time here is all too short.

What I've done serves mostly to show that nearly all limits are self-imposed, a false construct of the mind. You can take on mind-boggling challenges. It may cause you grief, it may test your relationships and cause you to question your sanity, but you *can* do it! Yes, a fifty-seven-year-old man can run across the United States and break a couple of records in the process. People of any age can accomplish what few others have done; we can endure the trials, overcome the obstacles, put up with the pain to realize our dreams.

Why not try?

Remember what the badger said: "I can teach you only to dig, and to love home." Consider me a badger, then. Being a runner doesn't make you a sage. It can give you a personal philosophy, test you and take your measure, and even save your life. But it doesn't make you a good person, or even a nice person. It doesn't guarantee a great marriage or success in business. Those achievements spring from your own character and your own experiences, and I wouldn't presume to tell you who to be or how to live.

But everyone can dig deeper and love more.

Crossing the United States on foot further enamored me of my home, of my country, and of its people. It emptied me out to the point where I could find peace and strength and endurance only by looking into my wife's eyes or feeling her hand on my cheek; it showed me where my heart is, and how to temper my soul, to give and accept acts of kindness and not be so quick to judge. It made me realize that my legacy resides in my children and the memory of those who've now vanished from our daily lives but remain vivid in recollection. It's all as it should be. I think about the past, perpetuating memories of those who made me who I am, to be passed on to my children, and to their children. Ours is a story of perseverance; all of us push on, in our sometimes awkward ways, and we make meaningful progress when we learn from those who've traveled before us, honoring them as we focus on the road ahead.

Running America

(for Marshall Ulrich)

This road is mine to meet.
White line my life, direct it.
This way is good and honest.
There are surprises
And fortunes
Like calves that come in pairs
And fathers, too.

This road is mine to meet.
It is not a way from, but to . . .
The greening of the spirit
With hills and bridges and rivers
Mapped out eternal.

This road is mine to meet.
A perpetual autumn,
But it will winter over
Yet not until some lessons are learned
And things picked up along the way . . .
A baby's smile
A fetish for luck
A face staring down fear
A partner holding me up.

This road is mine to meet.
This pain does not belong to me.
I will give it away,
And I will embrace instead the day
That brings the promise of sleep.

JOANNE V. GABBIN
February 15, 2009

Appendix A

Training Schedule

Serious training for the transcontinental run began in October 2007, about a year before we stepped off in San Francisco. Initially, we expected the run to start in mid-March 2008, and when that didn't materialize, we set our sights on May. Again it was postponed, because we needed to secure more funding and sponsorship. We had an August start date, too, which was rescheduled for September. Providence! These delays allowed me to train hard and taper several times before we ran "for real," which prepared me better both physically and mentally for the ordeal.

The training schedule, created for me by Ray Zahab, was designed to get me ready for the high daily mileage that would be required. Specifically, it was intended to improve my agility (and occasionally give me a rest from the pavement) with trail running; my core strength with tire drags and cross-training; my leg strength with hill repeats; my speed with tempo runs; and my endurance with long runs and multiple runs in a day, as well as long runs, back to back, on consecutive days. We also incorporated some ultrarunning races—the seventy-two-hour "Across the Years" race in Arizona, the Badwater 135, and the Leadville 100—to practice running extreme distances on consecutive days, with a crew, and with the added flavor of a real contest.

Lest anyone be tempted to follow this regimen, I'll caution that it was tailor-made for me, and I'm in no way suggesting this is a recommended routine for any other runner. In fact, while I was compiling this information to be included here, I asked Ray how many miles a week he ran while preparing his own four-thousand-and-some-miles run across the Sahara, and he reported that he typically did up to 118 miles per week. It's a good thing he didn't tell me that *before* I completed this schedule, including up to two hundred miles a week, and ran across the United States doing about four hundred miles a week, or I might have been jealous, or even mad at him. But in retrospect I understand perfectly, as he demanded of me a kind of rigor that suited my body type—sturdy, strong, compact, "a tank," some say—my many years of experience with extreme endurance sports, and the particular demands of running across the country, mostly on asphalt and concrete.

Following are some especially harsh weeks, cherry-picked from various parts of the year in training, just to give you a taste of what I did to prepare.

October 8–14, 2007 (50 miles/week)

MONDAY	TUESDAY	WEDNESDAY	THURSDAY	FRIDAY	SATURDAY	SUNDAY
OFF	**Tire Drag** On pavement or road: 10 mins warm-up, 90 mins pull tire at best pace, 10 mins no tire at easy pace. Post-run: core workout.	**Trail Run** 70 mins on technical trail: pick terrain that forces you to concentrate; worry less about speed, and focus on agility.	**Hill Repeats** Warm up at easy pace, run up 1 km hill at max pace, run back down very easy to recover. Repeat 5X, then run 10 more mins at very easy pace for recovery.	OFF	**Tempo Run/Stage Simulation** 3 hrs on road, running at best pace. Test hydration and fuel; focus on pushing yourself.	**Tempo Run/ Stage Simulation** 2 hrs on road, running at best pace. Test hydration and fuel; focus on pushing yourself.

November 5–11, 2007 (75+ miles/week)

MONDAY	TUESDAY	WEDNESDAY	THURSDAY	FRIDAY	SATURDAY	SUNDAY
Trail Run 80 mins on very technical trail: pick terrain that forces you to concentrate; worry less about speed, and focus on agility.	OFF	**Cross-Train** 60 mins mountain biking, hiking, or take the day off.	**Over/Under Tempo Run** Pick a hilly course. 10 mins easy pace, ramp up to 5K race pace for 5 mins, then 10K race pace for 5 mins. Repeat 6X for a total of 30 mins. Spend the next 15 mins at easy pace.	OFF	**Tempo Run/ Stage Simulation** 6 hrs on road, running at easy pace. Test hydration and fuel; focus on pushing yourself to maintain a consistent pace over the longer distance.	**Hill Repeats/ Tire Drag** Warm up at easy pace, run up 5,000-foot, 5K hill at max pace dragging tire, run back down very easy to recover. Repeat 4X, then run 20 more mins at very easy pace (no tire) for recovery.

May 12–18, 2008 (120+ miles/week, peak volume)

MONDAY	TUESDAY	WEDNESDAY	THURSDAY	FRIDAY	SATURDAY	SUNDAY
Cross-Train/ Strength Train 1 hr activity of choice. 1.5 hrs strength training, upper and lower body.	**Long Run** 3 hrs easy pace.	**Peak Runs** 2 hrs in morning, then take 45 min off. Run 2 more hrs in afternoon.	**Strength Train/ Late-Night Run** 1.5 hrs strength training, upper and lower body. 1.5 hrs late-night run at best pace.	OFF	**Peak Runs** 5 hrs in morning. 3 hrs rest. 5 hrs in afternoon.	**Long Run** 10 hrs total: 5 hrs, then stop to eat, taking no more than 1-hr break. 5 hrs more.

July 14–20, 2008 (150+ miles/week)

MONDAY	TUESDAY	WEDNESDAY	THURSDAY	FRIDAY	SATURDAY	SUNDAY
Badwater 135 Race Finishing Time: 36:44		OFF	**Mount Whitney** Summit, total elapsed time for 157 mi in Death Valley: 97:45.	OFF	OFF	**Road Run** 6 mi, easy pace.

July 28–August 3, 2008 (200 miles/week)

MONDAY	TUESDAY	WEDNESDAY	THURSDAY	FRIDAY	SATURDAY	SUNDAY
Road Run 50 mi	**Road Run** 50 mi	**Road Run** 50 mi	OFF	**Road Run** 20 mi	**Hilly Run** 10 mi	**Road Run** 20 mi

August 11–17, 2008 (125 miles/week)

MONDAY	TUESDAY	WEDNESDAY	THURSDAY	FRIDAY	SATURDAY	SUNDAY
OFF Massage	**Road Run** 4 hrs on the flat with support.	**Tempo Run** 1 mi at easy pace, 1 mi at best pace, repeat 5X on road.	**OFF**	**OFF**	**Leadville 100 Race** Finishing Time: 28:09	

August 25–31, 2008 (100 miles/week)

MONDAY	TUESDAY	WEDNESDAY	THURSDAY	FRIDAY	SATURDAY	SUNDAY
OFF Massage	**Road Run** 15 mi at easy pace.	**Road Run** 20 mi at easy pace.	**Road Run** 15 mi at easy pace.	**OFF**	**Road Run** 20 mi at easy pace.	**Road Run** 30 mi at easy pace.

September 1–7, 2008 (80 miles/week)

MONDAY	TUESDAY	WEDNESDAY	THURSDAY	FRIDAY	SATURDAY	SUNDAY
OFF Massage	**Road Run** 15 mi at easy pace.	**Road Run** 15 mi at easy pace.	**Road Run** 15 mi at easy pace.	**OFF**	**Road Run** 15 mi at easy pace.	**Road Run** 20 mi at easy pace.

September 8–14, 2008 (160+ miles/week)

MONDAY	TUESDAY	WEDNESDAY	THURSDAY	FRIDAY	SATURDAY	SUNDAY
Road Run 10 mi	**Road Run** 8 mi	**Road Run** 5 mi	**OFF** Travel to SFO.	**OFF**	**Run across the United States** Days one and two: 139.8 mi.	

Appendix B

Course Statistics

DAY	DATE	RUNNING TIME	WEATHER	CREW	END	ELEV. GAIN/LOSS	AVG. ELEV.	MILEAGE
1	Sept 13	5:12 a.m.–8:20 p.m.	Partly cloudy Low 55 High 82 Wind 6–28	Heather, Paul, Kathleen, Jesse, Roger	CA	1680/1834	173	69.7 mi
2	Sept 14	4:20 a.m.–9:46 p.m.	Sunny Low 52 High 90 Wind 5–26	Heather, Paul, Kathleen, Jesse, Roger	CA	843/472	181	70.1 mi
3	Sept 15	4 a.m.–10:59 p.m.	Sunny Low 51 High 84 Wind 2–10	Heather, Paul, Kathleen, Jesse, Roger	CA	9360/1453	4,434	70.0 mi
4	Sept 16	5:06 a.m.–11:15 p.m.	Sunny, cloudy in p.m. Low 53 High 90s Wind 1–20	Heather, Paul, Kathleen, Roger	NV	801/5020	6,444	70.0 mi
5	Sept 17	4:26 a.m.–11:45 p.m.	Sunny, Low 55 High 90s Wind 6–9	Heather, Paul, Kathleen, Jesse, Roger	NV	1273/1411	4,275	70.0 mi
6	Sept 18–19	4:59 a.m.–3:25 a.m.	Sunny, Low 55 High 90s Wind 6–9	Heather, Kathleen, Dave, Roger	NV	3192/1637	5,422	70.0 mi

#	Date	Time	Weather	People	State		Steps	Miles
7	Sept 19–20	7:07 a.m.–3:45 a.m.	Sunny, 90s Low 59 High 80s Wind 12–28	Heather, Paul, Kathleen, Roger, Dave	NV	2923/2582	6,606	60.0 mi
8	Sept 20–21	8:46 a.m.–5:28 a.m.	Sunny Low 46 High 80s Wind 6–21	Heather, Paul, Kathleen, Roger	NV	3156/2844	6,697	62.0 mi
9	Sept 21–22	10:26 a.m.–3:07 a.m.	Sunny Low 41 High 75 Wind 10	Heather, Paul, Kathleen, Roger	NV	1693/1286	7,090	42.8 mi
10	Sept 22–23	8:47 a.m.–2:19 a.m.	Sunny Low 37 High 67 Wind 7–15	Heather, Paul, Kathleen, Roger	UT	2674/4262	6,385	60.0 mi
11	Sept 23–24	8:55 a.m.–1:43 a.m.	Sunny Low 46 High 80 Wind 2–6	Heather, Paul, Kathleen, Brian, Roger	UT	2159/2434	5,379	50.4 mi
12	Sept 24	7:05 a.m.–11:14 a.m. (Injury/rest: Plantar Fasciitis)	Sunny Low 57 High 74 Wind 3–6	Heather, George, Paul, Roger	UT	26/200	4,588	12.8 mi

DAY	DATE	RUNNING TIME	WEATHER	CREW	END	ELEV. GAIN/LOSS	AVG. ELEV.	MILEAGE
13	Sept 25–26	7:06 a.m.–12:49 a.m.	Sunny, breezy Low 40 High 86 Wind 7–10	Heather, George, Kathleen, Colleen, Paul, Roger	UT	466/305	4,673	51.0 mi
14	Sept 26–27	6:56 a.m.–2:00 a.m.	Sunny, breezy Low 53 High 84 Wind 4–10	George, Kathleen, Colleen, Becky, Paul, Roger, Heather	UT	1716/1777	5,119	66.0 mi
15	Sept 27–28	7:06 a.m.–1:58 a.m.	Sunny Low 46 High 80 Wind 1–12	George, Kathleen, Colleen, Becky, Theresa, Paul, Roger, Heather	UT	5033/2365	7,003	64.2 mi
16	Sept 28–29	7:33 a.m.–1:05 a.m.	Sunny Low 53 High 81 Wind 8–10	George, Kathleen, Paul, Becky, Theresa, Roger, Heather	UT	1467/2033	5,471	62.0 mi
17	Sept 29–30	7:05 a.m.–1:20 a.m.	Sunny, dry and warm Low 46 High 81 Wind 4–7	Heather, Kathleen, Amira, Paul, Roger	CO	1864/1489	5384	60.2 mi
18	Sept 30– Oct 1	7:03 a.m.–1:05 a.m.	Sunny, warm Low 40 High 81 Wind 0–9	Heather, Amira, Kathleen, Todd, Roger	CO	2480/2081	6,265	61.4 mi

19	Oct 1–2	6:58 a.m.–2:08 a.m.	Sunny Low 28 High 75 Wind 10–22	Heather, Kathleen, Todd, Paul, Chuck, Roger	CO	4498/2350	8,332	66.7 mi
20	Oct 2–3	7:32 a.m.–1:26 a.m.	Sunny, light rain p.m. Low 30s High 60 Wind 9–20	Heather, Kathleen, Brian, Paul, Roger	CO	2966/2148	9,171	60.2 mi
21	Oct 3–4	7:25 a.m.–12:15 a.m.	Sunny, cloudy p.m. Low 30s High 60s Wind 4–26	Heather, Kathleen, Brian, Elaine, Amira, Paul, Roger	CO	43/4273	7,014	64.8 mi
22	Oct 4–5	6:53 a.m.–1:00 a.m.	Partly cloudy Low 41 High 73 Wind 1–14	Heather, Kathleen, Ali, Elaine, Taylor, Brian, Paul, Roger	CO	1014/1255	4,932	67.9 mi
23	Oct 5	7:03 am–2:22 p.m. (Injury/go to ER)	Partly cloudy Low 43 High 67 Wind 11–22	Heather, Elaine, Ali, Taylor, Paul, Roger	CO	105/675	4,572	18.0 mi
24	Oct 6–7	2:34 p.m.–1:22 a.m. (Injury/MRI: Tear in foot tendon, tendonitis, muscle strain)	Mostly cloudy Low 44 High 66 Wind 13–32	Heather, Brian, Paul, Roger	CO	636/606	4,211	32.0 mi

DAY	DATE	RUNNING TIME	WEATHER	CREW	END	ELEV. GAIN/LOSS	AVG. ELEV.	MILEAGE
25	Oct 7	7:17 a.m.–11:02 p.m.	Partly cloudy Low 44 High 70 Wind 7–17	Heather, Dave, Brian, Kira, Paul, Roger	NE	49/858	3,861	49.9 mi
26	Oct 8–9	7:12 a.m.–1:05 a.m.	Clear Low 44 High 73 Wind 6–22	Heather, Paul, Kira, Brian, Roger	NE	210/1082	3,030	60.4 mi
27	Oct 9–10	7:55 a.m.–2:37 a.m.	Partly cloudy Low 42 High 52 Wind 10–26	Heather, Kira, Paul, Dave, Roger, Brian	NE	531/926	2,433	60.4 mi Mile 38.5 this day was HALFWAY
28	Oct 10–11	8:07 a.m.–12:39 a.m.	Partly sunny, breezy Low 48 High 68 Wind 12–33	Heather, Kira, Dave, Brian, Paul, Roger	NE	584/752	2,242	60.5 mi
29	Oct 11–12	7:45 a.m.–1:22 a.m.	Mostly cloudy, light rain Low 45 High 65 Wind 12–21	Heather, Kira, Dave, Brian, Paul, Roger	NE	285/719	1,881	60.7 mi
30	Oct 12–13	7:57 a.m.–1:39 a.m.	Mostly cloudy, light rain, Windy! Low 66 High 79 Wind 20–43	Heather, Dave, Kira, Rick, Brian, Paul, Roger	NE	407/858	1,458	55.0 mi

#	Date	Time	Weather	Participants	State			Miles
31	Oct 13–14	8:12 a.m.–1:11 a.m.	Chilly rain, windy Low 43 High 58 Wind 14–26	Heather, Dave, Kira, Brian, Paul, Roger	IA	1214/1415	1,163	60.0 mi
32	Oct 14–15	8:11 a.m.–12:19 a.m.	Mostly cloudy, rain Low 39 High 53 Wind 0–8	Chuck, Dave, Kira, Brian, Paul, Heather, Roger	IA	1516/1457	1,094	62.0 mi
33	Oct 15–16	8:13 a.m.–12:33 a.m.	Partly sunny, light rain Low 38 High 57 Wind 10–28	Kira, Dave, Paul, Chuck, Brian, Heather	IA	1414/1587	1,099	61.0 mi
34	Oct 16	8:07 a.m.–11:59 p.m.	Clear and calm Low 42 High 43 Wind 0–7	Heather, Dave, Chuck, Brian, Paul	IA	807/1088	966	62.0 mi
35	Oct 17–18	8:08 a.m.–2:00 a.m.	Mostly cloudy, light rain, calm Low 41 High 53 Wind 0–6	Heather, Dave, Jenny, Kira, Paul	IA	778/1118	695	60.0 mi
36	Oct 18–19	8:09 a.m.–1:45 a.m.	Foggy, cloudy, clearing in p.m. Low 45 High 64 Wind 0–8	Heather, Dave, Brian, Jenny, Kira, Paul	IL	581/609	646	60.5 mi

DAY	DATE	RUNNING TIME	WEATHER	CREW	END	ELEV. GAIN/LOSS	AVG. ELEV.	MILEAGE
37	Oct 19–20	8:19 a.m.–12:21 a.m.	Partly cloudy Low 43 High 64 Wind 10–28	Heather, Brian, Jenny, Dave, Paul	IL	787/678	605	60.0 mi
38	Oct 20–21	8:23 a.m.–12:31 a.m.	Mostly cloudy, rain, windy Low 42 High 62 Wind 15–22	Heather, Kira, Paul, Brian, Dave, Chuck, Paul	IL	354/468	717	60.0 mi
39	Oct 21–22	8:25 a.m.–12:54 a.m.	Partly cloudy, windy Low 36 High 58 Wind 6–18	Kira, Jenny, Dave, Brian, Paul	IN	285/309	692	60.0 mi
40	Oct 22	8:55 a.m.–2:00 p.m.	Clear, windy Low 34 High 57 Wind 12–30	Chuck, Jenny, Dave, Paul	IN	285/237	693	15.4 mi
41	Oct 23–24	8:30 a.m.–12:47 a.m.	Clear, windy, cloudy in late p.m. Low 33 High 63 Wind 10–25	Dave, Jenny, Heather, Brian, Kira, Amira, Paul	IN	725/609	725	62.0 mi
42	Oct 24–25	8:18 a.m.–12:41 a.m.	Rain! Low 46 High 56 Wind 13–18	Heather, Amira, Paul, Kira, Brian, Dave Thorpe	OH	361/366	818	60.0 mi

#	Date	Time	Weather	People	State			
43	Oct 25–26	7:45 a.m.–1:00 a.m.	Mostly cloudy, windy, rain Low 41 High 52 Wind 10–25	Heather, Paul, Dave T., Brian, Kira	OH	440/412	877	60.0 mi
44	Oct 26–27	9:20 a.m.–1:30 a.m.	Mostly cloudy, windy, light rain Low 39 High 59 Wind 15–37	Heather, Kira, Alex, Brian, Bob, Paul	OH	1087/865	1,105	60.0 mi
45	Oct 27–28	8:40 a.m.–1:24 a.m.	Rain/snow, windy Low 32 High 43 Wind 11–29	Heather, Alex, Bob, Brian, Cole, Paul	OH	1601/1629	1,094	60.0 mi
46	Oct 28–29	8:15 a.m.–1:30 a.m.	Rain/snow, windy Low 37 High 42 Wind 14–37	Heather, Paul, Bob, Alex, Brian	PA	2572/2773	1,133	60.0 mi
47	Oct 29–30	8:15 a.m.–1:45 a.m.	Snow, cloudy Low 33 High 37 Wind 13–16	Heather, Bob, Kate, Paul, Brian	PA	2362/2286	1,120	60.0 mi
48	Oct 30–31	8:10 a.m.–1:00 a.m.	Partly cloudy Low 28 High 48 Wind 6–14	Heather, Michael M, Paul, Brian	PA	3077/2749	1,609	62.0 mi

DAY	DATE	RUNNING TIME	WEATHER	CREW	END	ELEV. GAIN/LOSS	AVG. ELEV.	MILEAGE
49	Oct 31–Nov 1	8:10 a.m.–12:47 a.m.	Clear, sunny Low 32 High 64 Wind 3–20	Heather, Tom, Paul, Amira	PA	2169/2626	1,570	61.0 mi
50	Nov 1–2	8:00 a.m.–1:00 a.m.	Mostly cloudy Low 34 High 64 Wind 0–7	Heather, Brian, Tom, Elaine, Paul, Kate	PA	1234/1901	991	62.0 mi
51	Nov 2–3	7:30 a.m.–12:51 a.m.	Overcast to clear Low 30 High 52 Wind 6–15	Heather, Brian, Elaine, Paul	PA	3458/3503	1,076	61.0 mi
52	Nov 3–4	7:15 a.m.–1:49 a.m.	Overcast Low 36 High 52 Wind 0–6	Heather, Brian, Elaine, Taylor, Tom, Mark, Paul	NJ	2208/2318	700	62.0 mi
53	Nov 4	7:46 a.m.–7:10 p.m.	Overcast to clear Low 49 High 63 Wind 1–12	Heather, Brian, Taylor, Elaine, Therese, Tom, Mark, Kathy	NY	971/1395	262	43.2 mi
Cumulative Mileage								3,063.2
Cumulative Elevation Gain								+84,430
Cumulative Elevation Loss								−84,385
Overall Average Elevation								3,135

Appendix C

Nutrition and Diet

Although my philosophy regarding sports nutrition is simply to eat real food to provide essential vitamins and minerals, I do supplement with a few pills and powders—nothing too out-of-the-ordinary, though. During my run across the United States, I took a daily multivitamin for general health, glucosamine and chondroitin to protect the joints, omega fatty acids for heart health, Endurox Excel Natural Workout Supplement to help the body burn fat more efficiently and reduce the need for carbohydrate consumption, probiotics to aid digestion, liquid vitamin B complex to fortify the immune system and provide energy, L-glutamine to aid in muscle repair, and Sustain tablets for electrolyte replacement.

Beyond that: just food. Real food, not special food for athletes, no gels, bars, fancy recovery mixes, or things like that. We figure that I ate as much as four men would normally eat, and I consumed only one "engineered" or sports-specific food supplement during the run—everything else was the normal fare anyone can buy in a grocery store. In ultrarunning, as in many sports, people are often looking for the silver bullet, the one thing you can consume to make it all easier. I'm here to tell you that nothing like that will make running hundreds of miles "easier." Or, for that matter, ten miles. Sure, you need to eat sufficient protein, carbohydrates, and other nutrients. But I like what Michael Pollan has to say: This is the first time in history that people are trying to figure out what to eat based on individual nutrients rather than just choosing *food*. That's a mistake in my book (and, to give credit where credit's due, he points out the mistake in his book, as well). Similarly, some tout a vegetarian diet, but I'm not buying that, either. I've read that our evolution— particularly, our ability to run and think fast—seems to be linked to obtaining protein (meat), and our body mass and brain size seem to be linked to eating meat and fat. Given our smaller, omnivore teeth and simple (not ruminant) gut, we're suited to digesting meat effectively. Theoretically, we do better as a species when we include decent-quality animal protein in our diets.

On an individual basis, that seems to be true, too. During one conversation I had with Ted Corbitt, he told me that he'd gone vegetarian for a few years in his forties, but then he'd developed anemia. On doctor's orders, he became a moderate meat eater from then on. Problem solved. Certainly, it's possible to eat a vegetarian diet without winding up with some kind of deficiency, but then you're back to shopping for nutrients instead of food.

Keep it simple.

At an ultrarunning training camp, I met a superb African runner, Jackton Odhiambo, a 2:12 marathoner who was tall, lean, and muscular.

I was giving a nutrition presentation and emphasizing a 60 percent carb, 20 percent fat, 20 percent protein ratio, when I turned to Jackton and asked what he did to make sure he got plenty of protein back home in Kenya.

His answer was unexpected: "We drink cow's blood."

That's a little over the top, even for me, but a balanced diet of whole foods—not manufactured "foodstuffs"—delivers what you need. When we're young and burning up the calories, we can get away with a lot, but age and wisdom guide us back to the basics. As humans, we're lucky to be able to survive on just about anything we put into our bodies (I call this my "incinerator theory"), but in the long run, we need to pay attention to what has been proven by the past: a balanced diet of real food.

During the run, I ate four meals a day and a ton of "mini-courses," or snacks, in between, and drank constantly, consuming somewhere between eight thousand and ten thousand calories in about sixty or more servings a day. I'm the first one to admit it wasn't exactly health food, either. A lot of it was, for convenience's sake, processed and packaged, cooked in a microwave or heated up on the RV's stove top. Yet the crew did such an amazing job of keeping me fueled up and hydrated that I lost only four pounds in the 52½ days I was traveling across the country on foot. That's pretty remarkable for a guy my size; I'm five feet, nine inches tall, and four pounds on my frame is nothing.

Breakfast

Initially, my first meal of the day would come at varying times, 5:30 a.m. if I was getting on the road early, or as late as 9:00 a.m. if I'd run all night and gotten only a few hours of sleep. After we established a regular routine somewhere in Nebraska, breakfast was served around 7:30 a.m. so I could be on the road by about 8:00.

Typically, breakfast included two fried eggs, sunny-side up; a few strips of bacon; and a couple of slices of toasted banana bread with butter. I'd eat while getting dressed, sitting down every now and then on the edge of the bed for a couple of bites at a time—a small luxury I didn't take for the rest of the day. Every other meal was eaten on the go.

Before walking out the door of the RV, I'd grab a thermos of oatmeal with sugar and butter, as well as more toasted banana bread, and eat that over the next couple of hours, or about eight miles.

Lunch

Usually, my lunch was served after the first marathon, no later than about 2:00 p.m. each day, and it would include the sort of thing we eat at home: a grilled ham and cheese sandwich, or spaghetti with sausage and sauce, tacos, pizza, or something like that—always packaged or prepared so that it was easily portable.

Dinner

After I reached forty miles, dinner would appear. Again, this meal would mimic something we'd have at home but was made to eat in hand rather than on a plate: fried chicken, pork chops, steak or a burger, or fish. I was especially fond of the fried clams and lobster bites from Long John Silver's, and I found that I didn't crave red meat at all, except in tacos or as an addition to spaghetti sauce. Whenever production brought us dinner, it usually came from the deli counter of a local grocery store or takeout restaurant: a pan of lasagna, Chinese food, various salads, bread, fresh fruit, vegetables, and so on.

Food from sit-down restaurants was, of course, more tasty: the kraut burger Elaine got for me in Colorado, pork burritos from El Jalisciense in Utah, and delicious chicken burritos Chris Frost brought me in Illinois, a full dinner, including a baked potato (!), in Indiana, and another home-style meal from a family restaurant in Pennsylvania. These were second only to some homemade dishes that friends or family members brought. Pot roast, chicken noodle soup, even baked desserts . . . heaven!

Happy Hour

We started a routine of eating hot food at the fifty-mile mark when the nights got cold, just before we reached Craig, Colorado, and then we kept it up all the way to New York. Somewhere in the Midwest, Brian started calling it "happy hour," and the name stuck. This "meal" always included some popcorn and a couple of O'Doul's nonalcoholic beers. I'm not normally much of a beer drinker, but during extreme events, I like this nonsweet drink as a change of flavor. I'd also have some kind of hot food, such as macaroni and cheese, soup or stew, or a microwaved frozen dinner.

Snacks

Between meals, I ate constantly. Yogurt. Fruit. Pudding. Cheese and crackers. Salads. Nuts. Trail mix. Cheez-Its. Granola. Cereal with milk. Ice cream. Milk shakes. Hot fudge sundaes. Homemade goodies that friends and family brought for us: banana or pumpkin bread, cookies, pastries, coffee cake, scones, cobbler. All delicious! And I really enjoyed the fancy rolled wafer cookies; they were so delicate, elegant, and fussy— so completely opposite of how I was feeling. Having them made me feel somehow special, like a patron in a restaurant where the chef comes out to say hello, or a child whose mother knows his favorite dish and serves it on a dreary afternoon.

Sometimes, Heather would bring me Andes chocolate mints as a signal that I could stop and soon put my head on the pillow. No check to pay, just my reward for finishing the day's mileage before turning in for the night.

Drinks

It's been said that caffeine isn't good for athletes, because it serves as a diuretic and can dehydrate you. It's also been said that it's beneficial to performance, so the jury is still out on this one, at least among the scientists. However, I've found that during my extreme events, caffeine's essential. As we made our way across the United States, I had coffee in the morning, and Red Bull in the evening. During the day, I often drank Starbucks DoubleShots and Frappuccinos in my Muscle Milk, a high-protein sports powder mixed with whole milk that I drank all day long (with or without a caffeinated boost). During the 52½ days on the road, I went through twelve 2.98-pound containers of Muscle Milk, a total of 228 ten- to twelve-ounce servings, or more than four servings per day. In addition, I drank Ensure, another high-protein "liquid meal."

Not one ounce of plain water crossed my lips, as every sip needed to deliver some of my calories for the day. I did enjoy orange juice every morning; throughout the day, I had various fruit juices, soft drinks, yogurt drinks, Kool-Aid "slushies" that the crew whizzed up (loved 'em!), and energy drinks like Fuze and SoBe; and I drank at least two O'Doul's at "happy hour" each night. And the pièce de résistance, the treat that always made my day: a root beer float.

Appendix D

Injuries, Ailments, and Treatments

In Roosevelt, Utah, Dr. Paul told me that he'd seen more ailments during our run so far than in the entire lineup of athletes at the Western States 100 and Badwater 135 combined.

"Are they worth shooting?" Joking, I was asking if our legs and feet were bad enough to warrant us being put down, like disabled farm animals.

He laughed. "Well, I told Charlie that he's lucky I'm not in veterinary medicine."

We were both lucky not to be racehorses, that's for sure. But I should speak only for myself: I stumbled, I hobbled, I broke down. Still, I maintained my form as best as I could, even walking into the hospital the one time we sought medical attention, strutting like there was nothing at all wrong with me. It was a point of pride: *Okay, I may be injured, but you're not going to tell me to stop running unless you can* prove *to me that I can't continue. I sure as hell won't give you your evidence.*

God, I'm hardheaded. Case in point: herewith a general log of the injuries and ailments, along with their treatments, while I was running across the United States.

Disclaimer: I'm not a doctor, so this is a layman's list, not medical advice. If you ever deal with any of these problems, consult your own physician to get proper, prompt treatment.

Joint Pain (Onset: Day 1)

While everything ached pretty much from the start, late during our first week, significant pain began in my right knee. Dr. Paul treated it with manipulation, and I wore elastic pullover knee braces to help stabilize the joint as I ran. I also wore a more substantial brace from VQ Ortho-Care for one day. About halfway across the country, I was able to ditch the braces and use them only occasionally if the knee flared up.

My hips became an issue during the second week. Tired and overworked back muscles and my tendency to over-pronate were likely contributors, as well as the length of my stride, quite long given my height. There wasn't much to do for this pain, and it stayed with me throughout the run. Unlike some of the other ailments, though, this one would come and go.

Heat Exhaustion (Onset: Day 2)

With temperatures reaching into the nineties during the first few weeks, I did my best to minimize the impact of the heat, but it was inevitable:

the heavy sweating, the paleness, the muscle cramps, the fatigue and weakness, the dizziness and headaches. My crew kept me hydrated, I replaced electrolytes using Sustain, and I sought shade wherever I could find it. The high temps ceased to be a problem on day twenty, when we reached cooler weather.

Muscle Cramps and Strain (Onset: Day 2)

Periodically, I experienced muscle cramps, involuntary and forcible muscle contraction, including severe cramps like a charley horse, when the muscle locked in spasm. At various times, my hands, the arches of my feet, my calves, and especially toward the end of the run, my back would cramp up. This is a common problem most runners face at some point or another, usually near the end of intense exercise, or a few hours later, and in the heat because sweat drains the body of fluids, salt, and minerals. These cramps were annoying, and the more serious spasms occasionally stopped me in my tracks, but this was probably one of the more minor issues during the transcon.

Perhaps every muscle and tendon in my legs and feet was strained at one time or another, or maybe even throughout the run, from overuse. One main area of strain was in my hamstrings, which tightened up every day. Strains are more likely to happen when one muscle group is stronger than its opposing muscle group, as with hamstrings and quadriceps. The quads on the front of the thigh are usually more powerful, so during endurance events, the hamstring can become fatigued faster than the quads, leading to strain. The problem with hamstring strain—aside from the immediate issue of pain in the back of the legs—is that it can compound into lower-back issues, which it did for me later in the run (see page 276).

During the first ten days of the run, I wore Zensah compression sleeves on my calves to increase circulation and oxygen blood flow. To deal with muscle strain and reduce inflammation throughout the run, we used ice therapy on various parts of my body, including my feet, ankles, calves, knees, and thighs. Whenever possible, we elevated my legs—in fact, every night except one, when she wasn't there, Heather put pillows under my legs and ice on the sore spots to treat injuries. Stretching and massage were both an effort to keep me as limber as possible to prevent minor strains from becoming major injuries.

Tendonitis (Onset: Day 2)

Various tendons in my feet, ankles, and legs were overworked from the start, and my Achilles became inflamed nearly immediately. Connecting the calf muscles to the heel bone, it's the largest tendon in the human body, and can withstand forces of one thousand pounds or more. Still, it's a vulnerable spot, a common area for an overuse injury among all types of athletes. It's likely that my Achilles tendonitis came from my tight and tired calves, bringing some severe pain, both while running and at rest, as well as terrible stiffness after sleep.

Another serious tendon issue was posterior tibial tendon dysfunction during the first eleven days of the run, when this tendon—which starts in the calf, stretches down behind the inside of the ankle, and attaches to bones in the middle of the foot—became inflamed and tight, causing pain and swelling in the inner ankle down into the arch in my foot. This gradually developed into pain on the outer side of my ankle and foot, and tenderness over the midfoot. It's hard to say if this ever resolved; it certainly contributed to, or maybe just graduated into, the plantar fasciitis described on page 274.

Late in the run, after I'd reached two thousand miles and crossed the Mississippi, I also experienced severe shin splints, a pain in the lower part of my legs, that was most likely medial tibial stress syndrome, an irritation to the tendons and the attachment of these tendons to the bone in the front of my lower legs. I worried that this would put me out of the running, just as it had Charlie. So we removed all pressure from the front of my shin, even pinning up the leg of my running pants, and I shortened my stride and iced it regularly. Luckily, I was able to stave off a more serious injury but continued to have lower leg pain on and off for the remainder of the run.

To deal with all these tendon issues, I fooled around with various orthotics and was very selective about shoes. I cut a notch in the back of my shoes and socks to keep them from rubbing against and irritating my Achilles. We iced various parts of my body, massaged my legs, and stretched. All of these efforts, and ibuprofen, helped some, but the Achilles continued to plague me until New Jersey, where Tom Triumph gave me a pair of soft, heel-cup inserts that helped immensely, not just with the Achilles pain, but also with other, more serious foot and lower back pain detailed on page 276.

Sleep Deprivation (Onset: Day 3)

Notable effects of lack of sleep—most pronounced during the earliest days of the run, when I was on the road up to twenty hours a day—included periods when I wasn't able to think straight or stay alert. It was most acute that night in Nevada, on day eight, when I was babbling incoherently and Heather pulled me off the road to get some sleep.

We used a prescription sleep aid to help me rest, because, aside from the fact that we allotted only a few hours for time in bed, it was difficult to actually sleep, as a result of my aches and pains. (The nightmares didn't help, either.) The Ambien was a mixed bag: It did help me rest, but because I often got up before the recommended length of sleep, I was groggy and disoriented.

The best treatment for this problem was more sleep, and it helped some when we instituted a naptime, just after I finished my first marathon of the day, which we started doing regularly in eastern Utah. After we decreased the daily mileage goal from seventy to sixty miles per day, I also got a little extra sleep. However, this issue persisted across the country, contributing to my emotional fragility. Rarely did I sleep more than five hours a night.

Blisters and Bloody Nose (Onset: Day 5)

The tiny annoyance of both of these is almost not worth mentioning, as I sustained so few blisters (prevented with Sportslick and ENGO patches, and easily treated by draining them), and only one bloody nose. The nosebleed happened when we were east of Fallon, Nevada, and it was probably brought on by the intense, dry heat of the day. It took a while to get under control, but it did stop. I had no more trouble with this during the rest of the way across America.

Canker Sores (Onset: Day 7)

Caused by constantly eating and drinking, my mouth became raw, and I developed open sores. At Dr. Paul's direction, we cut out salsa and citrus snacks for a while, and I rinsed my mouth several times a day for the next several days with a mixture of Mylanta and a squirt of Orajel. That did the trick, and I used the rinse occasionally throughout the rest of the run, as needed.

Plantar Fasciitis (Onset: Day 12)

Diagnosed by Dr. Paul in Delta, Utah, this injury to my right foot occurred after I'd run just over seven hundred miles . . . and still had more than 2,300 to go. A relatively common and painful runner's ailment, this affects the sole or flexor surface (plantar) of the foot when the fibrous band of tissue (fascia) that connects your heel bone to the base of your toes becomes inflamed. One of the primary causes is tight calf muscles, no doubt a contributing factor in my case. Usually, rest is the first treatment for this condition, but that wasn't happening. I did take some time off on day twelve; after running just 12.8 miles, I went to a hotel and stayed in bed for the rest of the day. Dr. Paul also administered Kenalog, an anti-inflammatory drug, by injection to my gluteus maximus. I wore a night splint for a couple of nights after that, then replaced it with the Strassburg Sock. We managed the pain with ibuprofen and frequent icing during the day, and Heather iced my foot (and other aching body parts) for me at night while I slept.

An injury that can take months to heal, and even stops some people from running altogether, the plantar fasciitis persisted the rest of the way across America. We learned later, when I had an MRI in Sterling, Colorado, to diagnose a different injury, that it was likely that I didn't just irritate the fascia but actually ruptured it. The injury caused persistent pain and swelling in my foot, made my toes go numb, and created a hard, golf ball–sized knot of scar tissue in the arch of my foot that remains unresolved.

Longitudinal Tear in Tendon Tissue (Diagnosis: Day 23)

After an MRI in Sterling, Colorado, the doctor advised me that I had inflamed tendons in my right foot, and that I'd torn the tissue along the length of a tendon on the outside of my foot—not a torn tendon, per se, but a tear "in" the tendon. (He also told us about some other mild strains to the muscles in my foot.) It wouldn't heal without rest, he said, and he was right. It did not improve as I ran, but I did get better at ignoring the pain. We upped my dosage of ibuprofen, and I disowned my foot.

Infection (Onset: Day 43)

The big toe of my left foot became infected when one of the few blisters I got didn't heal properly. Dr. Paul diagnosed the problem when I showed him the red, swollen, and warm toe, and prescribed a course of antibiotics. The infection cleared up.

Diarrhea (Onset: Day 44)

Although the antibiotic was effective in ridding me of the infection in my toe, it also caused an annoying side effect: diarrhea. Not too severe, but inconvenient: I had to stop frequently to relieve myself, and the diarrhea also caused some chafing, which I treated with Sportslick. The problem lasted about six days and then was resolved when I was off the antibiotic.

Dislocated Fibula (Day 45)

In Wooster, Ohio, I stepped off a curb and . . . snap! There was immediate, severe pain in my knee and calf. After Dr. Paul examined my leg, probing it to find the precise problem, he grabbed, pulled, and pushed and then—presto, change-o—I felt better! Heather iced the knee for me while I slept, and when I woke up, I was able to run without problems. Dr. Paul confided in Heather and Robert Spieler, but didn't tell me, that I had slightly dislocated my fibula, which he popped back into place.

Severe Back Pain (Onset: Day 38)

Throughout the run, I often experienced low back/lumbar pain, which Dr. Paul attributed to tight hamstrings. It didn't gain much of my attention, however, as other physical issues were more pressing and painful, and I seemed to be able to overcome some of this discomfort by just waiting it out. However, by day thirty-eight, my back began to spasm and couldn't be ignored any longer. Dr. Paul attended to it with stretching and manipulation.

The morning of our last day, waking up in New Jersey, my back was a complete mess—I thought I'd have to crawl into Times Square—but a chiropractor gave me an adjustment that completely eradicated the pain, and I was able to run to the finish.

Post-Run Recovery

After I stopped running, it took several months for my body to stop aching—it was always hurting somewhere, all the time. But I have recovered from nearly all my injuries. Every now and then, some of my joints ache, but whose don't? The plantar fasciitis and tendonitis have had the longest-lasting effects: There's still scar tissue in my arch, and I have

yet to regain feeling in either of my big toes. But that doesn't necessar-
ily mean I've sustained permanent damage, just that I need to give it
time. I've been hurt before and, even though it's taken years in some
cases, regained full sensation. The body has a miraculous ability to heal
itself.

Appendix E

Supplies, Clothing, and Gear

Most of my clothing and equipment was kept in the crew van and RV, as described here.

Shoes and Clothing

The crew kept a variety of shoes in the van for me, as I often switched them out during the day, depending on how my feet were feeling, the terrain (uphill or downhill), and how much cushioning or pronation control I felt like I needed. Usually, though, the shoe changes were about making sure that whatever was on my feet wasn't broken down, that the structural integrity of the shoe was intact. My favorites were from Pearl Izumi. I also wore, and wore out, at least fifteen pairs of Nikes supplied by Champs.

In the back of the van, the crew kept my "closet," a tall collapsible laundry basket that contained almost all of the clothing I would wear during the run. Heather kept a few items in the RV, like street clothes I would finally wear again after I finished, but most everything was in my closet. To make it easier for the crew to find what I needed, my clothes were put into large ziplock bags, labeled with black marker and separated into the following categories:

- Shorts, both loose-fitting running shorts and compression shorts
- T-shirts (cotton and technical)
- Long-sleeved technical shirts of various weights
- A light fleece shirt (one of Heather's that I found to be the right weight, although the periwinkle color wasn't very masculine)
- Fleece vest (one Kate bought in Iowa somewhere)
- Tights and running pants of various weights
- Raincoat (Heather's purple GoLite Gortex one, until Dave Thorpe bought me my own in Indiana)
- Warm fleece coat
- Hats (a lightweight skullcap was my favorite), gloves, and a Buff
- Socks of various types and weights, including Injinji tetra socks, Zensah compression leggings, and what came to be one of my favorites, Balega
- Non-cotton underwear from ExOfficio and GoLite
- Custom orthotics, as well as over-the-counter orthotic insoles by Sorbothane

This closet went with us at night, into the RV or hotel, to ensure that I would have access to all of my options in the morning.

Everyday Gear

Every morning, I strapped on my GoLite Slant pack, with one holder (I cut the other one off) for a GoLite water bottle to carry my Muscle Milk. In the pack, I kept my rescue inhaler in case of an asthma attack, a lightweight GoLite wind jacket, a pocket-pack of tissue for toilet paper, and hand sanitizer. My orange SPOT tracker hooked onto my Slant Pack belt, along with (most often) one of two Sirius satellite radios, which I usually kept tuned to The Spectrum.

The Murse

We had a medium-sized plastic container, with a lid, that the crew called my "murse," short for "man purse." Truth is, I didn't like that name much, but a crew person had come up with this the previous year at Badwater (the same year Dr. Paul started using the term "gimp"), and it just stuck. After all, it contained all of my daily necessities, frequently used items like those you'll find in most women's purses. Items in the murse included:

- Sportslick for friction protection/blister prevention (so, so very important!)
- "Lipshit": Neosporin and Carmex
- Ibuprofen
- Sustain electrolyte replacement tablets that I would take every hour when it was hot, or every two to four hours when cooler
- ENGO patches for blister prevention
- Small scissors and a kit for blister treatment (to cut them open to allow drainage)

- Large scissors for "shoe surgery," which I performed often
- Sunscreen
- My headlamp
- Extra batteries

The murse would also follow me for naps and at nighttime, as it seemed that I would always need something from it.

Crew Van Supplies

In the front of the van, the "wheelman" would keep the logbook, recording the following information:

- Exact start time and location.
- Crew at the beginning of the day, each crew change, and crew at the end of the day.
- Details of all rest breaks or stoppages, including time of each stop or break, what it was for (changing clothes, treatment by Dr. Paul or massage, blister treatment, icing, shoe surgery, changing orthotics, a nap ... whatever), and length/time back on the road.
- Time I received each or any of the following: electrolytes, ibuprofen, lip treatment, sunscreen, or mouth rinse.
- General location.
- Overall description of the day, including things like cities traveled through, significant events, how I was feeling, weather, crew thoughts and comments.
- Exact stop time and location.
- Total distance run that day.

The wheelman would get and follow the daily directions, provided by Kate and Amira. In the west, like on Highway 50 through Nevada and

Utah, the directions were simple: Head down the highway. But, in the east, especially through big cities and on the winding roads of Pennsylvania, following each and every turn, twist, landmark, or street sign became more of a challenge; thus the crew repurposed campaign signs, as well as balloons, to mark most turns.

The wheelman would also be responsible for keeping electronics charged: two Sirius satellite radios, which the crew would swap out for me, iPod, digital camera, video camera, and mobile phones so that the crew van could always be reached ... when there was cell service. I never carried my phone or BlackBerry; focusing on running, not checking calls or e-mail, was plenty for me to do. Heather took care of communications and "real life" stuff so I didn't ever have to think about it.

Behind the front seats, the crew kept a cooler of clean ice. They used a funnel to scoop ice from this cooler into my water bottle, which was filled with whatever Muscle Milk concoction I was having, or to put ice into my drink glass, always a red plastic Solo cup with a bendy straw. A second cooler held drinks: Ensure, DoubleShots, Frappuccinos, soda, juice, and food that needed to be refrigerated, like yogurt, deli salads, fried chicken, cheese, etc.

On the back bench seat, we kept a collapsible laundry basket of dry, non-refrigerated food items, like trail mix, crackers, and cookies. Within this basket was another basket with other supplies, including the cups and straws, paper towels, sanitary hand wipes, Kleenex packs (toilet paper), and ziplock bags, as well as medical-type supplies: the Mylanta and Orajel for my mouth rinse, the OTC elastic knee and ankle braces, and so on.

In the back of the van, a mesh laundry bag held night gear, including that stuff I hated to put on. We had headlamps for the crew, reflective vests, reflective leg and arm bands, and safety lights, including red flashers.

Also in the back of the van, under the closet, was some extra kitchen stuff (glasses, trash bags, paper towels), as well as a fanny pack that Dr. Paul used sometimes when he would run along with me while crewing. On the other side of the van, behind the backseat, were extra shoes, as well as a bag of sponsor-branded T-shirts.

Medical

I did take a few prescription medications during the run: a statin for high cholesterol, a hypothyroid medication, a twice-daily asthma prevention medication, and a prescription sleep aid. The only other prescription medications I took were the anti-inflammatory injection Dr. Paul gave me after diagnosing the plantar fasciitis in Delta, Utah, and a generic form of the antibiotic cephalexin for an infected toe in Ohio. I never took any kind of prescription, or narcotic, pain relievers.

We kept a variety of over-the-counter medical supplies on hand, including knee and ankle braces, the stuff we needed for my lipshit (Neosporin gel and Carmex), pain reliever (generic ibuprofen), and ingredients to make Dr. Paul's highly effective mouth-sore potion (Orajel and Mylanta). I also used the Strassburg Sock to stretch the plantar fascia at night.

One of our sponsors, VQ OrthoCare, provided us with proprietary products and on-the-road support, including two that proved invaluable:

- VQ CoolCare™, which we used almost every day, sometimes a few times a day, in the RV to "ice" my injuries. The system continuously pumped cold water into pads that could be wrapped around any part of my body, particularly my feet, ankles, shins, and knees.
- ArcticFlow™ Cold Therapy System was a portable device that we kept in the crew van, filled with ice water. It used gravity and a type of cast we wrapped around my foot, which made it a convenient way to ice my foot for ten to fifteen minutes while I caught a nap in the back of the van.

Robert Spieler from VQ OrthoCare also provided the following:

- Falcon Knee BRace (KBR) Hinged Wrap: In addition to elastic pullover knee braces, I also wore, for one day in Utah in particular, this more sophisticated knee brace to deal with severe pain.
- Night splint: After being diagnosed with plantar fasciitis, I wore this for a couple of nights and then replaced it with the Strassburg Sock.
- Electrotherapy: Occasionally, Robert would use some kind of electrotherapy on my leg and back.
- DeRoyal ankle brace: In addition to elastic pullover ankle braces, one day I wore a more sophisticated ankle brace made by DeRoyal.
- Blue-ice-type sleeves of various sizes to go over/around my ankles, legs, or knees.

RV Supplies

The RV was home base for Heather and the crew, so all of their clothing, some bedding, and personal stuff (which was limited: Everyone packed light!) was kept in the RV. GoLite provided sleeping bags and a couple of tents, and Pacific Outdoor Equipment provided sleeping pads, camping chairs, and inflatable pillows. Extra shoes from Champs were stored under our bed in the back of the RV. Food for my meals and meals for the crew, along with food and drink for the van, were constantly purchased and on hand in the RV, along with ice to fill the coolers in the crew van. The rented RV came with dishes and pots and pans, although we supplemented the supply with a few items, including the Vita-Mix, a toaster, and a coffeepot. Power cords and chargers to run cell phones and computers, as well as numerous road atlases and state road maps, were always floating around, especially when Roger was helping to track the route and preparing the daily planners.

Something that I always looked at in the RV was the NEW YORK HERE WE COME sign that Kathleen put up when we were in Nevada, above a map of the United States with "bubble" marks for each of the planned days of the run. As I went along, I crossed off each day, each chunk of seventy miles, a visual representation of how far I had to go, or how far I had come.

Appendix F

Charities, Sponsors, and Partners

Charities

The United Way "Live United" campaign was the designated charity for the transcon, in particular their programs to fight childhood obesity, a worthy cause. I continue to work with the organization to promote fitness.

I'd hoped to include the Religious Teachers Filippini in the fund-raising efforts associated with this run, but that didn't work out. However, I still support the sisters, and personal donations by friends and

family continue to help this cause. It's my charity of choice, and a por-
tion of the profits from this book will go to their project, AIDS Orphans
Rising. You can learn more about the charity's good work on my website,
MarshallUlrich.com, and at AIDSOrphansRising.org.

Ongoing Sponsorship

The following sponsors have supported my athletic career for several
years, largely by providing me with their excellent products to use during extreme endurance events. Those whose names appear in boldface
provided products for the transcontinental run; ENGO/Tamarack
Habilitation has continually provided financial sponsorship, including
money for the run across the United States.

> C.A.M.P. USA • Dermatone Laboratories, Inc. • **ENGO/
> Tamarack Habilitation Technologies** • ExOfficio • **GoLite**
> • **Injinji** • Larabar/Humm Foods • LaSportiva • **LEKI USA**
> • The North Face • **Pacific Outdoor Equipment** • **Pearl
> Izumi** • **Sportslick** • **Zensah**

Documentary Sponsorship

The companies below sponsored *Running America*, the documentary.
Those whose names appear in boldface continue to provide support for
me as an endurance athlete.

> Super 8 • AXA Equitable • **Vita-Mix** • **VQ OrthoCare** •
> **Crocs** • SpinVox

Transcontinental Run Sponsorship

The following were partners/product sponsors of Running America, the event:

CarbonFund.org • Celestial Seasonings • Champs • Gatorade • PowerBar • Sombra Professional Therapy Products • SPOT • Timex

List of Illustrations

After seventeen days of running and intermittent but intense feelings of isolation, I'm also eager to see family and friends who are planning to meet us.

Page 124. Fat foot, November 23, 2008: Three weeks after completing the run across the United States, my right foot is still significantly swollen from two major injuries, plantar fasciitis, and a tear in the tendon.

Page 142. Rumbling and rambling, October 9, 2008: Escorted by choppers through McCook, Nebraska, I'm enjoying the roar of the engines and the company of local easy riders, Mitch Farr (left) and Blaine Budke (right). *Photo courtesy* McCook Daily Gazette

Page 162. Amish Country, October 29, 2008: Trudging up endless hills in Pennsylvania with the snow falling in autumn, I'm in a mood that suits my surroundings: waning, withering. But I'm also feeling the pull of New York City. Now on day forty-seven, we're so close! *Photo courtesy Bob Becker*

Page 172. Can-do crew, September 30, 2008: Eighteen days into the run, early in the morning, and west of Maybell, Colorado, Kathleen Kane (on her supposed day off and wearing pajamas) works on my back. *Photo courtesy Kathleen Kane*

Page 180. Stray Dogs together again, October 4, 2008: My longtime friend and racing companion Mark "Mace" (left) and his son, Travis (right), come out to run with me near Fort Collins, Colorado, and head into the Pawnee grasslands of the eastern plains. Mace's company always means a lot of laughs, hours that pass like minutes, and sound counsel.

Page 199. Finish line, November 4, 2008: Heather, laughing and crying at the same time, embraces me on the portico of New York City Hall. *Photo © Sheri Whitko Photography*

Page 200. State of elation, October 21, 2008 : Running toward the Indiana sign on day thirty-nine, I'm excited to pass another important milestone and eager to resolve some troubles brewing behind the scenes.

Page 210. Small packages, October 13, 2008: Although I felt depressed and hopeless earlier on day thirty-one, when I lock eyes with the Beasley baby around midnight, just west of the Iowa border, it all falls away.

Page 220. Victory, November 4, 2008: Jumping for joy at the steps of New York City Hall, I'm finished running. *Photo © Sheri Whitko Photography*

Page 232. Over and done, November 4, 2008: After 117 marathons in 52½ days, it's time to take off my shoes. New York City Hall stands in the background as I wonder what's next. *Photo © Sheri Whitko Photography*

Page 247. What a drag! October 2007: In training for the transcon, I'm pulling a tire to increase strength, something I did off and on during the year of preparation, when I logged hundreds of miles each week. *Photo by Helen Richardson for* The Denver Post

Page 253. More road ahead, October 21, 2008: Fall in the Midwest, and I'm still running endless roads and hills in Illinois on day thirty-nine. *Photo courtesy Steve Shepard*

Page 263. Eat and run, October 2, 2008: Crossing the high plateau west of Maybell, Colorado, I'm sipping one of many "mini-meals" while on the move with Brian Weinberg. This is how I ate almost everything, at a quick walk, with no time to sit down.

Page 269. Heals on wheels, October 8, 2008: In Nebraska on day twenty-six, I insist the crew van be dubbed "Dr. Paul's Rolling Rehab Clinic," because everything, even medical care, has to be done on the go.

Page 279. Rest stop, October 25, 2008: Our RV and the crew van are parked in front of a grain elevator in Elgin, Ohio, where, as a farm boy myself, I felt right at home spending the night. (The vehicles would stop just about anywhere along the route, whenever necessary.) *Photo courtesy Dave Thorpe*

Page 287. Good habit, July 2008: As I run with Sister Mary Beth Lloyd of the Religious Teachers Filippini at the Badwater Ultramarathon, we talk about the work of the charity and the mission of the sisters: "Go and teach." (Sister Mary Beth did more than fifty miles that year and climbed Mount Whitney—all in her habit. I thought she deserved a finisher's medal for that, so I gave her mine.)

To view more behind-the-scenes photos of the 2008 run across the United States, as well as other adventures, visit http://www.MarshallUlrich.com/blog.

Acknowledgments

Thanks go first to my children, Elaine, Taylor, and Alexandra (Ali), for without them, I'd be incomplete; in each of them, I see facets of the future. I owe gratitude, too, to more of the family: my mom, my brother, Steven, his wife, Kathy, and their two children, and my aunt Irene Houtchens, all of whom came out to support me in Ault, Colorado. My sister, Lonna, and her daughter, Cris, were there both in Colorado and at the finish in New York City, along with my cousin Kathryn Amira. Heather's mother, Janis, and her sister, Laura, also watched me go. It's impossible to convey how much everyone's presence along the way meant to me.

Heather was instrumental in the run across the United States; that's evident on every page of this book. She was also critical to the accuracy and emotional honesty of this retelling, and she painstakingly reviewed the statistics, checked facts, and helped me describe some of the more difficult experiences. (Let me say, though, that any errors or omissions made here are mine alone.)

My agent, Stephen Hanselman, and his brilliant wife, Julia Serebrinsky, saw potential in this story and have helped me every step of the way. Megan Newman at Avery genuinely got and then bought into this book about running that's even more about life. Bart Yasso made an invaluable recommendation, and Frank and Nilsa McKinney have provided so much support, advice, and guidance over the years, pointing me in the right direction. Karen Risch brought magic and meaning to the words.

To all my racing and climbing friends from the Eco-Challenges, the Raid Gauloises, the Seven Summits, and the 120-plus ultramarathons with whom I've shared the roads, oceans, seas, mountains, and diverse terrain: I think of you all often, and I hope you'll forgive me for not calling special attention to each and every one of you, as there are just too many to mention. For all your friendship and support, I thank you. I'm especially grateful for having known Ted Corbitt and having the example of other past ultrarunners, bunioneers, and pedestrians.

In remembering years long past, I want to honor the memory of the late Gary Adams, who encouraged and studied me early on in my running career, photographing Death Valley and helping make it a National Park.

I must also mention Rosa Martinez, a part of the family and a godsend for all of us as the children grew up. She helped raise the kids and was there for us from the very beginning, becoming a surrogate mother to Elaine once Jean was gone. Peter and Susan Alpert, too, were comfort and support during Jean's illness and after her death.

Sister Mary Beth Lloyd and Sister Virginia Jamele have done so much for impoverished women and children around the world, and I'm honored to be a small part of the fund-raising that helps them do the real work of peace and justice. Ray Zahab believed in and encouraged me, providing the training and nutrition guidance, as well as shaping the mental attitude necessary to complete my journey. I owe my success to my mentor in New York, who wishes to remain anonymous, though I must at least reveal that she has been my guiding light, keeping me focused on the task at hand and allowing me to accomplish the impossible.

Certain people helped me overcome so many obstacles along the way. Dr. Paul Langevin, the magic man; Nancy Smith, who worked a miracle healing my back the very last day; and Robert Spieler from VQ OrthoCare, who was always a shout away during the run—each provided much-needed medical expertise. You kept me moving. Then there were the people who did most of the crewing: my dear friend and neighbor Roger Kaufhold, Kathleen Kane, Jesse Riley, Kira Matukaitis, Dave Pearson, Jennifer Nichols, and Chuck Dale; and Brian Weinberg, who would come out and pace me at all hours of the night, uplifting my spirit and staying with us till the finish.

My "Stray Dogs" Eco-Challenge teammates, Mark Macy and Dr. Bob Haugh, both came out to run with and support me, including Mace seeing me to the finish. Mace and Dr. Bob, you have been dear friends and mentors for decades, providing support and stability in my life. Corny as it may sound, you two are my heroes. Tom Triumph, who more recently became a close friend, oozes enthusiasm and support; he and his wonderful wife, Therese, and their daughter, Alexandra, and son, Tommy, opened their hearts and doors to the crew in New Jersey as we prepared to finish the run. I must also thank those who have given in the past and gave to me their crewing expertise and support: Theresa Daus-Weber, Todd Holmes, Becky Clements, Bob Becker, Alex Nement, George Velasco, Colleen Oshier, Cole Hanley, Michael Mezzacupo, and Kathy Farrell. I couldn't have done it without you.

My generous friend Chris Frost allowed me to train and stay at his house, and then came out to support me on this run—twice. Art Webb has always given his undying support, and both Chris and Art ran with me at the beginning, in San Francisco, helping me calm my nerves and settle in for the long haul. Penny and Bud Smith took care of Spike and Moxie, our dogs. Special thanks to Dave Thorpe for his kindness, crewing, and concern; you are a true friend. For the food and friendship you brought out for us, my hat's off to Deb Sensensey, Craig and Denise Parker, and Mike and Elaine Mullin. Gary Kliewer, Murray Griffin, Kari and Phil Marchant, Ben and Denise Jones, I thank you for your support over the years; it has meant so much to me. Lisa Smith-Batchen and Lisa Bliss provided communications and encouragement that helped me keep the faith.

Thanks to Jesus Gutierrez (El Jalisciense–Ricos Tacos); Blaine Budke and Mitch Farr (the chopper guys); David, Sam, Samuel, and Sylvia Beiler (David's Awesome Cookies); and Kathi Rogers (Rogers Pumpkin Patch). When I was feeling down, you raised me up.

Jim Simone, Sally Habermehl, and Jan Depuy, I can't tell you how much it meant to me that you arranged to have those young men and children come run with me.

Dana Offenbach was there in New York at all hours of the day sorting things out to make this run a success. Kevin Kerwin and his wife, Kate O'Neil, were on the ground and making sure the documentary *Running America* became a reality. Rick Baraff and Amira Soliman were part of the production group, but they also integrated into the crew more times than I can count. When we were short on crew, they always (along with Kate) came to the rescue. Andreas von Scheele, Steve Clack, and Cory Gegner rounded out the film crew, doing a terrific job and putting in long hours.

It was very special to have Todd Jennings, Ira Bellach, Jose Vargas, Irene Chin, Theresa Tokarowski, Sam Wright, Camille Pruvost, and Melissa Lin meet me as I came off the George Washington Bridge into Manhattan—it was fantastic to share the long journey's end with such wonderful people.

A special thanks to the runners who came out and experienced a part of Running America: Travis and Donavahn Macy; Steve and Barb Shepard; Melissa Burdick; David, Sydney, and Marcie Atwood; Caleb Beasley, along with his wife and beautiful baby; Doug Douillard; Abbey and Arden Habermehl; Nathan Depuy; Juli Goldstein; Michael, Paulette, Corrine, and Evan Hansen; Jennifer, Thomas, and Andree Langevin; Vanessa Loggins; Jim and Maggie McCord; Glen Turner; Cody Westheimer; Christine Wilson; Joel Rine; Pennsylvania state trooper Kevin Warren; and the many, many others who were there to help guide the way and share the road.

I'd like to award a virtual world's record to Mr. Tracy Pugh's students at Jackson Elementary in Greeley, Colorado, who ran a combined 3,078 miles together in P.E. class, doing laps and following our progress, too. I loved meeting you in March 2009—believe me, your young enthusiasm was as inspiring to me as I ever hope to be to you.

To Jerry, Linda, and Bethany Douglass: Chris watched over me out there and was a galvanizing spirit, keeping me on track. He will forever live in our hearts.

And last but not least, thank you to Frank Giannino, who set the transcontinental record back in 1980, for all your support and for coming to the finish to congratulate me. You are still the king of the road.

Bibliography

America: The Story of Us. The History Channel/A&E Home Video, 2010.

American Academy of Orthopaedic Surgeons, "Plantar Fasciitis," AAOS.org (http://orthoinfo.aaos.org/topic.cfm?topic=AA00149).

Bovsun, Mara. "Edward Payson Weston," Ultrawalking.net (http://www.ultrawalking.net/historia/weston.html).

Chase, Adam. "On the Trail with Yiannis Kouros," *Running Times,* April 2006 (http://www.runningtimes.com/Article.aspx?articleID=7582).

The Distance of Truth. Pageturner Productions, 2008.

Hunt, Linda Lawrence. *Bold Spirit: Helga Estby's Forgotten Walk Across Victorian America.* University of Idaho Press, 2003.

Kastner, Charles B. *Bunion Derby: The 1928 Footrace Across America.* University of New Mexico Press, 2007.

Lehrer, Jonah. "Depression's Upside," *The New York Times,* February 28, 2010 (http://www.nytimes.com/2010/02/28/magazine/28depression-t.html).

McNerthney, Casey. "Seattle's First Distance Hero Risked His Life to Run Race," *SeattlePI.com,* November 24, 2007 (http://www.seattlepi.com/local/341003_gardner24.html).

Murakami, Haruki. *What I Talk About When I Talk About Running.* Vintage Books, 2009.

Pollan, Michael. *Food Rules: An Eater's Manual.* Penguin Books, 2009.

Talpey, Tom. "The Pedestrian," RunningPast.com (http://www.runningpast.com/pedestrian).

Tingley, Joseph V., and Kris Ann Pizarro. *Traveling America's Loneliest Road: A Geologic and Natural History Tour Through Nevada Along U.S. Highway 50.* Nevada Bureau of Mines and Geology Special Publication 26, University of Nevada, Reno, 2003.

Weston, Edward Payson. "Weston's Auto Lost, Needs His Supplies," *The New York Times,* April 3, 1909.

White, T. H. *The Once and Future King.* G. P. Putnam's Sons, 1939.

Index

About the Author

Marshall Ulrich is a versatile, world-class extreme endurance athlete: an ultra-runner, Seven Summits mountaineer, and adventure racer. His prolific athletic career has earned him numerous wins, records, and firsts on some of the toughest courses in the world, and taken him to the top of the highest mountains, including Mount Everest—all in his forties and fifties. He defies the ideas of "too far," "too old," and "not possible."

In 2008, at the age of fifty-seven, Marshall clocked the all-time third-fastest crossing on foot from San Francisco (or L.A.) to New York City, and set new records for the masters and grand masters divisions.

The proud parent of Elaine, Taylor, and Ali, he lives with his wife, Heather, in the mountains of Colorado.

To contact Marshall and learn where and when you can attend one of his training camps, climb mountains with him as your guide, or hear him speak about his adventures in person, please visit MarshallUlrich.com.

dreams in action
discover what you're made of